DATE DUE

THE SOCIAL CONSTRUCTION OF VIRTUE

The Social Construction of Virtue

The Moral Life of Schools

George W. Noblit
and Van O. Dempsey

WITH
BELMIRA BUENO
PETER HESSLING
DORIS KENDRICK
REEDA TOPPIN

State University of New York Press

Published by
State University of New York Press, Albany

For information, address State University of New York Press,
State University Plaza, Albany, N.Y. 12246

Production by M. R. Mulholland
Marketing by Fran Keneston

Library of Congress Cataloging-in-Publication Data

Noblit, George W.
    The social construction of virtue : the moral life of schools /
George W. Noblit and Van O. Dempsey : with Belmira Bueno ... (et al.)
        p.   cm.
    Includes bibliographical references and index.
    ISBN 0-7914-3079-0 (ch : alk. paper). — ISBN 0-7914-3080-4 (pb : alk. paper)
    1. Moral education—United States.   2. Moral education—United States—Case studies.   3. Education—United States—Philosophy.
4. Educational sociology—United States.   5. School management and organization—United States.   I. Dempsey, Van O., 1960–
II. Bueno, Belmira Oliveira.   III. Title.
LC311.N56   1996
370.11'4'0973—dc20   95-39477
                                                                           CIP

10   9   8   7   6   5   4   3   2   1

This book is dedicated to our children,

BEN, CLAY, MARY VAN, TARA, AND TYLER

CONTENTS

ACKNOWLEDGMENTS

Educational reform has become a national pastime. Politicians have found that there are careers to be made in attacking and making policy to reform schools. The American public is all too ready to let schools bear the brunt of the failures of our economy and democracy, and educators seem all too willing to accept the charges leveled at them. The rhetoric of reform, however, has kept the definition of the problem curiously narrow. Policymakers, the public, and educators frame the problem with schools as insufficient achievement, and have used test scores as the legitimator of the problem and the efficacy of proposed solutions. Policymakers, educators, and the public purposely avoid the real issue.

Schools have not been, and are not, as much about learning knowledge as they are about morality. What we want schools to do most is develop morality and do this well. We want our children to have our values and to behave in responsible—indeed, virtuous—ways, and we are not sure that schools help with this. Policymakers avoid this issue because it is usually confounded with religion, because policymakers need a connection to test scores, and because it is not clear what policy might do to deal with this messy situation.

In fact, the situation is much worse than this. We are captives of our own ideas about education and morality. These ideas lead to educational reform recycling again and again. These ideas also blind us to the possibilities that everyday life offers us. In this book, we attempt to address both of these consequences in an effort to allow us to be participants in, and not pawns of, our culture and moral life. The social construction of virtue is about reclaiming moral life with schools.

We could not have begun such an ambitious project, let alone finish it, without the help of many colleagues and friends. The research this book is based on was collected as a team effort. The team also wrote numerous professional papers and repeatedly discussed the meaning of what we were learning. Belmira Bueno, Peter Hessling, Doris Kendrick, and Reeda Toppin all contributed in these and other ways. This book was written with them. They deserve much of the credit for whatever is good about this book, but they do not deserve criticism for what is wrong (that is our province).

A number of people and organizations supported our work. We thank Richard Phillips for putting us together and for his unwavering belief in our efforts. When we started this project, Frank Brown, as Dean of the School of Education at the University of North Carolina at Chapel Hill, funded the transcription of some of the interviews and travel to present preliminary findings. John Shelton Reed, Director of UNC's Institute for Research in the Social Sciences, awarded us a summer grant for the initial analysis of the data. Ronald Butchart contributed not only his very useful book on doing local school histories but also much of his time as a discussant of papers and symposia and as a helpful critic of our overall efforts. Kathryn Borman and Sally Lubeck critiqued our preliminary papers from a more ethnographic perspective. Together they helped us articulate an ethnohistorical perspective. Michele Foster and Vanessa Siddle-Walker helped us better understand Rougemont School and Community. Brian Matney and Gail Davis helped with our work in Cedar Grove School, allowing us to deliver on promises all too easily made. Paul Bitting, Kathy Hytten, and Warren Nord all read an early draft of this book and helped us better understand our own arguments and their weaknesses. Paul Bitting, Lynda Stone, Alan Tom, Jonathan Sher, Brian McCadden, Dwight Rogers, Mary Kay Delaney, and Warren Nord, as the "moral education" group at UNC–Chapel Hill, all critiqued the final chapter of the book and developed our ideas more generally. Lynda Stone, Kathy Hytten, and Michael Gunzenhauser made important contributions to our critique of Dewey. Our colleagues Jill Fitzgerald, Catherine Marshall, and Dwight Rogers at UNC, and Anne Nardi, Rogers McAvoy, Sam Stack, and Gwen Jones at WVU all have been patient listeners and concerned critics of our musings and writings. Writing a book consumes vast amounts of time, and we would like to thank our deans, Donald Stedman and Jane Applegate, for being tolerant of absences and absent-mindedness. Finally, this book would not have been completed without Amee Adkins and Sofia Villenas. They read, critiqued, and edited the final drafts and insured that all the incidental tasks of book writing were accomplished. They worked long, hard hours, and we owe them a great debt of gratitude. Finally, we would like to thank Jaci and Mary for their love, patience, and support through the trials and tribulations we have created.

1

Education and the Social Construction of Virtue

It is time to face the inescapable conclusion. We are unable to reform American education. Even with all the changes in the past fifteen years, this remains true. These changes probably *have* led to some improvements—not always seen (in hindsight) to have been worth the costs. Indeed, historians of education (Kent 1987; Cuban 1988; Tyack, Lowe, and Hansot 1980) recount the recycling of reform in this century, including the waves of our current reform era. Cuban sees "the inevitable return of school reforms" (1990: 3) as due not to the failings of schools or of reform initiatives but to "conflicts over values" (7). He argues that reform recycles because value shifts in the larger society lead the schools to accommodate; to adjust rather than fundamentally change. This is because the implementation of reforms are limited by the same value conflicts that stimulate reform. Kent sees the issues of the 1980s (the concerns for standards and accountability) as recycling the issues of the 1950s because "the familiar demand pattern for reform, namely a short burst of intense action followed by longer periods of inaction and neglect" (1987: 148), is unable to resolve issues of fundamental values. The recycling pattern helps perpetuate the value conflict by periodically recreating "crises" in education. Whereas Cuban (1988) sees the fundamental value conflict as being excellence versus equity, we will argue that these are modern manifestations of more deep-seated ideas, "oratorical" and "philosophical" (Kimball 1986), about education in our culture.

The last one hundred years shows a lineage to our recycling of reform. The Committee of Ten report in 1893 (NEA), the reforms of the late 1950s, and the reforms of the 1980s express an oratorical conception of excellence. The "Cardinal Principles" in 1918 (Commission on the Reorganization of Secondary Education), progressivism in the 1920s through the 1940s, and new curricula and programs of the 1960s and 1970s express the philosophical conception of equity. These sets of reforms are not pure in their adherence to any single value. The value conflict is so ingrained in our society that any reform contains elements of both values. Because each reform value contains elements of its contrary, initiating reform around one sows the seeds of its own capitulation to the other.

All of this demonstrates that we are conservative about education in that we conserve the existence of an essential value conflict. These values and their opposition are reified, taken-for-granted assumptions that unconsciously shape how we think and act regarding education, and we have thus become pawns of this value conflict. We play out one idea then the other—viewing each reform as unique and new, uncognizant of their lineage, legacy, and historical pairing. Unknowingly we recreate the value conflict in each generation, in each reform, in each educational crisis. We do not reform education, we only recycle our educational reforms.

There have been two waves to the 1980s reform efforts (Zeichner 1991) that reveal how the expression of one value about education is soon tempered by another. Each wave of reform is an artifact revealing our value conflict. *A Nation at Risk* (National Commission on Excellence in Education 1983) prompted a series of top-down initiatives that are now looking less promising than they did in the early 1980s. *A Nation At Risk* justified a call for excellence by declaring that education had failed the nation, undercutting our economic competitiveness by "an unthinking, unilateral educational disarmament" (1). The problem was portrayed as a retreat from standards concerning content, expectations, time, teaching, and leadership. Eight solutions were offered: (1) an increase in the number of courses required for graduation, (2) more rigorous standards and higher expectations for students, (3) more time devoted to instruction in the basic coursework, (4) higher standards for entering teaching, (5) rigorous evaluation of existing teachers, (6) a career ladder for teachers, (7) educational leadership that develops school, and (8) community support and state and local responsibility for implementing the proposed reforms. In this we see the value of excellence rhetorically defined as a return to the standards of the past, recreating a past educational and economic glory for the United States.

The Carnegie report, *A Nation Prepared: Teachers for the Twenty-First Century* (1986), signaled a partial swing of the pendulum away from excellence by warning that the early reforms have undercut *the* fundamental requirement of equitable education—a teacher's ability to adapt instruction to the specific needs of the student. The proposal shows that this was only a partial step away from *A Nation at Risk*, balancing a call for rigorous national standards for teaching and teacher preparation with restructuring schools to allow for more teacher autonomy in deciding how to teach. Even this balance is one-sided. Teacher autonomy concerned only site-level autonomy, primarily the means of instruction. They were still accountable for student achievement. Just as the American public readily agreed with *A Nation at Risk,* it just as quickly gave its assent to *A Nation Prepared.* While the reforms of the 1980s led to increased centralization and standardization, the reforms of the 1990s are now beginning the swing to decentralization or "restructuring" of education (once again), supposedly to allow education to be more responsive to ways in which children actually learn.

How all of this will eventually sort out remains to be seen, but we believe it is safe to project that both kinds of reform will continue for the forseeable future. They will continue to vie for the public's attention and support, will continue to alternate between these seemingly contradictory logics, not because the public is duplicitous, uninformed, or comprised only of blind followers of educational leaders; nor even because the reforms themselves are inherently inadequate or technically deficient on either side. Reform will recycle for two reasons, the first and foremost being that the American mind is "closed." Bloom (1987) has argued that the American mind is closed because we have failed to inculcate Western values in our youth. For us, the American mind is closed because Western culture has been inculcated quite effectively into the American mind—so effectively, in fact, that most Americans simply play out their culture unthinkingly. We are unknowingly pawns of our culture and its most prevalent beliefs about education.

Cuban's (1988) notion of ingrained value conflict highlights a second reason why we are unable to reform schools. Educational reforms are also framed in the language of technical rationality (Collins 1982; Mannheim 1936). To reform schools, we restructure the school organization, design curricula, train teachers, set standards, and monitor compliance. However, education ultimately is not about these things, as important as they are. Reform recycles because we repeatedly misspecify the essential nature of education in this way. Schooling is fundamentally a moral, not a technical, enterprise. Schools, as social institutions, express our values more than achieve goals. Reforms based in instrumental rationality ignore both the value conflict and its essential message that schools are less about instructing facts and more about constructing morality. Until we understand what this means, reform itself will be a captive of our fundamental value conflict. Therefore, as a second reason, reform recycles because we repeatedly misspecify the essential nature of education. We repeat: Schooling is fundamentally a moral, not a technical, enterprise.

The Ideas That Bind and Blind

What Cuban terms values of excellence and equity have a long history in Western society. Indeed, Kimball's (1986) ambitious history of the idea of liberal education documents the ubiquity of the value conflict we have been discussing. Before we discuss his work in more detail, we will translate the key terms we have been using for the value conflict into those used by Kimball. "Excellence" is a modern term for the oratorical idea, and "equity" for the philosophical idea. Each idea is fundamentally moral, as all ideas are (MacIntyre 1981). In this case, each idea explicitly offers a moral conceptions of the good and true.

Kimball characterizes the oratorical idea as follows:

(1) Training citizen-orators to lead society (2) requires identifying true virtue (3) the commitment to which (4) will elevate the student and (5) the source for which is great texts, whose authority lies in (6) the dogmatic premise that they relate the true virtues, (7) which are embraced for their own sake. (1986: 228)

For the orators, the source of virtue and morality is in the distant past, and we must strive to recapture it so that we may approach the ideal of a virtuous life.

Kimball defines the philosophical idea in noticeably different terms: (1) Epistemological skepticism underlies (2) the free and (3) intellectual search for truth, which is forever elusive, and so all possible views must be (4) tolerated and given (5) equal hearing (6) with the final decision left to each individual, (7) who pursues truth for its own sake. (228)

For the philosophers, the good and true are located in the future. This requires values of tolerance, individualism, and freedom.

Kimball argues that these ideas are inextricably linked since the time of ancient Greece and that their opposition has led to successive attempts to accommodate each other. Thus, rarely do we see either idea in a "pure" form. Yet these ideas, in our culture, are taken for granted. We take them as assumptions that structure our actions, and are usually not aware of them or their effects on our actions. Moreover, their opposition is also assumed and implicit. These ideas and their opposition are reified in our culture. They blind us to alternatives and bind us in the recycling of educational reform.

It is difficult to become aware of deep-seated moral assumptions. A first step is to make the implicit explicit. Yet this does not lead us to challenge such ideas. We only become aware of what we value. Bowers (1984) argues that one way to problematize ideas is to focus on their history and human authorship, and the text of Kimball's book is devoted largely to chronicling the human authorship and social conditions affecting the relative popularity of each idea.

Kimball locates the founding of the oratorical idea in ancient Greece. Isocrates, a famous rhetorician, wished to wed the Sophists' emphasis on rhetoric and its expression with a concern for values drawn uncritically from the traditional virtues associated with the Homeric heroes. Isocrates was highly skeptical of Socrates' and Plato's dialectical search for the truth, seeing endless speculation as wasteful. For Isocrates, the goal of education was better defined: as Kimball quotes, "to speak well and think right" (1986: 18). The Isocrates–Plato opposition was the first known instance of the opposition of these moral ideas. The concern was how to understand what *was* truth and goodness. Isocrates turned toward tradition and the eloquent expression of the wisdom to be found in rhetorical argument, while Plato located truth and goodness in the future, to be discovered only as the result of diligent search. Each mode of thought spawned disciples and sponsors, who eventually created firm institutional bases and intellectual pedigrees for each of these ideas about education.

Generally speaking, Isocrates was more successful than Plato in promoting his agenda in their time. The oratorical idea found favor with the elites for both education and public life, and in turn was embraced by the Roman Empire's educational thinkers: Varro, Cicero, and Quintilian. While the oratorical idea was dominant, the philosophical approach, owing perhaps to the immense prestige of Plato and Socrates, was now equally well ensconced in educational thought. This led the Roman thinkers (and their successors) to develop arguments that subsumed the philosophical idea under the oratorical, ironically institutionalizing both ideas. As Kimball notes, "Manifest in this lineage is the orators' perpetual conflict with the philosophers" (33). In the latter years of the Roman Empire, it would seem that educational theory became inextricably linked to two important political struggles. There was the constant threat of the dissolution of the empire coupled with the ethnocentric assumption of Roman cultural supremacy. This somewhat paradoxical combination meant that the Romans were "more sympathetic toward the oratorical tradition with its concern for law, order, noble virtue, and public expression" (Kimball 1986: 32). Second was the Christian conversion of the empire. Christians had originally opposed the ideas of the Roman orators, and were ultimately charged with undermining classical culture. After some four centuries of persecution under the logic of Roman orators, Christians came to consider the modes of classical study and its dominant oratorical idea as necessary for the study of Christian theology. As Christians ascended to high offices in the

Roman Empire, Augustine legitimated the oratorical idea to justify the reliance on teaching of Scripture for all Romans.

This subsuming of the orator-philosopher educational argument into medieval Christian casuistry all but silenced the debate, as the empire slowly faded away, and with it any serious interest in classical education. What did survive was largely in Christian monasteries. Charlemagne began an educational revival when he brought Alcuin (A.D. 730–804) from England to be master of his palace school. Alcuin argued persuasively for education based on the ideas of Cicero, thereby successfully reviving the dominance of the oratorical over the philosophical idea. The final breakup of empire by the ninth century was followed in the eleventh century by an economic revival, paralleling a revival of interest in education and an expansion of cathedral and parish schools. This set the stage (along with the rediscovery of the works of Aristotle and the Greeks) for a revival of the interest in the philosophical idea among those scholastics who employed the dialectical method to their subject matter. Kimball notes, "The archetypal scholastic was Abelard" (1079–1144) (57). Abelard reversed the hierarchy of ideas about education that Cicero established, subordinating rhetoric to logic. The orator-philosopher debate was fully and heatedly engaged throughout the twelfth century, leading to the battle between the clerics and scholastics in the thirteenth century and the supremacy of the philosophical idea in the fourteenth century.

Kimball argues that the meaning of the Renaissance is best understood here as a successful revival of the oratorical idea. Just as the rediscovery of Aristotle boosted the prestige of the philosophical idea in the twelfth century, the rediscovery of Quintilian and Cicero fueled a similar revival of the oratorical idea on the part of Renaissance humanists. Kimball portrays the influential Erasmus (1469–1536) as a powerful orator who broke with other Renaissance humanists when he argued that oratorical studies need not be reserved for the elite. We will see this split revisited in the differences between modern orators Allan Bloom and Mortimer Adler. The Protestant Reformation provided a further boost to the oratorical idea with a scathing criticism of scholasticism. Martin Luther advocated the reform of education to include the oratorical arts, especially grammar and rhetoric. The Catholic Church, attempting to regain its status in the face of the Protestant onslaught, also expanded its seminaries, which embraced an oratorical curriculum. In the sixteenth and seventeenth centuries, the battle between the philosophical idea and the oratorical idea continued, with the oratorical idea being dominant.

The origins of American education were oratorically dominated as well. The first universities—Harvard, William and Mary, and Yale—had largely oratorical curricula, and so did the schools, existing primarily to groom students properly for university study. The gentlemanly ideal soon crossed the sea to America, helping further to justify an oratorical curriculum, the notion that merit and moral worth were connected to education. Education came to be defined as both worthy in itself and capable of transferring that worth to the person so educated.

Kimball sees, in the rise of experimental science and the Enlightenment, a resurgence of the philosophical idea. Emerging from the Renaissance and the empirical research of Copernicus (1473–1543), Kepler (1571–1630), and Galileo (1564–1642), the new science and new philosophy revived Socratic criticism and mathematical sciences. John Locke (1632–1704), Thomas Hobbes (1588–1679), René Descartes (1596–1650), David Hume (1711–1776), and Jean-Jacques Rousseau (1712–1778) all reemphasized the philosophical idea's endless "search for truth," its critical tradition of thought, now coupled with startling new ideas about freedom and egalitarianism. True, most of these thinkers worked outside the established (and more oratorical) educational institutions of their day, but their thought did lead to a degrading or rhetoric in eighteenth-century England to simply the proper form and style of expression. The European universities were largely in decline by then, but later managed to join with established religious orders to resist the inclusion of the new sciences in their curricula.

In colonial America, the major activity involving the new philosophy and science was also taking place well outside established institutions. Championed by Benjamin Franklin (and others), the American Philosophical Society was organized independent of educational organizations. The American Revolution imbued the new United States with Enlightenment thought, including associating liberty, equality, and progress with learning; science and experimentation; and promoting an abiding suspicion of authority and tradition. Yet with all this, most schools and universities experienced little change until after the War of 1812. In the 1820s and 1830s, German universities, with their attitude of free inquiry, were increasingly influential to Americans, and this led to some curricular change, including what we would now call tracking of students, departmentalization of faculty, some student choice in course selection, instruction in modern languages, and teaching via lectures. It is more accurate, however, to understand this as a continuation of the struggle between the two ideas. Indeed, as the new sciences were added to requirements for admission to universities, the standards for classical studies were simultaneously being raised, a pattern that has been repeated numerous times in American educational history, each time noticeably increasing the burden on secondary schools to better prepare students for higher education.

In any case, it is clear that the firm embodiment of the philosophical idea in science was gaining status and that the oratorical idea was being forced to accommodate to its new—lower—status, an accommodation that resulted in the ingenious argument that classical studies were ideal for "training" the intellect. This was clearly a step away from the previous oratorical assertion that classical studies created virtuous gentlemen. Another accommodation was for classical studies to embrace an increasing specialization of research and study, which, in the end, both protected classical studies from the intrusion of the philosophical idea and enabled the oratorical idea to share in some of the new status accorded to the sciences. In any case, it was not until after the end of the Civil War, the passing of the Morrill Land Grant Act of 1862 (which was seen as a move against the oratorical curriculum), and the publication of Darwin's *On the Origin of Species by Means of Natural Selection* in 1859 that the philosophical idea actually gained a stronghold in American education. American pragmatism and progressivism soon carried the philosophical idea to new heights, expanding the applicability of the term "science" to a wide range of disciplines, including education, and thereby encouraging increased disciplinary specialization and elective coursework.

Pragmatism, as developed by George Herbert Mead, Charles S. Peirce, and William James, reframed Darwin's notion of natural selection to include the human animal's ability to shape the environment, thus undercutting the misuse of Darwinism by elites to justify the often oppressive status quo. John Dewey fashioned this radical notion into educational progressivism "oriented against affirming the certitide of any absolute standards and values and toward appreciation of the individuality of each human being and reliance on a free experimental approach to every new situation encountered in life" (Kimball 1986: 169). Politically linked with Populism early in this century, Progressivism evolved into a broad movement of critique and educational reform. Arrayed against this unexpected development were the Neohumanists, such as Alexander Meiklejohn, who argued with renewed vigor for a course of study based on the so-called Great Books, a strategy he justified as helping to sharpen mental discipline and the critical processes. Meiklejohn further pled for universal education based on the idea that, in a democracy, all must have the *same* education, much as Adler and Hirsch now argue. Indeed, it is telling to note that Adler (with Robert Hutchins) led a Great Books course of study at the University of Chicago that closely followed Mieklejohn's basic plan. According to Hutchins, "Education implies teaching. Teaching implies knowledge. Knowledge is truth. The truth is everywhere the same. Hence education should be everywhere the same" (quoted in Kimball 1986: 179).

After World War I, the conflict between the two ideas seemed to be promoting too much scholarly disunity, and various efforts were made to force an accommodation. This time it was the philosophical idea that accommodated; and, as Kimball argues, the accommodation was really a covert commitment to elitism, achieved by establishing a hierarchy of knowledge in which the pursuit of scientific knowledge was seen as the highest calling—which in turn became linked to graduate study, meritocratic criteria for selection to advanced courses, and highly competitive examinations. Progressivism adopted this accommodation rather freely into constant calls for vocational education and other forms of student tracking and testing.

World War II led to an enormous emphasis on technical training, and those few orators who objected to such education were often unfairly critiqued as not being clearly in support of the cause. In any event, the war ended with the battle still engaged over which idea would dominate American education. Kimball does not develop a detailed postwar history of this debate, but argues that the conflict has continued unabated. Kimball ends his book by saying that "the Ciceronian and Socratic conceptions of liberal education continue to stand in tension, as they have since antiquity, like two foci of an ellipse whose locus includes the varying approaches to liberal education of any particular time" (241).

To continue Kimball's analogy of an ellipse, we can see that two recent reform foci, excellence and equity, are, respectively, the oratorical and philosophical ideas. The term "excellence" signals an emphasis on reclaiming past, but now eroded, standards. Isocrates and Cicero would see their ideas in this. The term "equity" signals tolerance and the democratic values associated with the search for truth and virtue. Individuals should be free and unhampered in the search for elusive truths. Socrates and Abelard would recognize equity as akin to their ideas. The tensions between excellence and equity are in large part the tensions between the ideas from antiquity.

Understanding that our modern reforms are not new ideas but manifestations of ideas that have been in opposition for centuries also allows us to conclude that the failures to reform education are not due simply to failures of will, inadequate resources, and the recalcitrance of educators or educational organizations. Rather, our reforms recycle because of the tacit assumptions that undergird them, including the assumptions that these ideas are the central ideas about education and that they are opposed to each other. Taking these two assumptions for granted limits the possibilities for reform and makes us blind to alternatives that may exist in our society. We cannot recognize and value alternatives, because they violate our assumptions about what is and ought to be.

Possibilities

We have painted a somber portrait of the current state of educa-tion, but there are possibilities for escaping the reified ideas that bind us to a recycling of the history of educational reform. The possibilities lie in understanding these ideas and revealing their human authorship, social bases, and implications, as we have started to do in this chapter (Bowers 1984). Yet this in itself is not enough. Critique problematizes and debunks ideas, but it does not replace them. All too often, critique creates a void, and the ensuing struggle to fill that void leads to repro-ducing the very ideas critiqued, for these ideas have powerful backers and considerable cultural force, and, in the absence of any other ideas, are the "options" at our disposal. Critique must be coupled with con-struction so that, instead of filling the void with what we are given, we create alternatives. In the presence of powerful reified ideas, simply asserting a theoretical alternative will not suffice. Alternative ideas in this sense tend to end up as "occulted knowledge" (Southworth 1988) and shunted aside as esoteric sideshow freaks. A better prospect is to look to everyday life and try to discern what people do that we normally do not see because we are blinded by reified ideas. In everyday life, there are countless possibilities for cultural construction—the problem is to recognize them.

The critique of ideas and the search for alternative possibilities are both projects in the sociology of knowledge (Berger and Luckmann 1967). This perspective sees knowledge as constructed through human actions, and reveals the processes by which ideas become legitimated as knowledge. Knowledge is taken to be not a proven body of fact, as in positivistic disciplines, but a set of ideas that become socially regarded as facts. At any point in history there are myriad ideas, many of which fail to become legitimated as knowledge. Berger and Luckmann (1967) argue that, while most early treatises in the sociology of knowledge were concerned with the history of thought, there are also knowledges present in everyday life that need investigation. They write expansively: "The sociology of knowledge must concern itself with everything that passes for 'knowledge' in society" (14–15). In their efforts to promote this expansive view, they even argue that "commonsense 'knowledge' rather than 'ideas' must be the central focus for the sociology of knowledge" (15). While we will address both intellectual ideas and commonsense knowledge in this book, it is important to understand why Berger and Luckmann are emphasizing the latter. They are doing so because it is the commonsense knowledge that people take to be reality in their everyday lives. It becomes taken for granted. The practical program that Berger and Luckmann are proposing is to allow everyday people to understand how their lives are shaped by such assumptions so that "a taken-for-granted 'reality' congeals for the man in the street" (3).

We will take Berger and Luckmann's practical program for the sociology of knowledge a step further. In doing so, we will reclaim both sociologies of knowledge—the intellectual and the everyday. We will explore the intellectual ideas that are reified in our debates over educational reform. We will do this because these ideas are "realities" for theorists and policymakers. Moreover, these ideas, we argue, are so imbued in our culture that everyday people use them rhetorically at least to comment and complain about schools. These ideas are so powerful that they blind us to the alternative possibilities that we construct in our everyday lives. We will continue to be pawns of them until we dereify them.

Habermas (1971) proposes that one way to dereify ideas is to engage in a critique of ideology. This, he argues, can take place in an ideal speech situation. Free and uncoerced dialogue about our lives and the forces that dominate us can reveal the ideas that we take for granted, making them subjects for critique. Bowers (1984) argues that in everyday life we experience cultural transitions that give us moments of liminality when we experience being "betwixt and between" (van Gennep 1975: 21) established ways of thinking and doing. In these moments, we recognize our taken-for-granted's. As noted above, mere recognition of taken-for-granted's is not enough to promote change. Instead, they must be seen as somehow problematic and therefore inadequate as a depiction of reality.

Cuban (1988), Kent (1987), and Tyack, Lowe, and Hansot (1984) have all helped to make explicit the value conflict that promotes the recycling of reform. We can now recognize it, but much more is needed if we are to dereify it. This is the central task of this book. We have briefly examined the history of ideas that blind and bind us, and understand that these are not actually modern ideas but ideas as old as Western culture—many date from ancient Greece. This sets the stage for a more detailed analysis of the modern manifestations of these ideas. The goal of these analyses and critiques is to problematize these ideas *as ideas*. This is an ambitious task in itself, but it is insufficient for our purposes. We wish to wed critique to construction. In doing so, we want also to avoid reproducing the original problem of reified ideas by looking not to theory but to everyday life for alternative possibilities. The reified ideas are present in everyday life, but not to the extent or in the way that those who promote these ideas would have us believe. People in everyday life do something more and something other than what these ideas propose. The people we worked with on an oral history of two schools (which we will discuss in detail) engaged in a social construction of virtue. These people suggested interesting options for overcoming the seemingly timeless value conflict over education. We intend to use what they taught us to go one step further with the sociology of knowledge than Berger and Luckmann's (1967) practical project. We want to do more than "congeal" a taken-for-granted reality: We want to reveal that people in everyday life offer new possibilities for understanding the moral nature of education and thus how we might reform schools.

The Social Construction of Virtue?

We will examine education and morality from a unique perspective. Much recent thinking tends to frame morality as a problem of behavior and belief that can be remedied by curricula that exhort one or more ethical positions or processes that teachers and students should assume (cf. Purpel 1989; Sichel 1988; Straughan 1982; Jarret 1991). In themselves, these approaches all seem worthy of consideration and discussion, but we also see an irony here. Most of these approaches lament the increasing instrumentality of education but in the end succumb to it, as do so many of our reform attempts, by focusing on curricula and a goal of moralizing the youth of our society. The result of this instrumentality is that these recent works end up defining morality as a short-term goal, even when it is clear to us that all these authors are ultimately concerned about how schools play into the moral nature of adults and the society as a whole. What is needed are investigations that look to the moral influence of schools directly on adults and communities. A rather different approach to education and moral life may result.

We are much closer to, though still profoundly different from, the work of Philip Jackson and his associates that produced *The Moral Life of Schools* (1993). Both our similarities and our differences with their work are critical. Their work, like ours, is ethnographically based in schools. But whereas they are focused specifically on classrooms, we look at classrooms as only one part of a much broader context in which morality is constructed. They look at the activities, interactions, and relationships that go on in classrooms, as do we. But we do so primarily historically and also primarily from the standpoint of seeing the classroom as one location in a social context that includes the school, the community, the family, and the relationships that are constructed across them. Obviously both their work and ours is about morality. Jackson and his associates say that their book "is about moral matters as they impinge upon the work of the school" (xi). They further state, reiterating our point above about our differences, "What we offer instead is *a generalized way of looking at and thinking about what goes on in classrooms,* one that highlights the moral significance of much that occurs there" (xi–xii). As will be evident below, our project is of a different sort.

Following our discussion of reified ideas, we will examine how adults use their elementary school experiences to construct moral views. We will discuss the histories of two schools in this endeavor. Cedar Grove School is traditionally white but now desegregated. Rougemont School was traditionally African-American but was closed when Cedar Grove School was desegregated. In interviews with us, the people in each of these communities did much more than recount history. They were engaging in the construction of moral narratives. These were not simple recountings of facts but a recollecting and selecting of those values they saw as being important in the present. That is, the moral narratives tell us as much about the values of these peoples today as they do about the nature of the schools then. Further, inasmuch as these narratives were constructed as part of an oral history project, these tales were constructed to be carried into some future discourse about these schools and communities and possibly about education more generally. We were writing a history of the schools that was solicited and sponsored by Cedar Grove School. The project was a collaborative venture. This means that the tales were more than individualized stories. People talked to each other and to us, and, in so doing, constructed collective moral narratives, narratives in which they located themselves (MacIntyre 1981) by their relationships with the schools, the communities, and with historical figures whom they have made into icons of virtue.

We argue that the moral significance of schooling is found not so much in what is taught to children nor in the oratorical and philosophical ideas as in what children and adults *do with their schooling experiences.* The moral and the virtuous are created with, more than learned in, schools. This view is at odds with some views in moral philosophy and ethics. We signal this in our title: *The Social Construction of Virtue.* Traditionally, "virtue" refers to features or qualities in people that confer superiority: distinction, excellence, merit, goodness, effectiveness. Frankena describes virtue as "dispositions or traits of character" that people acquire over the course of their experiences. He is careful to distinguish dispositions from the principles upon which they might be based. The former guide action, the latter justify the actions. The former defines "what we are to be," not just what rules we are to follow (1963: 49).

"Virtue" traditionally is defined in somewhat absolute terms, based on some set of principles that justify the terms and make them universal. Our concern is with what this definition of virtue excludes or denies. We define virtue as an assignment of moral traits to individuals by others as well as by themselves. We make moral meaning by creating people whom we regard as virtuous. Our use of the term "virtue" is grounded in four points: (1) We reject the reified way in which virtue is usually discussed. Absent its human authorship, it fails to inform us about how to create moral action. (2) As above, virtue is a social construction. People make morality when they construct narratives of virtuous people. (3) Virtue is interpretive. It refers to the meaning of things and less so to actions that virtuous people are said to have engaged in. (4) What constitutes virtue is contextually specific. The schools we studied constructed their own sets of virtues. These virtues can teach us much about how schools are implicated in moral life. Yet the tales of virtuous teachers constructed through our work with these communities are situated in communities and temporally located. Moral tales are deeply embedded in their contexts. They are not just about the past of these schools and communities, nor just about pursuing a moral future, but also about what is the moral today.

The social construction of virtue has implications beyond the above proposals for moral education. The perspective critiques our reified ideas about education in general, suggests new possibilities for understanding the moral nature of education, and offers a different approach to educational reform—one that may allow us to escape recycling reform again and again.

A Perspective on Oral History

Oral historians have long been besieged by their colleagues who wish a more "objective" basis for history. The traditional historian wants evidence based in some record of an event, and then seeks evidence to corroborate this record. When sophisticated, such objectivist historians also question the availability and intent of the record itself. They ask why a record would have been made, under what conditions, and to what end. They would then ask about the extent to which the production of the record alters the factuality of the event in question. Such historians are in pursuit of a factual history, a history of things that did occur. This is an elusive goal. Ultimately, we cannot know to what degree the record has altered the event being recorded. Records are the province of the privileged, who have their own reasons for keeping a record. An objective history is also selective. Nonliterate peoples value oral traditions and, in any case, cannot write a journal. The poor have few resources to expend in producing a record of their existence, and records made by the stigmatized are not likely to be preserved, for they are not as valued by those privileged to preserve records.

The oral historian bucks this tradition by arguing that, given these and other conditions, we should seek another view of history. This view values an oral tradition, recognizes that without the efforts of oral historians there would be little record at all (and that selective) of some peoples, and cautions that all records are fundamentally subjective accounts that become objective only when people treat them as such. The efforts of oral historians are a healthy corrective to the more traditional history and to the disciplines that rely on history. Oral history is documentary, seeking to create a record where none would otherwise exist. We know much more about the less privileged because of oral history. It is clear, for example, that we would know much less about the lives of women textile workers if Jacquelyn Hall and her colleagues (1987) had not done an oral history of them. Their stories would have been lost in history.

We laud the efforts of oral historians. Indeed, our initial project was to create an oral history of two schools, and to create a document that allowed the people associated with these schools to consider their histories. In itself, this was a valuable and important enterprise that, as we will discuss, had some significant effects on these communities and schools. Further, the social construction of virtue that we recount in this book is derived from this attempt at oral history.

Yet any oral history, including this one, is imbued with the context of its creation. The oral histories of these two schools were not an academic enterprise for these people, done simply to create a record where none existed; rather, oral history was a moral enterprise through which people constructed the meaning of their schools for their own lives and the lives of their communities. The central project of this book is to understand these constructions. Here we depart from the usual meaning of oral history. Instead, we are building on the work of anthropologists (Vansina 1985; Finnegan 1992) who locate oral history in the context of oral traditions and sociologists of knowledge (Halbwachs 1992; Berger and Luckmann 1967; Dilthey 1977) more than in the discipline of history. In our view, oral history *and* story telling are both "ultimately based in, perhaps constituted by, social processes" (Finnegan 1992: 2). Further, when people recount their histories, they are not just reporting history but also constructing meaning out of those lives past and present. As Vansina writes: "Reminiscences are then not constituted by random collections of memories, but are part of an organized whole of memories that tend to project a consistent image of the narrator and, in many cases, a justification of his or her life" (1985: 8).

The social constructions of virtue (as we term them) for the schools we discuss in this book are not only of the past but of the present. They are products both of memory and of current beliefs. As Halbwachs puts it:

> Social thought is essentially a memory and . . . its entire content
> consists only of collective recollections or remembrances. But . . .
> only those recollections subsist that in every period society, working
> within its present day frameworks, can reconstruct. (1992: 189)

Oral history and our sociology of knowledge approach share an important characteristic, even if some oral historians will argue that we put an "interpretive veil" (Carlton 1991: 13) over the accounts told to us. Both oral history and the sociology of knowledge owe a debt to historicism (Berger and Luckmann 1967: 7), the idea that historical events have to be understood within their situation. For Dilthey (1977), this means moving history from the study of overarching periods of history to the study of the history of lived experience. Giddens sees it as a "consciousness" of how time is related to the development of social life by those living that life (1979: 199). Both oral historians and sociologists of knowledge are dedicated to capturing historicity, if to somewhat different ends. The oral historian seeks to capture it, while the sociologist of knowledge studies what people are accomplishing with the historicity they construct. The oral historian is rightfully concerned that scholars who use oral history analytically may be misrepresenting the historicity of people's accounts. Often this can mean that the oral accounts are distorted to fit grand theoretical schemes. However, the implications of historicity for the disciplines is now better understood. A long-standing feature of the sociology of knowledge, history has found new purchase in the explorations of postmodernity. Lyotard sees the "postmodern as incredulity towards metanarratives" (1979: xxiv).

Our approach is probably best expressed by Marcus and Fischer, who, writing about anthropology, argued that the social sciences have reached an "ethnographic moment" that signals a change in views of the nature of social research. This moment is concurrent with an "experimental moment" in anthropology which "marked the practical suspension of its grand nineteenth century vision of a science of man." The root of both moments is an "intense concern" with the "way social reality is presented" and "the acutely felt problem of description" (Marcus and Fischer 1986: 165). In response to these concerns, the authors argue:

> The only way to an accurate view and confident knowledge of the
> world is through a sophisticated epistemology that takes full
> account of intractable contradiction, paradox, irony, and uncer-
> tainty in the explanation of human activities. This seems to be the
> spirit of the developing responses across disciplines to what we
> described as a contemporary crisis of representation. (14–15)

As a result, there has been a "shift in stress from behavior and social structure, undergirded by the goal of a 'natural science of society,' to meanings, symbols, and language, and to a renewed recognition, central to the human sciences, that social life must fundamentally be conceived as the negotiation of meanings" (26).

Our use of oral history in this book is clearly not that of an oral historian, but we share the concern with being representative of people's lives. Further, whatever disagreements oral historians have with us, we believe they will share our belief that our work is to foster people becoming moral participants in their culture. As Freire writes: "We need to be subjects of history, even if we cannot totally stop being objects of history. . . . As active participants and real subjects, we can make history only when we are continually critical of our very lives" (1985: 199).

The virtues that the communities and schools discussed in this book created in their recollections are both historical and current. They are constructing with us a view of the past that has relevance to the present, including how we think about educational reform. Yet, for us, these accounts are also about the future. When we met with these people and recorded their recollections with the promise of some product that would be available to a wider audience and preserved over time, their accounts were also contributions to the future. This notion of continuity is truly noteworthy and will be discussed further in the final chapter.

Reclaiming and Reconstructing Values: Research Methods

Our study is qualitative in nature (Patton 1992; Goetz and LeCompte 1984). It employs research techniques borrowed from history, oral history, and ethnography. Taken together, the research methodology may best be termed "ethnohistorical" (Precourt 1982). Our interest is in capturing what the peoples of College Park and Rougemont (all place and personal names are pseudonyms) would "recollect" when we asked them about the histories of their schools. We discovered they were telling moral tales. However, this masks the real research process and the experiences that led to this framing of the study. In fact, this study is based on two studies that seemed at the time to be conceptually separate, but were not and are not.

Our original involvement with the school was the result of the newly appointed principal coming to talk with us about how we might create some sort of university–school partnership. He had taken courses at the university and we had become acquainted. He had both altruistic and practical reasons for our original discussions. First, he wanted to be able to serve Cedar Grove School truly well. The school, an inner-city school, was remarkably successful. With 70 percent African-American students, it tied with another school, 70 percent white, for the top test scores among elementary schools in the district. This school broke the low performance stereotype associated with African-Americans so common in the South and in the inner city (Sizemore 1987) The principal, who was white, respected this achievement and wanted to figure out ways to work with the teachers that did not imply that he judged them as "needing improvement." He also clearly did not want to do anything that would "mess this up." It seemed to him that one way to bring some new resources to these able teachers was to create a new link with the universities in the area. He also had some practical interests. He was the fourth principal for the school in three years. The personnel manager for the district joked when giving him the post that he was being sent to the "graveyard of principals." Indeed, the school had a powerful, white-dominated Parents and Teachers Association and a powerful (60 percent) African-American teaching staff. They had repeatedly "ejected" (as one parent put it) principals who did not understand or respect what was going on with the school.

The school, while majority African-American, was jealously guarded by College Park, the white community in which the school was located. It was their traditional neighborhood school and they were still proud of it. They saw it as a central institution for their affluent community's survival in the inner city. They sent their children to the public elementary school, and promptly withdrew them from the public schools for middle and high school. The white community's promotion and defense of the school was legendary in Treyburn, the city in which Cedar Grove and College Park are located. They were reputed to have a "direct, white line to the school board," in the words of an African-American we interviewed. As we will discuss in some detail, there were historical reasons for such attachment to the school. The new principal, Mr. Michaels, understandably did not want to be the next principal to be "ejected." Practically, he had to find a way to demonstrate his leadership, avoid damaging the high levels of achievement, and satisfy the white community and the African-American and white teachers. In the end, he came up with a number of initiatives to accomplish his successful walk on this tightrope.

In collaboration with us, he designed his first initiative: doing an oral history of the school. It seemed a way to celebrate the school, allow him to learn more about the school and community, and to establish the school–university link. We were well aware that such a project was not threat free. Learning one's history may bring back things that you want forgotten. Mr. Michaels was also clear that the history could not deny the history of the African-American community who attended Cedar Grove School and whose Rougement School had been closed during desegregation.

We started the oral history project in the Fall of 1987. Our explicit agreement was that in exchange for doing an oral history of the school and writing a documentary and celebratory history, the research team would have the right to use the data for professional research and writing. We also designed the project, as we will discuss in chapter 3, to include students from the fourth- and fifth-grade Junior Historians Club. We helped the students design a interview guide that was of interest to them, and, with the help of the PTA, the students arranged and conducted interviews. Our interview guide was less concerned with dress codes and lunch menus than was the students', and more concerned with eliciting names of people, descriptions of classes and the school, curricula, and the community. We wanted to generate all the remembrances of the schools that we could. In the course of two years of data collection, we interviewed more than seventy people: current and former teachers, principals, students, and parents of both schools. They included people who had attended the schools as early as 1924 and teachers who had taught them as well. We talked with people who had lived in the communities in the 1910s. We talked to current teachers and parents, and so on. We used a snowball sampling design, asking each person who else we should interview. We also took people who walked in off the street and offered to be interviewed and people we met as we moved around the town in the course of our private lives.

We sought out more traditional historical sources as well. Guided by Butchart's *Local Schools* (1976), we searched widely for documentary evidence. At Cedar Grove School we found a wealth of documents covering much of the school's history. The PTA had, since the 1920s, compiled scrapbooks of memos, letters, photographs, newspaper articles, and other archival materials concerning the school. We had access to scrapbooks from the 1920s, 1930s, 1940s, and the 1960s. There were minutes of the PTA meetings from the 1920s and 1930s. We examined Board of Education minutes from 1915 through the present. We made repeated forays into the Southern Historical Collection at the University of North Carolina and into the public library collections in Treyburn. Interviewees also lent us their personal documents. At Rougemont School we were less fortunate. While we searched all the records above for materials and found some, the legacy of segregation and racism meant that materials were scarce. Further, after the school closed in 1975, much of the documentary data was either destroyed or lost. We were able to peruse church records in Rougemont, had the advantage of a history of churches prepared by a Rougemont resident, and found some references in the Board of Education minutes.

In addition to the oral history and historical studies we had ethnographic studies. This was due in part to the research team having more members drawn from sociology and anthropology of education than from history of education. We kept ongoing field notes of our interactions in and with the community during the oral history project. These enabled us to contextualize the history in the ways we will do in this book. We had regular research-team meetings to interpret these data, and wrote a series of professional papers that melded our developing historical understanding with our interpretations of the cultures of the schools and communities. Moreover, after the two years of historical data collection, and as we were writing the documentary and celebratory history of the schools, we also embarked on what we thought at the time was a separate ethnography of classrooms in Cedar Grove School. For an academic year, the ethnographers (Dwight Rogers, Margaret Terhaar-Yonkers, Reeda Toppin, Jaci Webb, and the authors) spent one day a week in the school. Each of us focused on one or two classrooms, took running notes, and wrote up field notes as soon as possible after the observations. Again, the research team met weekly to review findings and develop preliminary interpretations. These also have led to a series of professional papers and publications. As it turns out, this year also gave us important data on the effects of the written history of the school and a school play written and produced from the written history, and allowed us more fully to contextualize the historical study for our purposes here.

We had several mechanisms by which we could corroborate our findings which would in some qualitative studies be seen as indicators that our story is representative. Yet we argue that studies such as ours have few facts that can be confirmed through triangulation or member checks. Instead, what we have is a constructed tale or set of tales. The tales are constructed by those who talked to us, by ourselves, and by the mechanisms we used to check out our findings. Instead of insuring validity, our feedback mechanisms fed the process of social construction. Each was simply another scene for negotiation and for meaning-making. Reframed in this manner, we can see each interview as a cultural performance rather than a recitation of historical fact. People in our study saw "history" as something apart from them and apart even from those they knew in the past. When pondering the schools' pasts, they did not see their memories as part of "history." They felt that they did not "know any history" of the schools to tell us. These people saw their memories as "stories" rather than as history. Moreover, in many cases they also portrayed the schools' pasts as unified morality tales rather than as a collection of isolated facts or fragments. The interviewee was offering a story or set of stories that was their contribution to the larger effort of the oral history project. Each interviewee was creating a view of the schools' histories that promoted some values and ignored others. The interviewer was part of this process also, constructing with the interviewee the tale by the questions asked, the sentiments shared, and nonverbal cues, and often even by providing additional information. The interviewees, we now understand, were creating moral tales that, through being shared with us, would be carried into the wider discourse within and beyond the communities. They used the past as part of making a present (in the interview) moral view that would be carried into the future. It took us a long time to understand this. This is the essential lesson of this book. Everyday people have a conception of morality that encompasses and critiques a millennium of intellectuals' work. While few of them could articulate either the oratorical or the philosophical idea, their practical understanding of how to socially construct virtue goes a long way toward dereifying these ideas.

Our other venues for social construction included weekly meetings with the principal, our day-long ethnographic participant observations in classrooms, regular meetings with the advisory boards to each study, periodic faculty meeting reports, and informal conversations with teachers, community members, parents, and students, past and present, over the course of four years. Our research-team meetings should also be understood as meaning-making enterprises. Virtue was being negotiated and constructed throughout these processes, and we were partisans in its construction. We had our own, varied views that are now intermixed in the chapters that follow.

We also had more dramatic moments of' meaning-making. In March 1988, we shared some of our preliminary findings in an evening program for the PTA of Cedar Grove School. People from both Rougemont and College Park attended. This led to a series of informal conversations to help us "get it right." During the summer of 1989, we wrote a ninety-page documentary and celebratory history of the two schools. This was read by a set of readers selected by the principal representing both communities, and comments were fed back to us. The final version was printed in the autumn of 1989, and elicited sufficient comments for the principal to issue an errata sheet to be included in each copy. Social construction clearly did not end with the written product. The principal decided to go one step further and, with a grant from the local arts council, hired a playwright to script and produce a play for the children to perform, based on the history. The play was performed by the students and several members of the Rougemont and College Park communities in January 1990. The play was attended by more than six hundred people. This was impressive, since Cedar Grove School had some three hundred students and twelve staff. This was a powerful event we will return to in the final chapter, and one more opportunity for the social construction of virtue that led to a number of discussions with staff, parents, and community members. We continued to work with the school through 1989–1990, mostly in our capacity as ethnographers. During 1990–1991, we met occasionally with individual staff members and the principal, and conducted two faculty meetings reviewing the results of classroom ethnographies.

An interesting, and sometimes perplexing, component of our study was *Good Morning, Miss Dove*, written by Francis Gray Patton in 1947. Patton depicts the life of a teacher, Miss Dove, and her moral influence on students, teachers, and the community. Stern, strong willed, and most traditional, Miss Dove was the archetype of the school teacher during the postwar period. Cedar Grove School, with good reason, believed that Miss Dove was modeled after a former teacher at the school. The "real" Miss Dove, whom we will call Mrs. Gregory, was the moral icon of the school, but the attribution concerning the accuracy of the book was contested. We were careful not to lead our interviewees to talk about Miss Dove or Mrs. Gregory, letting them introduce the subject if they wished, and those who were aware of the connection almost always did. As we will discuss in chapter 5, *Good Morning, Miss Dove* was more than simply a written account. With it, the Cedar Grove School and the College Park community had a cultural artifact that was more concrete than their memories and in many ways more reliable, fiction or not. While our interviewees saw their memories fading with time, the book provided "hard copy." At times, it was difficult to distinguish whether we were being told about the book, the school, or some combination of both. In chapter 5, we will offer an interpretation of the meaning of this book for Cedar Grove School and offer a text for Rougemont School.

While Rougemont School did not have a book written about it, the accounts of the school did offer a number of moral icons that rivaled Mrs. Gregory, if not Miss Dove. These social constructions were significant parts of the moral tales of the schools. In this book, we will treat the accounts of the moral icons as "emblematic narratives." As Peacock argues, a life history is a "collective, public structure" organized around "making history" (1984: 95). Quinn and Holland (1987) see life histories as both constituting a culture and revealing the cultural models people use to construct their social lives. These teachers, regardless of the schools they taught in, were entrusted with sets of virtues that symbolized those of the community. People "recollected" them in the process of collecting the oral histories of the two schools. Let us be clear here, for the point is central to this book. The paragons of virtue that each school and community created for us may or may not in real life have had the virtues assigned to them. We suspect there are good bases for the portrayals, but that is not the point. The point is that the virtues and the emblematic narratives were constructed in 1987–1989, long after the teachers had retired from teaching. Further, the accounts are constructed with some imagined audiences in mind, and thus are fashioned in some respects for the performance of the remembrance for the interviewer, the school community, and even education as a discipline. As Vansina argues, such remembrances are about both the specific thing being remembered and a generalized sense of all such things experienced throughout life:

> It [a remembered observation] usually translates an opinion also held by the community, whether the facts substantiate it or not. Therefore actual statements about situations or trends need not in fact relate to actual events or observations. Often they derive from generalizations made by contemporaries or later generations. Such data testify then to opinions and values held, to mentalities, and that is their value, not as testimony of fact. (1985: 31)

We treat the accounts of the schools and the emblematic narratives of virtue in this manner. Virtue is a social construction for the people of these communities that speaks to now and the future as well as then.

Discussions of research methods in most studies make it appear that the study being authored was the only one considered and that the process of moving from a set of data to a book was not problematic. We cannot speak for others, but this was hardly the case for us. Indeed, we have struggled through a series of book ideas. In each case, the book idea failed because of what we have made the central thesis of this book. Faced with a mass of seeming historical data, we continually conceptualized a book about "the way it was" only to be thwarted by our understanding that we did not quite have it the way it was. We had what they and we constructed. For books concerned with the facts of history or cultures, this was a problem. For this book, however, our socially constructed tales are our strengths.

There are problems with our research methods. Clearly, we did not anticipate this book when we started, or we would have more carefully tracked the complete negotiation process, including our own parts in it. Second, while we had a multiracial research team of men and women, we cannot approach what African-Americans could have achieved. We look at the account of Emilie Siddle-Walker (1993) with envy. Finally, we ritually abuse ourselves with the complaints that we should have been smarter, more diligent, more careful, and so on. Even with these problems, however, we believe that this study has much to offer the ongoing discourse on education.

Critique and Construction

In the following chapters, we will continue our engagement in the two projects of the sociology of knowledge, the critique of ideas and the construction of possibilities found in everyday life. In chapter 2, we will explore the modern orators and philosophers. Our intent is not to be exhaustive, for this would be an endless task, but rather to concentrate on a few popular favorites in education. To that end, we will examine Mortimer Adler, Allan Bloom, and E. D. Hirsch as recent exemplars of the oratorical idea, and Dewey as a modern philosopher. We will explore and critique their ideas as well as the opposition between them today.

In chapter 3 we will give our account of Cedar Grove School's social construction of virtue. First, We will recount the oral history of the school and how people portrayed the school. Then we will turn to Cedar Grove School's paragon of virtue, the real Miss Dove, and explore what virtues they were constructing as emblematic of their moral beliefs. We will also identify when oratorical and philosophical ideas penetrate the moral tales, revealing that they are a small, yet not incidental, part of the social construction of virtue for Cedar Grove School.

The community of Rougemont portrayed their history rather differently. They were segregated from the white community and Cedar Grove School, which was but a few blocks away. They were also isolated from the more influential African-American communities in Treyburn. They both suffered from segregation and took advantage of it to invent their own social institutions. Rougemont offered not one but many emblematic narratives of virtue, in itself a revealing characteristic. In chapter 4 we will identify the virtues being socially constructed and the penetrations of oratorical and philosophical ideas in their moral tales about the school.

In chapter 5 we will revisit the orators' ideas about "great books" and philosophers' notions about the meaning of texts in ways of developing a different theory about the power of narrative. Since Cedar Grove School had *Good Morning, Miss Dove*, this is not an academic enterprise but an exploration of the impact this text had on the social construction of virtue. Rougemont had no book written about them, but we think it is worth speculating about what such a book might teach us about the social construction of virtue in the education of African-Americans. *Mary*, by Mary Mebane, is our offering to this discourse. This autobiography is located temporally and geographically near to Rougemont and is the story of a girl's struggle to lead a moral life through her school years. While it would not be taught in an orator's great books course, *Mary* suggests a way to view education that productively uses the opposition of the oratorical and philosophical ideas. Moreover, both books demonstrate the power of narrative in the construction of morality and virtue.

We will begin the final chapter by returning to the stories of Cedar Grove and Rougemont Schools. We first look at the effects of school desegregation on these schools and what this meant for continuing moral discourse for these communities. In many ways, both communities experienced a tragic loss, even though Rougemont School's closing was more devastating to its community. We then move to 1990, when a play based on the oral history was produced by the desegregated Cedar Grove School. The play and its effects suggest ways for us to work at the reform of education that do not entail the reification of ideas and that allow us to reclaim education as a moral enterprise. This leads us to a critique of educational policy and reform—and to suggest some possibilities for reclaiming moral life with schools.

2

Ideas That Bind and Blind

The American mind has been much lamented in recent years (Bloom 1987; 1988; 1990). Seemingly gone is the belief that the American mind is superior to other minds in particular ways. Americans used to believe that our minds were especially distinctive in innovativeness and initiative. We had a pioneer spirit and a "can do" mentality. Certainly, this American mind was somewhat anti-intellectual: It wanted less to consider an idea than to do something with it. It also was exceedingly ethnocentric. The American way of thinking was the best way. We were the fittest. We were more than surviving. We were surpassing the achievements of the old world and far ahead of the developing, or "third," world.

Given the recent developments in Eastern Europe and the subsequent spawning of capitalism and democracy in many parts of the world, the American mind should be even further vindicated. Our ideas and ways are ever more emulated. But the American mind does not believe this. It believes that the United States is in decline. It attributes this decline largely to our educational system, although in due course the family, religion, the government, and the economy all get their share of the blame.

In education, people point to "golden years," the 1950s or the 1920s or the 1960s, depending on who is being nostalgic. In those "golden years," students were interested in learning, teachers enforced discipline, parents supported the teachers, and so on. Now, though, these things are believed not to be true characterizations of schools, in part because people live and create a more complex world than we wish were the case and wish to remember. Education in America has always been a source of controversy and a field on which the contests of diversity in ethnicity, religion, race, gender, and status have been played. The "golden years" were never so glittery as they seem now—now that we believe we are in decline.

Our nostalgia, and our experiences with the contests over diversity, make the years in which only elite young men received higher education, or when each ethnic group or race or neighborhood had its own school, or whatever was our personal experience in school, seem better than whatever is happening now. Almost to a person, education was better then than it is now, regardless of when was "then."

This is the essence of our belief in our decline and of the role education has played in it. Yet from where does this nostalgia and the belief in decline come? It comes from a long-standing value conflict. Americans have seen educational reforms again and again (Cuban 1990), and they now have a cynical perspective that is hard to shake. Yet, cynical or not, Americans seem to have little understanding that the recycling of reform and our cynicism is the consequence of our ideas.

In the Mind?

There are those who would say that decline is more objective than we have portrayed it as being here—it is not just in the mind! Certainly, we can point to more "objective" indicators such as a decline in economic power or in inventions of new technology or other indicators. Yet the point is just that. These are just indicators, which require minds to assign meaning to them. Moreover, only in minds can such abstractions as "national decline" be understood or created. Only with our minds can we conceptualize how it is that education has failed us.

What's in a mind? Ideas. Ideas about the nature of things, about their importance and significance, and about how ideas relate to each other. We can alternatively refer to ideas as concepts or constructs or notions. Indeed, these words lead us to be cautious about the value of ideas. Ideas are made up by minds, and some ideas are believed to be of more lasting value than others. Contrasting concept with notion portrays this well. Some are explicitly more temporal or experimental: constructs, for example. In the end, though, ideas will do as the answer to the question, What's in a mind?

The idea that we are in decline has been around for a long time. In every epoch, some minds see decline as an idea that characterizes the state of society. When ideas have champions, however, who spread this idea and persuade others of its accuracy, an idea can become a belief, garnering a new significance as it is assumed to be true. Beliefs can become ideologies when justifications are constructed and treated as convincing or definitive. The belief in America's decline is just that: a belief that is becoming increasingly shared. The danger is that this belief will become an ideology, and those who have argued that education is to blame for America's decline play an important role in creating convincing justifications for an ideology. In our society, to posit a cause for something is a powerful justification for the salience of the something. To convincingly portray educational failure as a cause of national decline is to undercut the debate over whether we are in national decline in favor of who or what is to be blamed. In the "can do" American mind, the solution is to deal first with the supposed cause. As a result, the issue of national decline becomes taken for granted, as does the link between education and national decline. Beliefs easily become ideologies with such conceptual turns.

This still begs the question, From whence do ideas and beliefs come? In important ways, they come from culture. Culture provides us with assumptions, ways of thinking, and ways of doing things. But this image is much too static. It is better said that ideas and beliefs come from being cultural actors in the context of existing cultural discourse. Rather than the culture being transmitted to people and people being socialized to it, the cultural discourse and action is going on around people, and people use what they get from this discourse and action as the material for them to create ideas and actions. In this they both play out their culture and create anew from the base their culture gives them (Giddens 1979).

In cultural discourse and action, all actors are not equal. Some have more power, legal and otherwise, to control the beliefs and actions of others. Further, some have more status than others as credible spokes-people. The former are largely the politically influential, in and out of government. The latter are the intellectuals. The belief in decline and education's responsibility for it has been created and promulgated by elements of both groups, for in this, as in all human action, diversity is the rule, not the exception. In America, not all politicians believe the nation is in decline and not all intellectuals are busy promoting this belief and justifying it by blaming education. Indeed, this is one purpose of this book. Our tactic is to examine the case made by politicians and intellectuals for this belief and to look at its basis. To us, the authors of the belief in national decline due to the failure of education protest too much. They propose that we follow their lead to remedy this unfortunate state of affairs. We propose that it was following their lead that created the belief in decline in the first place. Their ideas both bind and blind Americans; they constitute a cultural trap difficult to escape.

The Pinnacle Is Past

The idea that we are not at the pinnacle of the world has many proponents, and their arguments are compelling. It is clearly true that our standing vis-á-vis the rest of the world is changing and that other nations are proving to be able competitors for the title of "world leader." Paul Kennedy sees the threat as one of losing our position at the pinnacle. He writes of the lessons of history:

To remain number one, the country concerned needs not only adequate and efficient armed forces; it also needs a flourishing economic base, productive and modern manufacturing, efficient plant and infrastructure, an enormous commitment to education at all levels, and a healthy, properly nourished, and decently housed population whose potential talents and energies are not sapped by deprivation. (Kennedy 1989: 38)

Kennedy's analysis should give us cause for concern. The United States has problems in each of these areas. Yet what is of most concern is how Kennedy has phrased the essential question. The title of this article is "Can the U.S. Remain Number One?" He is more judicious than the other intellectuals we will discuss, but, even for him, we achieved the pinnacle sometime in the past.

The idea that the pinnacle is past is even more prominent in those who wish to argue that the reason for national decline falls more squarely, although not exclusively, on education. The American public knows these authors well: Mortimer Adler, Allan Bloom, and E. D. Hirsch. Their works have been exceedingly popular. People of seemingly all walks of life have read or read about or have something to say about their ideas. In many ways, it is heartening to know that the United States citizenry would so avidly take to books about education.

Mortimer Adler's book, *The Paideia Proposal* (1982), is in many ways the keystone work of a distinguished career devoted to education. He worked most closely with Robert Hutchins at the University of Chicago, and with him championed the Great Books curriculum at the University of Chicago. This, in turn, led to editing a series of Great Books for *Encyclopaedia Britannica* and to more than a half-century of thought and writing on education.

In *The Paideia Proposal*, Adler argues, quoting Hutchins, "The best education for the best is the best education for all" (7). He addressed this treatise to a range of constituencies and their concerns about the fixture of the schools and of the nation, arguing that the time was ripe to deliver on the promise of democracy by embracing an educational system that has "the same objectives for all" (15) and "the same course of study for all" (21). This has been a popular work and has led to numerous schools attempting the proposal. Yet, in many ways, this book is the keystone of Adler's life's work of bringing elitist nature of the oratorical idea to a modern fruition.

A selection of his writings has been edited by Geraldine Van Doren (*Reforming Education: The Opening of the American Mind* [1990]). These works reveal Adler's commitment to the oratorical idea and his depth of understanding of this tradition. In this work, we also see that Adler is somewhat unlike Bloom and Hirsch in his understanding of the pinnacle being past. Adler wishes not to be associated with Bloom in particular on many counts. He argues that Bloom is an elitist, employs a "doctrinal style" (xxiii) in his teaching of the Great Books, and misdiagnoses the causes of relativism and skepticism about moral philosophy. He is clear that Bloom's locating of the latter causes in the 1960s is a mistake, for Adler wrote of the same malaise in the 1930s and 1940s. For Adler, the real cause is philosophical positivism and the relativism of sociology and cultural anthropology which he argues pre-dates the arrival of Nietzsche, who Bloom sees as one of the major causes, on the American scene. For Adler, the pinnacle of our society is much further in the past (around the turn of the century) than it is for Bloom or Hirsch, even if the situation is understood substantially in the same ways. Adler wrote in 1939 what Bloom echoes today. He argues that students "do not take *any* moral issues seriously. . . . Their only principle is that there are no moral principles at all" (7). He goes on to argue, "We are losing our moral principles" (20).

Adler's position is that of a classic humanist, even though he accommodates the philosophical idea considerably in *The Paideia Proposal*. He has consistently argued that there are "absolute and universal principles" (1990: 54) on which to base education:

I say the ends of education, the ends men should seek, are always and everywhere the same. They are absolute in the sense that they are not relative to time and place, to individual differences and the variety of cultures. They are universal in the sense that they are invariable and without exception. (1990: 57)

He goes on to argue that there are two ends to education: proximate and ultimate. He writes:

The proximate ends of education are the moral and intellectual virtues. . . . The ultimate end of education is happiness or a good human life, a life enriched by the possession of every kind of good, by the enjoyment of every type of satisfaction. (1990: 60)

His emphasis on virtue locates him quite close to Bloom, while his antipathy to Dewey he shares with both Bloom and Hirsch. In 1939, he critiqued *Democracy and the Curriculum*, a publication of the John Dewey Society:

They want freedom to such an extent that they wish to be rid of a curriculum as a prescribed course of study. Because it is prescribed, because it expresses the authority of teachers imposed upon students, because it makes the teacher and student unequal, it is regarded as undemocratic—as if democracy did not depend, as does every good social order, on leaders and followers, rulers with authority and subjects, not submissive, but well ruled. Throughout their writings they confuse authority, which is nothing more than the voice of reason, with autocracy, which is the violent imposition of a will by force; they confuse discipline with regimentation; they convert the equality of human beings as persons, sharing in a common nature and a common end, into an equality of individuals, despite the differences in their capacities and their merits. This is not the liberty and equality which constitute democracy as the social order in which popular sovereignty is most fully realized because, through the discipline of reason, men have the authority to govern themselves and use the freedom of self-government. This is the romantic libertinism and egalitarianism of Rousseau. (49)

While this shows the degree to which the modern orators such as Adler share a critique of the philosophical idea, it is even more revealing of Adler's thinking about the primacy of reason and knowledge in determining virtue. It is through reason that Americans have achieved the "most fully realized" democracy—not through revolution, voting, the Bill of Rights, or other historical events.

Adler argues that reason is the basis of moral thought and, consequently, virtue. The primacy of reason in determining values results from its basis in tradition. As Adler writes, "moral thinking commands assent to its conclusions because they are drawn from self-evident first-principles traditionally known as natural moral law" (1990: 15). He sees this as a direct contradiction to Dewey and what he calls "pragmatic liberalism" which has encouraged "familiar denials—of the objectivity of moral standards, of the rationality of men, of any method for answering questions except that of empirical science." These denials, he asserts, are the result of "corruption" that begins in the public schools that are "Deweyized" and continues through to the university. This corruption is of a "false philosophy, the destructive philosophy of positivism" (16–17). This is Adler's contribution to the cultural trap about education. He re-creates the dichotomy between the orators and the philosophers and argues that the two positions are mutually exclusive and contradictory. One cannot be true if the other is. We will return to this problem repeatedly, for it is essential to understanding our approach to the social construction of virtue. For Adler, a contradiction can be resolved only by revealing or proving one side to be true and the other false. In this he replicates the opposition of the oratorical and philosophical ideas, forcing us to take sides, as we have done throughout Western history. Yet contradictions can be resolved in other ways, as both Socrates and Dewey acknowledge with the concept of the dialectic, in which seeming contradictions yield a new synthesis. Socrates and Dewey (and Hegel and Marx) conceive of the dialectical process as progress, resolving the contradictions of history to face those of the current epoch. There are problems with this understanding, leaving us to argue in this book that, rather than synthesize the oratorical and philosophical ideas into a new thesis or argue for one over the other, we should instead try to expand the field of participants in the moral discourse about education in our society.

Given Adler's position on the evils of positivism and progressivism and correctness of "natural moral law" based in tradition, one can see why he puts his faith in a program of studies based on the Great Books. He argues that this is "the ideal minimum" (325) for a curriculum. For the early grades "junior great books" are recommended, leading to more difficult books and ultimately a lifetime of reading and rereading them. Yet we must be clear that Adler does not want these books read as history. He and Hirsch share an interest in what ideas these historical works convey:

> The educational purpose of the great books program is not to study western civilization. Its aim is not to acquire knowledge of historical facts. It is rather to understand the great ideas. (1990: xxxii)

There are "no better books" (327) for this, he argues, because:

> by everyone's admission they are the repository of whatever insight, understanding, and wisdom Western man has so far accumulated. By everyone's admission they set forth the ideas, the problems, the principles, and subject matters of the arts and sciences, which made our culture what it is. (1990: 327)

We argue that he is overstating when he resorts to the phrase "by everyone's admission." Indeed, he uses this justification after he has tried to respond to the criticisms that others have made of the Great Books program. The objections he addresses include how the books are selected, the paucity of modern works and works from other cultures on the list of Great Books, the need to master current thought also, the dogmatic imposition of a single philosophy via the program, the existence of great errors as well as great ideas in the books, the existence of better ways of studying the books, and the corollary claim of Great Books proponents that they have the best program. Clearly, the Great Books are not "by everyone's admission" what the modern orators claim them to be.

Adler is also careful not to promise that the Great Books will solve all the ills of education and society by themselves, but rather that they offer the "best opportunity" (328). He does claim two benefits rather clearly—one for the individual and one for our culture. For the individual, the great ideas contained in the Great Books are fundamental to how someone needs to think today:

> They are the ideas with which any individual must think about his own life and the world in which he lives. They are the problems which any society must face. They are the subject matters which represent the things worth inquiring into and learning about, certainly for anyone who wishes to understand a little about the nature of the world, of society, and of himself. (1990: 328–9)

Here we see expressed the dogmatism, absolutism, and universalism of the oratorical idea. The great works of the past are fully sufficient to guide our actions today and in the fixture. There are no "new" problems, ideas, or social arrangements that are worthy. The "old" ideas "must" be used to understand current affairs. There is, of course, a reason for this. Like all orators, Adler's primary interest is in containing our culture and transmitting it with integrity, for it is "worth saving from dissipation and neglect" (1990: 328).

> To the extent that the great books constitute the monuments of our culture, the substance of our intellectual tradition, the more individuals who in any degree actually possess some of the culture through the reading and discussion of the great books, the more favorable are the conditions for its transmission and progress. (1990: 328)

However, many argue that the Great Books and the canon of readings taught in English departments convey a selective view of what our culture is. Women and minorities are woefully underrepresented, and the criteria used by Adler and others are arbitrary and self-serving. They are arbitrary and self-serving in that "the test of time" (Adler 1990: 333) is a test devised by those whose expertise and status is based on having studied them extensively. It has been the orators throughout history who have been working to ensure that these works are seen as classics and required readings. The underrepresentation of women and minority authors is justified by Adler (1990: 334) as a "fact" rather than a judgment: "In the Western tradition until the nineteenth century, there simply were no great books written by women, blacks or non-Europeans." The controversy over what is to constitute the canon in college and university English departments reveals that even among the most learned in our society there is disagreement about what should be included. However, in some cases this is infighting among orators, not a challenge to the oratorical idea itself. The philosophers who engage in this debate are more likely to argue that our heritage is not as uniform as proposed by the orators, and suggest including works that represent the real diversity of our heritage. Yet here we see the elitism of both ideas. The decision about what is great is to be made by intellectuals. In this way, both orators and philosophers are self-serving. What they miss, and what we will return to repeatedly in this book, is the fact that the key cultural construction in all this debate about educational ideas occurs in deliberating what should be included. Both orators and philosophers want the citizenry to be pawns of their culture, to be left to read and be taught the Great Books rather than to participate in the decisions about what should be part of our culture. By requiring that the Great Books be always beyond the readers initial level of understanding, Adler ensures that they are pawns of the teacher, but more importantly he also ensures that the Great Books do not speak to the world the reader currently lives in without the mediation of intellectuals.

Adler does have a participation scheme for students. It is reserved to a particular teaching method, the seminar. This is actually one of Adler's accommodations of the philosophical idea. In fact, we see two accommodations here. First is the allowance of critique and critical thinking as one of the goals of education. Adler repeatedly argues that the study of Great Books enables the development of the mind: "Our task in reading and discussing them must, therefore, be to judge for ourselves where the truth lies and by the development of our critical faculties to make up our own minds on most basic issues" (1990: 323). Adler, of course, is not the first orator to make this accommodation. Kimball (1986) reveals that this was a common accommodation of the Renaissance humanists as they recaptured the ancient tradition. Today we see this accommodation rather commonly among modern orators. But we must also put this into the larger context of Adler's argument. Critique has its limits—it must serve the ultimate goal of transmitting our cultural heritage.

The second accommodation that Adler makes to the philosophical idea concerns how to teach. The traditional methods of instruction in rhetoric involved recitations, declamations, and disputations (Kimball 1986: 155). The seminar method, as well as lectures and laboratory studies, came to America from the German universities in the late nineteenth century and were associated with the development of the philosophical idea, especially experimental science. Adler himself attributes the seminar method to Socrates. He advocates an emphasis on the teacher asking questions that should be balanced with telling the students what they should have attended to in their reading and thinking. Here we see where Adler departs from the philosophical idea and from Socrates, who emphasized a more freewheeling search for truths. Adler explains the purpose of his emphasis on teacher-declarative speech in seminars as "always for the purpose of leading up to the critical questions that the student must try to answer" (1990: 303). The oratorical dogmatism is evident in his use of the seminar. To be fair, his *Paideia Proposal* represents an even broader accommodation in incorporating the study of the "organized knowledge" of the disciplines via didactic instruction, the "development of intellectual skills" (reading, writing, etc.) via coaching and practice, and the "enlarged understanding of ideas and values" via Socratic questioning about books and works of art and active participation in the arts (1982: 23). This accommodation is interesting because it replicates the historical superiority accorded oratorical studies, but it does reveal Adler's understanding that the philosophical idea is not going away. He works largely to contain it in this accommodation.

The late Allan Bloom's *The Closing of the American Mind: How Higher Education Has Failed Democracy and Impoverished Today's Students* is a masterful work, revealing his deep knowledge of classical works and of elite university students. He has carefully thought through what he sees as the failure of education. One should be careful, though, in drawing conclusions about universities and their failures. Bloom specifies his limits to be "the kind of young persons who populate the twenty or thirty best universities" (22). Moreover, his treatment of the failure of universities is more a personal lament and diatribe against changes in what counts as knowledge in this century, especially in the aftermath of 1960s and 1970s campus rebellions. His initial thesis is better understood as what is wrong with the elite youth of our country, for this is what he discusses in part 1 of the book.

Understood this way, he is concerned that our youth are improperly socialized in the home and in primary and secondary school and that this is not remedied by universities. The second part of the book is his lament of the changes in the knowledge base, especially the derogation of "reason" as the prime vehicle for virtue. In part 3 he turns to the university, chastising it for its behavior during the 1960s and 1970s even as he explains that the derogation of reason was the ultimate and long preceding cause.

Bloom is clear as to cause and the disease. Openness and cultural relativism have led our youth to no longer be concerned with moral virtue, reason, and natural rights:

> The recent education of openness has rejected all that. It pays no attention to natural rights or the historical origins of our regime, which are now thought to have been essentially flawed and regressive. It is progressive and forward-looking. It does not demand fundamental agreement or abandonment of old or new beliefs in favor of the natural ones. It is open to all kinds of men, all kinds of life-styles, all ideologies. There is no enemy other than the man who is not open to everything. But when there are no shared goals or vision of the public good, is the social contract any longer possible? (27)

He sees our society lurching toward an "indiscriminate freedom" that is "exempt from legitimate social and political regulation only by contracting the claims to moral and political knowledge" (28). Knowledge in such a society loses its status and becomes relativized as opinion, according to Bloom. Bloom reveals relativism's long intellectual history but attributes its most disastrous effects to the 1960s, when universities faced challenges from minorities and women by "hastening to fold up their tents'"; required courses were dropped and "doing your own thing" became the rule (321). Yet the violation, to Bloom, is twofold. Not only did universities surrender their authority and responsibility, but they also embraced a form of knowledge that is unconscionable—the social sciences. Of course, the social sciences were on the scene long before the 1960s, but we take Bloom's complaint to be the new popularity enjoyed by these "young" disciplines during and after the 1960s. No longer were the classics, and especially philosophy, seen as necessary to the education and lives of young people.

The social sciences, and indeed the natural sciences, are not acceptable to Bloom because they are relativistic. Reason is not absolute as it is in his philosophy. These disciplines find that in different situations similar events have different meanings. Moreover, the comparison of different cultures show they accomplish rather different things, and, for example, it is difficult to show that Western culture would better resolve the issues faced by Trobriand Islanders (Malinowski 1922) than the culture they already had, even though the anthropologist would have been much relieved by being in a culturally familiar situation. Yet it is not just the social sciences (and by implication the natural sciences, which also proceed from the relativistic framework of cause and effect) that Bloom wishes to indict. He sees that it was "the German connection" with American thought, especially Kant, Goethe, Nietzsche, and Weber. In part, Bloom's objection is to the influence of the Left on the university, Marx with his heirs and reconstructionists, but this is far too simplistic. Indeed, it is clear that Bloom has high regard for Nietzsche and Marx. The former, unfortunately in Bloom's mind, has an analysis of the human condition much like Bloom's view of today's youth. Marx has the saving grace of being a rationalist, believing that a false way of knowing can be revealed through reason, even if it could be overthrown only by revolution. It is the New Left that melded a Nietzsche with Marx, of which he is especially derogatory, for they relativized Marx's absolute.

This is more than sin to Bloom, for relativism negates, for him, the distinction between good and evil, and enfeebles reason from discerning the natural and the virtuous. He writes:

> It is not the immorality of relativism that I find appalling. What is astounding and degrading is the dogmatism with which we accept such relativism, and our easygoing lack of concern about what it means for our lives. (239)

In one sense, this to Bloom is the greatest failing of American society. We no longer believe that we have to make difficult choices, to stand for something, to martyr ourselves for something that we believe is truly vital. He bemoans the emphasis on conflict avoidance, seeing it as an indication that we no longer hold strong beliefs and/or have no faith that we can reason our way to virtuous resolution as opposed to a popular or acceptable one.

It is clear to Bloom that the university has failed—failed in that it did not hold to philosophy as the primary discipline. In part, this is because of the German connection which liberated the natural sciences from philosophy and established the possibility of the social sciences. Bloom argues that this fragmented the unity of knowledge, on the one hand, and, on the other, legitimated reductionist and deterministic thought. From the pinnacle of the 1950s, American universities lost both their vision and their intellectual unity without which they could not withstand the challenges to academic freedom from mass movements. The result was this: "Commitment was understood to be profounder than science, history than nature, the young than the old" (314). Universities responded by dropping course requirements and by establishing new curricula and departments. The result, according to Bloom, was that the students lost the opportunity to understand the "transhistorical" (308) truths taught by the Great Books and philosophers.

It is interesting that Bloom opens his book with a description of what students are now like at elite universities and posits that they have changed, and ends the book by blaming the universities for this change when it is as likely that the nature of students is due to other educational and familial experiences. Nonetheless, Bloom's argument is that the universities have failed to take advantage of the opportunity that a student presents when going to college:

> He had four years to discover himself—a space between the intellectual wasteland he has left behind and the inevitable dreary professional training that awaits him after the baccalaureate. In this short time he must learn that there is a great world beyond the little he knows, experience the exhilaration of it and digest enough of it to sustain himself in the intellectual deserts he is destined to traverse. He must do this, that is, if he is to have hopes of a higher life. (336)

In this Bloom likens the teacher to a "midwife": "No real teacher can doubt that his task is to assist his pupil to fulfill human nature against all the deforming forces of convention and prejudice" (20). But the midwife has given up all pretense to do this, according to Bloom. The students will remain as they come to the university.

Bloom blames "values clarification" in the schools and the family and divorce for the current moral plight of university students. While he mistakes a once-popular book for an implemented educational innovation, it is clear that he is well within the mainstream of moral philosophy. He, and many more who study philosophy, agree that in the absence of strong religious influences there is little that resembles moral reasoning in everyday life. The issue here, of course, is how wedded philosophy is to religion, a belief to which Bloom pays great testimony. In any case, the students that Bloom teaches offer "less soil in which university teaching can take root" (61). Students have lost both their "practice" and "taste" for reading (61), starting in the late 1960s:

> Students cannot imagine that the old literature could teach them anything about the relations they want to have or will be permitted to have. So they are indifferent. (66)

The result is that they have "no recourse whatsoever against conformity" (67). Bloom is clear that students do not have "any notion of the serious life of leisure" (77). Because values are empty for these students, there is little but immediacy and the self-centeredness it implies. While he sees sex as particularly indicative of this, the central issue is that students' "primary preoccupation is themselves" (83). Bloom is eloquent in his characterization of what openness in education has created:

> This indeterminate or open-ended future and lack of binding past means that the souls of young people are in a condition like that of the first men in the state of nature—spiritually unclad, unconnected, isolated, with no inherited or unconditional connection with anything or anyone. They can be anything they want to be, but have no particular reason to want to be anything in particular. (87)

They are "nice" but "not particularly moral or noble" (82).

The second characteristic that Bloom notes in today's students is egalitarianism. Students believe that everyone should be given equal opportunities to learn and to be. They have no strong opinions about making everyone alike as the result of socialization or education. Coupled with egalitarianism is meritocracy, the belief that each should be rewarded according to their individual achievements. Race and gender should not affect how people are rewarded for their achievements. That Bloom should complain about this, of course, is the basis of many of the critiques of this work. Yet Bloom is arguing that the net result is that people feel groundless without a heritage or a "natural" role. Individualism leaves only separateness in its current form. "We are social solitaries" (118), resulting in a "psychology without the *psyche*, i.e., without the soul" (136).

If Bloom is vitriolic about African-Americans and feminism in his critique, it is to his credit that his proposals for improving education are not a direct attack on either's beliefs. Indeed, a criticism of his work is that he provides little guidance at all for how education might be improved. It is true that he is less than sanguine about the prospects:

> It is difficult to imagine that there is either the wherewithal or the energy within the university to constitute or reconstitute the idea of an educated human being and establish a liberal education again. (380)

> One cannot and should not hope for a general reform. The hope is that the embers do not die out. (380)

His pessimism should not be interpreted as indicating he has no program for change. He clearly does. It is true it is a nostalgic program, one that wishes to return to a time when philosophy was the master discipline and when reason was believed to be the key to living a good life. This requires a focus on basic beliefs about the education and knowledge, not on the technical apparatus that so often is the focus of reforms.

Our present educational problems cannot be seriously be attributed to bad administrators, weakness of will, lack of discipline, lack of money, insufficient attention to the three R's, or any of the other common explanations that indicate things will be set aright if we professors would just pull up our socks. All these things are the result of a deep lack of belief in the university's vocation. (312)

To Bloom, the essence of the solution is twofold. First, there must be emphasis on thought, not on research or publication. The problem is fundamentally philosophic, and a good place to start is in "the contemplation of Socrates" (312). For Bloom, thought puts reason at the center, for reason can provide a transhistorical unity to mankind. The use of reason is "the fulfillment of humanity" (292) in that it allows the investigation of "the question, 'What is man?,' in relation to his highest aspirations as opposed to his low and common needs" (21). In Bloom's mind, this enables people to develop shared values, goals, and visions and thus a meaningful social contract. The second part of Bloom's solution is a return to tradition. Tradition, for Bloom, is a basis for future action and includes religion, our nation's founding and originating documents, and great books. Education should be the place where these traditions are examined and where our common culture is wrought via reason. Universities have a special tradition that must be rekindled in order for this to take place: a tradition of rationalism and freedom of thought. In this it should be distinctive not only compared to other educational institutions but also compared to the wider society, especially in regard to demands for relevance or practicality. An essential part of this distinctiveness needs to be a renewed belief in books and the truths they provide. He writes:

Of course, the only serious solution is the one that is almost universally rejected: the good old Great Books approach, in which a liberal education means reading certain generally recognized classic texts, just reading them, letting them dictate what the questions are and the method of approaching them—not forcing them into categories we make up, not treating them as historical products, but trying to read them as their authors wished them to be read. (344)

Bloom is optimistic that such a curriculum will win the minds and interests of the students, feeding "the student's love of truth and passion to lead the good life" (345).

E. D. Hirsch, in his *Cultural Literacy: What Every American Needs to Know* (1987), turns his attention to the educational institutions that are responsible for creating the homogenized students about whom Bloom is so concerned. While Bloom, Adler, and Hirsch share much, it is clear that Hirsch puts much more stock in the recent scientism, especially language research, than does Bloom. In fact, Hirsch uses it to justify the reasonableness of his approach. Moreover, Hirsch is much more sensitive to the charges of elitism, sexism, and racism than is Bloom, and spends considerable effort to refute such charges. However, Hirsch does share with Bloom and Adler the fundamental belief that education is no longer serving the nation's interests and that what is needed is a shared, common body of knowledge.

Hirsch sees waiting until the university years to be much too late, arguing that by the age of thirteen "basic acculturation should largely be completed" (30). Hirsch surely shares Bloom's concern over the effect of relativism, but has focused his critique of education more squarely on educational thought of this century. He dates and characterizes the problem differently. He opens with the observation that what were acceptable literacy levels in the 1950s will not do now. This is because the world requires higher levels than ever, and other countries have surpassed the United States in their levels of literacy. Hirsch sees "high universal literacy" (2) as necessary for greater economic prosperity, social justice, and effective democracy. He asserts:

> During the period 1970–1985 the amount of shared knowledge that we have been able to take for granted in communicating with our fellow citizens has also been declining. More and more of our young people don't know things we used to take for granted. (5)

For him, the implication is clear. Our nation is in jeopardy because of education's failure to impart high levels of cultural literacy.

Historically, Hirsch finds the culprit to be the *Cardinal Principles of Secondary Education* (Commission on the Reorganization of Secondary Education 1918), which, according to Hirsch, rejected the traditional focus on subject matter for a focus on social adjustment, utility, direct application of knowledge, and good citizenship. He has two substantive criticisms of the *Cardinal Principles*. The first concerns educational formalism. In this critique we see Hirsch's scientism. He asserts that an emphasis in the report on the diversity in our society and the individual differences in student performance required reliance on formalism. In this case, formalism involves a focus on the "fundamental processes" (Hirsch 1987: 120) involved in reading, writing, and mathematics and conceives of them as skills that can be developed independently of the content being mastered. His review of recent research leads to another conclusion: that "we cannot treat reading and writing as empty skills, independent of specific knowledge" (8).

Hirsch decries two theoretical developments as especially damaging to establishing a national culture. First, he rejects educational formalism. He argues that research has brought doubts that are any "general or transferable cognitive skills" (60). This, of course, flies in the face of much research in reading, for example, which has emphasized the skills as the building blocks of learning to read. Hirsch proposes that there are severe limits to this theory. In general, he argues that skills are only transferable to similar or analogous configurations of a task. Moreover, skills do not lead to the acquisition of relevant knowledge. It is the other way around: "Once relevant knowledge has been acquired, the skill follows" (61). What is important is the schemata the children have for interpreting words and symbols. To paraphrase Hirsch though we have a bad memory for words, we have a good memory for meaning.

The issue here is how important is the substance of what we already know for that which we will come to know. For Hirsch, it is everything. We use what background knowledge we have to interpret what new information we experience. In his words, schemata not only enable us to recognize symbols, but they also enable a "constructive" process:

> We construct an elaborated model of what the words imply and store that. . . . [W]e always go beyond a text's literal meaning to supply important implications that were not explicitly stated by the words of the text. (39)

The "two-way traffic" between the words read and a person's schemata means that we use background knowledge as a way to interpret the less-than-explicit and/or -complete texts with which we come into contact (53). Schemata then enable both the storing of knowledge so it can be retrieved and the efficient organizing of knowledge so it can be quickly and aptly applied.

His objection to educational formalism is that their focus on generic skills is scientifically unsound and has contributed to the United States' inability to promote universal literacy. As we will discuss, however, Hirsch has some sympathy with the notion of seeking a generic solution. His search has been for generic background knowledge and thus schemata, enabling students to share a high level of literacy.

The second theoretical development that Hirsch finds problematic in the *Cardinal Principles* concerns what he sees as the conjunction of

European romanticism and American pragmatism that John Dewey championed. He argues that the 1918 report "implicitly accepted" romanticism and an attack on rote learning of abstract knowledge and added Dewey's ideas about social utility as an educational purpose (Hirsch 1987: 117). The long-term result of this, Hirsch argues, is today's focus on the educational needs of the child and of society.

Hirsch is clearly more tentative about the effects of this second theory than the first, even though he goes on to link them as "romantic formalism" (121). While noting Dewey's emphasis on the uniqueness of the individual and the use of schools for practical social purposes, he also notes that Dewey was "appalled" at the use of scientism by educational administrators in implementing and institutionalizing progressive theories. Moreover, Hirsch says Dewey assumed high literacy would be the result of implementing his ideas. Hirsch is also careful not to blame Dewey for open schools, indicating that pragmatism was shed in favor of romanticism. In this, Hirsch foreshadows some of our concerns that the history of ideas, even educational ideas, is not identical to the history of education as practiced in the United States. Nonetheless, it is clear that Hirsch lays the blame for the current levels of literacy firmly at the feet of romantic, pragmatic, and formal educational theories. The net result has been a fragmented curriculum.

For Hirsch, decline is based in our inability to create a national language and therefore a national culture. The fragmented curriculum inhibits such developments. His argument follows Gellner (1983). The thesis is that modern nations and their complex economies require widespread literacy: "At the heart of modern nationhood is the teaching of literacy and a common culture through a national system of education" (Hirsch 1987: 73). This requires, on the one hand, a standardized language and, on the other, mass literacy. Hirsch sees our language as having three distinct domains. First is a knowledge of terms and referents "known by literate people everywhere in the world" (75). Here he posits that, regardless of language, there are some words that are shared universally, and these should be promoted via national educational systems. Second is the vocabulary of the English-speaking world that is shared by such nations as Great Britain, New Zealand, India, and so on. Part of this is due to classics in literature and to significant historical developments. Third, the vocabulary of one's nation, derived from literature, history, and customs, completes our language and makes one literate. Significantly, a national language transcends particularistic dialects due to region, class, race, and the like.

Creating a national language is contrived, to be sure, but, to Hirsch, it is essential to stabilizing a culture, which in turn enables the nationalism he regards as essential to economic success. Hirsch expands on these notions in his concept of cultural literacy:

The need for culture is really just another dimension of the need for a language. A nation's language can be regarded as a part of its culture, or conversely, its culture can be regarded as the totality of its language. (1987: 83)

In this, Hirsch sees himself as creating a useful corrective to the theories of Rousseau and Dewey: "an anthropological theory of education" (xv) focusing on "acculturation, the transmission to children of the specific information shared by adults" (xvi). Breaking from Bloom not only in valuing anthropology, he accepts the relativity of cultures and the arbitrary nature of national languages and cultures. The universal, for Hirsch, is the establishment of a nationally shared symbol system. He sees this as necessary to stem the decline of the United States.

Cultural literacy is defined as

the network of information that all competent readers possess. It is the background information, stored in their minds, that enables them to take up a newspaper and read it with an adequate level of comprehension, getting the point, grasping the implications, relating what they need to the unstated context which alone gives meaning to what they read. (2)

Cultural literacy includes knowing the shared conventions for spelling, grammar, and vocabulary of the nation put in the context of associations, referents, and shared meanings that have been historically attached to the vocabulary. He posits that high levels of universal cultural literacy should be the goal of education.

This, of course, is a demanding goal. Hirsch proposes that the place to start is with the curriculum. In this, he wishes to preserve both flexibility and commonality. Even though his emphasis has been on the nation, he does not wish to sacrifice our state and local control of schools. He is in favor of schools sharing a common goal with diversity in how that goal is achieved. His curriculum has two parts: an extensive curriculum and an intensive curriculum.

The extensive curriculum includes traditional literate knowledge which should be taught "as a vivid system of shared associations" (127). Hirsch understands that for more literate people this information is extensive in that it covers a broad range yet is limited in the depth of knowledge about the associations. He argues that this kind of information is essential as preliminary building blocks for children to acquire more detail. This curriculum should be known by all children and be common to all schools in the nation. He argues that this material can be taught in a variety of ways from traditional to progressive. However, Hirsch does essentially see "piling up of information" as the only way to enable students to become culturally literate (xv). Moreover, he points to cross-cultural precedents for memorization as the main vehicle for literacy, and argues that even untraditional schools have not been able to avoid rote learning. In any case, his argument is consistent with traditional curricular thought for determinate knowledge. This information can be fixed and the content expressed in ways that educators can adapt for instruction. It is this part of the curriculum that Hirsch sees as innovative. It establishes a common culture.

The intensive curriculum "encourages fully developed understanding of a subject, making one's knowledge of it integrated and coherent" (128). Here he sees himself as incorporating Dewey's emphasis on intensive engagement with cases of things. It is also here that Hirsch sees pluralism in his proposal, since the cases so examined can be determined by the teachers and students even as he posits a limit to the flexibility of the intensive curriculum. His argument is that the local community should establish what domains the cases are to represent while leaving the choice of specific cases to teachers and students. He also sees the strength of adding the intensive curriculum to the extensive as a way to avoid a core curriculum of subjects that each student would have to take.

In the later years of schooling, Hirsch proposes more emphasis on broad survey courses within subject areas. These should have specific factual content to continue developing the national language and culture. His focus here is on facts about which he is unashamed:

> But it isn't facts that deaden the minds of young children, who are storing facts in their minds every day with astonishing voracity. It is incoherence—our failure to ensure that a pattern of shared, vividly taught, and socially enabling knowledge will emerge from our instruction. (133)

Finally, Hirsch turns himself to the practical issue of how to get the content he has advocated available for schools. There are historical precedents for his proposals. He greatly admires textbooks, especially those such as Blair's *Rhetoric* in 1783 (1965), which he argues was essentially a "dictionary of cultural literacy for those who were not born to English literate culture" (Hirsch 1987: 85). He argues that all national systems of education rely on textbooks and readers as subtle means of promoting a national language and culture. He sees modern textbooks as lacking an emphasis on national character and insufficient as compendia to introduce students to literate culture. The result is his collaboration on *The Dictionary of Cultural Literacy* (Hirsch et al. 1993), which not only defines words and terms but also gives their historical and literate association and meanings. He also suggests an increased emphasis on factual narratives for children's learning to read and new textbooks that follow his conception of cultural literacy. He argues for replacing the SAT with tests based on general knowledge that has been commonly agreed upon. All these proposals are part of his practical plan to bring the literacy of Americans back to the forefront of the world.

These modern orators, Bloom, Hirsch, and Adler, clearly have some differences in their respective approaches, but we think they are relatively minor. Of the three, Bloom is the most condemnatory of the philosophical idea, whereas Hirsch and Adler seek strategic accommodations. Hirsch accommodates theoretically by proposing an anthropological theory and practically on his creation of new texts and leaving curricular decisions to our state and local educational agencies. Adler accommodates theoretically by embracing a goal of critical thought, albeit limited, and practically in his inclusion of modern subjects of the social sciences and in allowing an emphasis on developing intellectual skills, both as part of his *Paideia Proposal*. These differences clearly excite the passions of the modern orators but are often missed by their critics who see their overwhelming similarities. The critics, however, tend to focus on surface similarities, such as the ignoring of gender and race differences.

The modern orators share much deeper ideas than these. First, the modern orators agree that the pinnacle of our society is past. The Great Ideas have already been thought, the essential truths already discovered. The fixture of our society, for them, is in trying to regain the ideas that we now value less than we once did. Second, and related, the greatness of our nation is seen by the orators as linked to our ability to recapture the now past pinnacle. Our nation was greater, according to the modern orators, when we had less diversity and more agreement about what was to be valued. They are after a common culture that perpetuates the ideas of the past. Third, the common culture can be created through education, but only through education guided by the oratorical idea. While there may be some accommodation to the philosophical idea, the oratorical idea must lead and dominate if we are to reclaim our pinnacle and our national greatness. Fourth, the current decline of our nation and culture is due to the overwhelming success of the philosophical idea in education. In their minds, Dewey won and we have suffered because of this. Fifth, the modern orators agree that education is fundamentally about values. This should outshine the technical and the scientific. The moral virtues are based in absolute and universal principles. The first principles and thus our virtues are to be discovered in the Great Books, Ideas, and Works and through rational thought (i. e., logic and reasoning). Knowledge and reason are, and should be, the bases of our values.

In this book we will respond to some of these elements of the modern oratorical idea, arguing that they have some fundamental flaws. Yet we want to be careful not to reproduce the reification of the opposition of ideas we are so concerned with by simply using the philosophical idea to critique the oratorical one. The former must be subject to the same consideration we have given the latter. We must turn our eye to Dewey and his powerful play on the philosophical idea. Once this is accomplished, we will move forward in our project to reclaim moral life with schools.

The Pinnacle Ahead

For those in the philosopher's camp, the key is not that we are in a state of decline. For the philosophical position, the question is the extent to which we are effectively conducting our search for truth. "Decline," under philosophical terms, would be directly associated with locking ourselves into the thoughts and ideas of the past, failing to exercise them in the search for a better society to come. In modern times, this theme has been notably argued by John Dewey. For much of his career, Dewey attempted to extend the discussion beyond the content of the pinnacles of the past to how that content might serve us in our quest for the pinnacle to come in the future and how education would bring us to that pinnacle. It is in that quest—the process of what we do with the knowledge of all ages—that we find truth.

To offer an understanding of the educational philosophy of Dewey, we present a summary and critique of one of his most noted works, *Democracy and Education* (1916). Dewey states the following as the purpose for this book:

> The following pages embody an endeavor to detect and state the ideas implied in a democratic society and to apply these ideas to the problems of the enterprise of education. The discussion includes an indication of the constructive aims and methods of public education as seen from this point of view, and a critical estimate of the theories of knowing and moral development which

were formulated in earlier social conditions, but which still operate, in societies nominally democratic, to hamper the adequate realization of the democratic ideal. (iii)

Dewey opens *Democracy and Education* with the argument that education is a continuation of social life that was accomplished by the transmission of knowledge from one person to another through communication, "the process of sharing experience till it becomes a common possession" (9). People are born into social groups, and the "aims and habits" (3) of the group have to be passed from the preceding to the succeeding group. This process of passing on the culture, necessary for the reproduction of the group, must be a deliberate transmission. Experiences, then, are educative to the extent that they are social, shared, and allowed for the participation of incoming and existing group members. Community maintains itself through the renewal accomplished in this process with the education of new members:

By various agencies, unintentional and designed, a society transforms uninitiated and seemingly alien beings into robust trustees of its own resources and ideals. Education is thus a fostering, a nurturing, a cultivating process. (10)

This transformation occurs, according to Dewey, in the context of an individual's social environment, which he defines as "those conditions that promote or hinder, stimulate or inhibit, the *characteristic* activities of a living being" (11). Moreover, this environment should be used as a tool for the education of the young. Dewey suggests that schools take three approaches to exploit this social environment in the process of educating. First, the social environment should be broken up into transmittable pieces, given the difficulty of transmitting a complex social environment in its entirety at one time. Second, schools should eliminate undesirable elements of the current environment, thus allowing for an enhanced environment in the future. Third, schools should balance elements of the social environment such that each individual can escape the limitations of his environment and access the broader social environment around him (20).

As the young are brought into the social group, according to Dewey, they have to be "directed" toward the aims and beliefs of the group into which they are born. This direction requires bringing the interests of the young into orderly continuity with those of adults, which means that the young have to come to understand the relationship between their actions and the means they were to exercise and the ends they were to achieve as members of the social group. This continuity Dewey refers to as "like-mindedness" requires people to "be really members" of the social group; "otherwise, there is no common understanding, and no community life" (30). The primary means of this continuity and of establishing community—and direction for the young—is through language. The young come to this direction through the like-mindedness they create by seeing the "prevailing habits of others" (32) and by developing similar habits through connections with others. Dewey sees this experiential process of developing like-mindedness as critical:

> The net outcome . . . is that the fundamental means of control is not personal but intellectual. It is not "moral" in the sense that a person is moved by direct personal appeal from others, important as is this method at critical junctures. It consists in the habits of *understanding*, which are set up in using objects in correspondence with others, whether by way of cooperation and assistance or rivalry and competition. *Mind* as a concrete thing is precisely the power to understand things in terms of the use made of them; a socialized mind is the power to understand them in terms of the use to which they are turned in joint or shared situations. *And mind in this sense is the method of social control.* (33)

The young learn through joint activities with others. Schools, therefore, as the institutions formally charged with educating the young, should provide children primarily with "direct and continuous occupation with things" (38) in shared activities. Only through such joint activity, according to Dewey, could social direction be attained.

Dewey also argues that we tend to look, in education, at the immaturity of an individual as a lack of some set of characteristics or traits—a bias born out of seeing children "comparatively" as opposed to "intrinsically" (42). When seen as a comparative state, immaturity has negative implications, but when looked at as an intrinsic state, immaturity implies possibility. This intrinsic view of immaturity offers educational possibilities in terms of "dependence" and "plasticity" (43–44). Immaturity as dependence presents possibilities in that dependence involves interdependence, the opportunity to become involved with others. Immaturity as plasticity involves the ability to learn through experience and to transfer lessons learned in one experience to another to guide action. In the context of immaturity, Dewey sees life as a process of development, and vice versa. Growth in this sense is, as Dewey describes it, an end in itself and not merely a means to other ends, with the same being true for education. This understanding had been distorted in schooling, with growth and education seen as *"having* an end, instead of *being* an end" (50). In contrast to the educational process described above, Dewey argues that this means–ends distortion leads to three educational fallacies, all attributable to the oratorical idea:

> First, failure to take account of the instinctive or native powers of the young; secondly, failure to develop initiative in coping with novel situations; thirdly, an undue emphasis upon drill and other devices which secure automatic skill at the expense of personal perception. In all cases, the adult environment is accepted as a standard for the child. He is brought up *to* it. (50)

Dewey contrasts this description of education as growth with three contrary descriptions: education as preparation, education as unfolding, and education as training in "formal discipline." When education is viewed as preparation for adulthood, Dewey argues that "children are not regarded as social members in full and regular standing. They are looked upon as candidates; they are placed on the waiting list" (54). By deferring the purpose of education to the future, a key source of motivation is sacrificed, because children live in the present. Also, such a view places the focus of education on a far-off future, and expectations become ones of what the child would be, not what the child is. Dewey believes that

> the mistake is not in attaching importance to preparation for future need, but in making it the mainspring of present effort. Because the need of preparation for a continually developing life is great, it is imperative that every energy should be bent to making the present experience as rich and significant as possible. Then, as the present emerges insensibly into the future, the future is taken care of. (56)

Dewey also criticizes the view of education as an "unfolding of latent powers" (56) toward some sense of developmental perfection. The significance of such unfolding is found in the end product, not in process, and also implies a movement away from something, a reiteration of immaturity as a negative state. The third contrary view—formal disciplines—treats education as training to do something better than it was done prior to training. The problem, for Dewey, is that the powers to be trained become the aims of education rather than the result of growth. It also implies the innate existence of such powers in an undeveloped state within the individual. Education as training in formal disciplines refers to "both the outcome of trained power and to the method of training through repeated exercise" (61). Dewey cites as examples of these mental faculties such things as perception, retention, association, and thinking. Education, according to the view, is a process of the mind, through repetition, such that such mental faculties are made mental habits. In his time, Dewey had the same worries about formalism as Hirsch has.

Dewey further highlights different views in the educational process by categorizing them according to their conservative and progressive characters. He describes two views as being conserving: education as formation and education as recapitulation and retrospection. Education as formation emphasizes the role of subject matter to the exclusion of the existence of mental faculties mentioned earlier. Dewey describes formation in this sense as a connection of mind with subject matter. "Education proceeds by instruction taken in a strictly literal sense, a building into the mind from without" (69). The key issue here, presentation of subject matter from outside the mind, has three educational implications: (1) The mind is formed through presentation of material to it; (2) educators are to find appropriate material for original stages of formation, and then progress to the next stage on the basis of the previous; (3) method of teaching is preparation by bringing previous presentations back into consciousness, creating interaction between old and new presentations, then applying the newly formed content to a task. Such methodology was appropriate for "all subjects for all pupils of all ages" (71). This view of education as formation, according to Dewey, has one fundamental theoretical defect": that of "ignoring the existence of a living being of active and specific functions which are developed in the redirection and combination which occur as they are occupied with their environment"(71).

Education as recapitulation and retrospection, the second conservative view, focuses on education as biographical and cultural capitulation to the past. Dewey dismisses biological ontogeny as not important, but expands on cultural ontogeny. This cultural recapitulation begins with the child at a mental and moral stage of "savagery" which focuses on the material world as proper subject matter, and progressed from the savage to "contemporary life" (72). Education as retrospection underlies this view, in that

it looks primarily to the past and especially to the literary products of the past, and that mind is adequately formed in the degree in which it is patterned upon the spiritual heritage of the past. (73)

The problem with recapitulation and retrospection, according to Dewey, is that ontogeny is more than mere repetition; it includes change and going beyond what had come before. Development requires a "short-circuiting" (73) with the past, as does education. In the process of education, the young have to be freed from the passé. "The business of education is rather to liberate the young from reviving and retraversing the past than to lead them to a recapitulation of it" (73).

But, as Dewey asserts, parts of the past could be useful and wise to maintain, this being due to their use in the *present* environment and as a resource for present needs. But again, Dewey reminds us that subject matter located in the past provides another process–product dichotomy of growth as discussed earlier. Education should keep the process of growth alive, and ensure its future survival as well. Individuals live in the present, and

> the study of past *products* will not help us understand the present, because the present is not due to the products, but to the life of which they were the products. A knowledge of the past and its heritage is of great significance when it enters into the present, but not otherwise. And the mistake of making the records and remains of the past the main material of education is that it cuts the vital connection of present and past, and it tends to make the past a rival of the present and the present a more or less futile imitation of the past. Under such circumstances, culture becomes an ornament and solace; a refuge and an asylum. (75)

Dewey describes this view of education-as-reconstruction as "progressive." The basic question in this reconstruction is how to bring what had gone before into the realm of present experience. Both unfolding from within and formation from without could educationally be a reconstructing of experience, with the end result being a "direct transformation of the quality of experience" (76). Dewey defines the quality of experiences as that which is learned from it:

> We thus reach a technical definition of education: It is that reconstruction or reorganization of experience which adds to the meaning of experience, and which increases ability to direct the course of subsequent experience. (76)

Dewey qualifies his discussion of society and groups thus far as a generic discussion, and charges that the quality of education varies with the quality of group life. Societies based in change formulate different aims compared to those societies that wish to avoid change. Therefore, the application of general ideas of education to practice have to be done with an understanding of the current life of the society.

But "society" has multiple meanings and implications. Individuals can associate in a variety of ways, individuals can simultaneously be members of different groups, and major social groups can be composed of minor groups. Yet we tend to associate unity with society: "Society is conceived as one by its very nature" (82). In fact, societies contained many different kinds of associations, "good and bad" (82). Education by a group tends to socialize to the group, "but the quality and value of the socialization depends upon the habits and aims of the group" (83).

Dewey suggests that we avoid two approaches in measuring the value of a given mode of social life. First, we should not search for an ideal, since ideals are unattainable. Second, we should avoid overemphasis on what is here because problems exist in the current mode. We should pull out the desirable, use that to critique the undesirable, and seek social improvement. And in seeking the desirable, we should give deference to those desirable traits held in common. And to attain these common traits,

> all the members of the group must have an equable opportunity to receive and take part from others. There must be a large variety of shared undertakings and experiences. Otherwise, the influences which educate some into masters, educate others into slaves. (84)

Lack of social intercourse of values and interests between classes restrict diversity and lead to more rigid class lines, further limiting social intercourse. Such limitations tend to make activity routine for the disadvantaged classes and "capricious, aimless, and explosive" for the materially advantaged (85).

Dewey also criticizes isolation and insulation of groups which lead them to focus solely on the interests of their own. The main goal for such groups becomes protection from outsiders, not wider social relationships. Such isolation rigidifies and institutionalizes; it sanctions selfishness, self-centeredness, and static ideals. To invite social intercourse with others would endanger tradition or custom. To this same point Dewey argues that expansive eras in history had coincided with the dissolution of distance between peoples. The objective was to take advantage of the dissolution of space.

Dewey extends his discussion into the "democratic ideal" of education, restating two elements that point to democracy. One is the variety of points of view and interests and reliance on the recognition of mutual values and interests in social control. Second, social intercourse provides for readjustment through new situations created in the interaction, making subsequent interaction more easily accomplished. Dewey characterizes this sense of democracy as one that goes deeper than education to create an enlightened electorate.

> A democracy is more than a form of government; it is primarily a mode of associated living, of conjoint communicated experience. (87)

The more diversity in contact that occurs, the more diversity in stimuli that is possible, which ultimately puts a "premium" on diversity of action. Again, Dewey sees this diversity as characteristic of democracy, and the sustenance of diversity of action and interests necessary to avoid stratification, to seek adaptability, and to learn to live with change. Dewey concludes this discussion of the democratic conception as it relates to education by describing the historical development of the relationship between forms of social control and the nature of the society controlled. Beginning with Plato's philosophy of education and working through the eighteenth- and nineteenth-century notions of educational philosophy, Dewey argues that the fundamental breakdown in the creation of such a philosophy was the overattention to institutions and social groups at the expense of the individual, thus subordinating the individual and individual development. Dewey included the caveat that "the conception of education as a social process and function has no definite meaning until we define the kind of society we have in mind," and within that the belief that education is "a freeing of individual capacity in a progressive growth directed to social aims" (97–98).

At this point, Dewey shifts the nature of his discussion to "aims" in education, his primary concern being with the location of aims, be they intrinsic to the activities in which one is engaged or imposed from without. To determine whether aims exist, Dewey suggests four areas of questioning: (1) the presence of "intrinsic continuity" in activity, (2) the presence of direction to activity due to "careful observation of the given conditions" and the discovery of "hinderances" in the way, (3) the "proper order or sequence in the use of means," and (4) the possibility of choice in alternatives (101–102). Dewey summarizes the process to claim that having an aim is tantamount to having intelligence, and, further:

> To have a mind to do a thing is to foresee a future possibility; it is to have a plan for its accomplishment; it is to note the means which make the plan capable of execution and the obstructions in the way,—or, if it is really a mind to do the thing and not a vague aspiration—it is to have a plan which takes account of resources and difficulties. Mind is capacity to refer present conditions to future

results, and future consequences to present conditions. And these
traits are just what is meant by having an aim or a purpose. (103)

Aims, according to Dewey, are the result primarily of people's
desire to alter defects and address needs of immediate situations and
given time periods. Aims are also the results of desires to bring about
changes or alterations to situations. Aims exist in at least three different
forms: those based in nature, those based in social efficiency, and those
based in culture. Nature as the basis of aims was most notably articu-
lated in Rousseau's attempts to base education in the natural context in
which children grow and develop. Nature provides the "standard" for
development, and the task of educators is to follow that standard.
Dewey, while supporting the emphasis on the natural context of the
child as the basis for learning, finds too little structure in Rousseau's
perspective, and counters that the learning environment has to be organized to some degree for the most appropriate learning to take place.
"The moral," according to Dewey, "is not to leave [children] alone to
follow their own 'spontaneous development,' but to provide an environment which shall organize them" (115). In opposition to the overemphasis on nature, social efficiency aims at education as the development
of habits such that individuals are subject to social rules and social
control. This is accomplished by providing structures to bring into line
"native individual capacities" such that they contribute to "occupations
having a social meaning" (118–9). The danger of such efficiency lies in
becoming so vocationally narrow that those with differing capacities are
stratified and in becoming so civically narrow as to eliminate the benefits
of economic and vocational progress. To maintain such a balance, Dewey
argues that "it must be borne in mind that ultimately social efficiency
means neither more nor less than capacity to share in a give and take of
experience" (120). Where culture becomes an aim in education, Dewey
claimed that culture is first a personal cultivation of appreciation of
"ideas and art and broad human interests" (121). The meaning of
activity, according to Dewey, is critical, as is the distinctiveness of traits
that each individual develops that make her/him unique. This distinctiveness could then be the basis for social service in the quest for social
efficiency. Again, Dewey warns that such efficiency should be defined
broadly to escape narrow associations with economic or vocational
concerns and to build a stronger association with democratic living.

When social efficiency as measured by product or output is urged
as an ideal in a would-be democratic society, it means that the
depreciatory estimate of the masses characteristic of an aristocratic

community is accepted and carried over. But if democracy has a moral and ideal meaning, it is that a social return be demanded from all and that opportunity for development of distinctive capacities be afforded all. The separation of the two aims in education is fatal to democracy; the adoption of the narrower meaning of efficiency deprives it of its essential justification. (122)

Dewey believes it essential that the development of social efficiency and personal culture be brought together into one process rather than perpetuated as a dichotomy. People could develop their capacities as individuals in such a way as to bring those unique personal cultures to bear on social concerns and needs. One did not necessarily exclude the other.

Dewey next turns to "interest" and "discipline." He connects interest to aims as well as to purpose in the educational process. Interest is the substance of connection that a person made with the parts of the world that s/he had reason to know about, "that self and world are engaged with each other in a developing situation" (126). "Discipline" is the product of will, the result of one who strives to accomplish an aim. Discipline not only includes the consideration of aims but also considers the process to achieving those aims and the commitment to carrying them out. Dewey holds that the difference between being weak willed and being strong willed and thus exercising discipline is an intellectual difference "consisting in the degree of persistent firmness and fullness with which consequences are thought out" (128). Further, he asserts the connection between interest and discipline:

A person who is trained to consider his actions, to undertake them deliberately, is in so far forth disciplined. Add to this ability a power to endure in an intelligently chosen course in face of distraction, confusion, and difficulty, and you have the essence of discipline. (129)

Interest is a measure of the degree to which one disciplines oneself to action, and, conversely, the degree to which one is willing to exercise discipline is a measure of interest.

Dewey then uses this connection between interest and discipline to argue that subject matter had been illegitimately treated as an objective reality, separate from those who use it for some purpose. Dewey claims that subject matter existed only to the extent that it was put to use "to respond to present stimuli on the basis of anticipation of future possible consequences." He further contends that "the things, the subject matter known, consist of whatever is recognized as having a bearing upon the anticipated course of events, whether assisting or retarding it" (130–1). This he contrasts with the more traditional notion of "discipline," which refers to traditional areas of study and methods of teaching where students are forced to learn knowledge in which they have no interest. Dewey sees the connection in his sense of discipline to interest as vital to the learning process, and he sees the more traditional notions of discipline and interest as corruptive. A "genuine" theory of education, he argues, requires this connection in his terms:

> To organize education so that natural active tendencies shall be fully enlisted in doing something, while seeing to it that the doing requires observation, the acquisition of information, and the use of a constructive imagination, is what most needs to be done to improve social conditions. To oscillate between drill exercises that strive to attain efficiency in outward doing without the use of intelligence, and an accumulation of knowledge that is supposed to be an ultimate end in itself, means that education accepts the present social conditions as final, and thereby takes upon itself the responsibility for perpetuating them. (137)

Dewey next moves to a discussion of the relationship between thinking and experience. This relationship, he argues, is between our actions and our thoughts concerning the consequences of these actions. Not to reflect on the possible consequences of action is to fail to think. Experience, according to Dewey, requires both the thought about considered action and the enacting itself. The essence of thought is the link between action and its consequences. Such thought leads to reasoning about what action to take, what the consequences of such action might be, the action itself, and scrutiny of the nature of the action's outcomes. He summarizes the position:

> While all thinking results in knowledge, ultimately the value of knowledge is subordinate to its use in thinking. For we live not in a settled and finished world, but in one which is going on, and where our main task is prospective, and where retrospect—and all knowledge as distinct from thought is retrospect—is of value in the solidity, security, and fertility it affords our dealings with the future. (151)

Dewey then uses his idea of thinking to form the basis of "method" in education. He claims that thinking has to be connected to "efficiency of action" (152) and to a better understanding of our experiences in the world. Experience is the method by which we learn, when experience means our acting and then the acting having an impact on us that we understand. Dewey contends that we learn from experiences when we react to the world around us in a problem-solving mode. To solve problems we must think effectively, and to think effectively we must be able to make use of our experiences to build intellectual resources to solve problems at hand. We must therefore be able to be perceptive and to make useful observations of the world around us such that we can harvest from our experiences resources for thoughtful action. From these resources and observations we develop solutions to problems, and then we apply solutions to test them (154–62). This process, Dewey asserts, recognizes the integration of mind with body and of our intellectual existence with the experiences in the physical world around us.

Before moving on to a more specific discussion of subject matter within curriculum and schools, Dewey extends his discussions of method and subject matter in general and further argues the inseparability of the two: "Method means that arrangement of subject matter which makes it most effective in use. Never is method something outside of the material" (165). He further contends, "Method in any case is but an effective way of employing some material for some end" (166). Dewey argues that treating method and subject as if they were isolated entities leads to four problems in education: (1) Such separation leads to a neglect of experience, which means method cannot be discovered without cases in which it is grounded; (2) as has already been noted, an inappropriate conception of discipline and interest are promoted; (3) learning is separated from the subject matter out of which learning supposedly occurs, and it is removed from activity; (4) because the mind is separated from the material of experience, method tends to become routines—a series of steps—separated from its experiential base. In opposition to this perspective, Dewey claims that method arises from subject matter, and its development should be solidly grounded in the experiential base in which learning takes place. Such a relationship requires a view of method based in "straightforwardness," or what a person is most directly interested in knowing or what problem needs to be solved; "open-mindedness," or a consideration of all possibilities that illuminate an experience; "single-mindedness," or maintaining a clear focus on the task at hand; and "responsibility," or the clear consideration of consequences for action taken (173–9).

The separation of subject matter and method presents another set of problems rooted more directly in subject matter itself. Not only does subject matter typically become disconnected from method, but it also tends to be treated as separate from the social context in which it has meaning (181). Subject comes to be treated as if it has inherent knowledge and value to be mastered for its sake rather than for socially derived meanings. This also means that the value of subject matter is not born out of the needs and interests of the student. It then becomes the job of the educator to bring these two entities together, and this serves only to highlight the distinctiveness between knowledge and the knower (student). More appropriately, as Dewey asserts, "the teacher should be occupied not with subject matter in itself but in its interaction with the pupil's present needs and capacities" (183). To recognize the value of subject matter as something inherent to the learner requires several concessions. First, the knowledge that means the most to a person is the knowledge of how to do something (as opposed to knowing for knowing's sake). Second, knowledge gains in value as it grows out of the problems we confront and the experiences we have (185–7). Otherwise, knowledge becomes the property of different intellectual domains of study. Third, knowledge that is of most respectable use is that which has stood the test of scientific rigor and has become certain knowledge rather than opinion or speculation:

> Without initiation into the scientific spirit one is not in possession of the best tools which humanity has so far devised for effectively directed reflection. One in that case not merely conducts inquiry and learning without the use of the best instruments, but fails to understand the full meaning of knowledge. For he does not become acquainted with the traits that mark off opinion and assent from authorized convicion.

But Dewey continues with a caveat:

> On the other hand, the fact that science marks the perfecting of knowing in highly specialized conditions of technique renders its results, taken by themselves, remote from ordinary experience—a quality of aloofness that is popularly designated by the term abstract. (189–90)

Fourth, and finally, Dewey contends that subject matter must be social and must be socially pertinent in the broadest sense of being socially shared. He places this above the knowledge of "specialized groups and technical pursuits" (191), and warns against such application of the term "social."

> But those who utter the saying frequently have in mind in the term human only a highly specialized class: the class of learned men

who preserve the classic traditions of the past. They forget that material is humanized in the degree in which it connects with the common interests of men as men. (191)

Subject matter, according to Dewey, is that which helps us solve the problems and understand the experiences of being social.

Dewey moves on to a discussion of "play and work" in the curriculum and then on to a discussion of the place of geography, history, and sciences in the curriculum. His central point on the study of geography and history is that experience becomes more important when one can connect lessons from any given experience to contexts outside that experience. The more of these connections one can make, the richer the learning that an experience can produce. Communication across these experiences comes from shared interests and a give and take between experiences. Geography and history, Dewey believes, are the best resources for creating and enhancing this connection of experiences. Dewey argues the particular importance of history in this process:

It is an organ for analysis of the warp and woof of the present social fabric, of making known the forces which have woven the pattern. The use of history for cultivating a socialized intelligence constitutes its moral significance.

And:

The assistance which may be given by history to a more intelligent sympathetic understanding of the social situations of the present in which individuals share is a permanent and constructive moral asset. (217)

Science, according to Dewey, is the culmination of the perfection of knowledge, "the office of intelligence" (228), and a liberating force in man's life (226–7). It is science, according to Dewey, that represents the pinnacle of man's intellect and that fuels the engines of progress for humanity. Science is also knowledge that separates conscious, directed knowing from reckless knowing based on happenstance.

To sum up: Science represents the office of intelligence, in projection and control of new experiences, pursued systematically, intentionally, and on a scale due to freedom from limitation of habit. It is the sole instrumentality of conscious, as distinct from accidental, progress. (228)

Dewey moves from this disciplinary-based discussion to a more general commentary on what is valued in education and how that affects the process of schooling. An examination of values, Dewey posits, offers an opportunity to bring aims in education in general in line with aims, through curriculum. One of Dewey's points here is that, because there are two different forms of valuing in education—intrinsic and instrumental—curriculum has been segregated into parts, with the differences being determined according to the type of value knowledge is perceived to have. Knowledge with intrinsic value is that knowledge which is valuable in and of itself, valuable to be known, "appreciative" knowledge (249). Instrumental knowledge is knowledge that can be put to use toward some objective beyond the knowledge itself. Out of this separation comes not only the segregation of knowledge into the different and distinct content areas found in schools but also the hierarchy of value we put on different forms of knowing. Dewey summarizes the problem this way:

> Business is business, science is science, art is art, politics is politics, social intercourse is social intercourse, morals is morals, recreation is recreation, and so on. Each possesses a separate and independent province with its own peculiar aims and ways of proceeding. Each contributes to the others only externally and accidentally. All of them make up the whole of life by just apposition and addition. (247)

Dewey argues further that this segregation is responsible for our separation of studies into those associated with labor and those associated with leisure. Certain forms of knowledge have historically been available for those who were located socially in leisure such that the knowledge most valuable for them has been what we came to call a liberal education. Others were socially positioned such that a more vocational form of knowledge in labor was made available. Dewey argues that such a segregation created not only classes of knowledge but classes of people as well, and finds such segregation (on both counts) undemocratic:

> The problem of education in a democratic society is to do away with the dualism and to construct a course of studies which makes thought a guide of free practice for all and which makes leisure a reward of accepting responsibility for service, rather than a state of exemption from it. (261)

In continuing his discussion of segregation, Dewey claims that there has historically been a tension between intellectual and practical studies based in the nature of "empirical" knowledge. Pointing back to

Plato and Aristotle, Dewey argues that experience had been coupled with the practical and with the material. It was treated as a lesser form of knowledge than that associated with reason based in abstract thinking. Mainly through Greek philosophy, reason came to be held as the standard of intellect, and experience was rejected as the realm of the earthy and practical. "Truth," in this thinking, was truth precisely because it was unsullied by the distorting influences of physical existence. Modern thought, represented in the work of Bacon, rejected reason as an abstract process usually constrained by dogma, and embraced experience as the basis of the highest form of knowledge. Experience became associated with "something intellectual and cognitive" (267) and with knowledge based in our understanding and mastering of nature as opposed to intellectual exercise. Bacon's contribution was to break us out of the tyranny of abstraction and idealistically based knowledge and signaled a transition to knowledge based in experience. Dewey adds one more stage to the refinement of experiential knowledge by claiming that experience has to be treated as not only cognitive but also practical (due mainly to work in psychology, industrial method, and scientific method). By making experience commensurate with the practical, experience becomes a matter of "doing and undergoing the consequences of doing" (274). He further states:

> When trying, or experimenting, ceases to be blinded by impulse or custom, when it is guided by an aim and conducted by measure and method, it becomes reasonable—rational. When what we suffer from things, what we undergo at their hands, ceases to be a matter of chance circumstance, when it is transformed into a consequence of our own prior purposive endeavors, it becomes rationally significant—enlightening and instructive. (273)

Dewey attributes another segregation in education to the Greeks, that of the separation of physical studies and social studies. Like the intellectual and practical segregation, the social and the physical are segregated along the mind–world dichotomy. According to Dewey, the ultimate aim of Greek philosophy was knowledge of human ends. As the Romans adopted the Greek legacy and modern man the Roman's, knowledge of nature was important only to the extent that it could enhance the aim of the conquest and control of man, not nature (279). Dewey tracks this development of the segregation of science from literature throughout the Renaissance and the Enlightenment, arguing that as science gained its position of supremacy, the rift between the two forms of knowledge was increased. He again cites Bacon as a central figure in this rift, given Bacon's emphasis on man's control of his own ends that would come with his control of nature. And here Dewey raises a pivotal point. The progress subsequent to Baconian philosophy failed to include a moral discourse, according to Dewey. In the progress that ensued, human exploitation that had long been a subject of philosophical study had, if anything, been intensified by the progress of science. As we moved from feudalism to capitalism and through the industrial and scientific revolution, we did so at the expense of human interest.

Naturally, this application of physical science (which was the most conspicuously perceptible one) strengthened the claims of professed humanists that science was materialistic in its tendencies. It left a void as to man's distinctively human interests which go beyond making, saving, and expending money; and languages and literature put in their claim to represent the moral and ideal interests of humanity. (283)

Dewey argues that there is no such thing as a division between man and the physical world in which he lives, and there can be no legitimate view of knowledge of the world as if there were two distinct physical and human entities.

The obvious pedagogical starting point of scientific instruction is not to teach things labeled science, but to utilize the familiar occupations and appliances to direct observation and experiment, until pupils have arrived at a knowledge of some fundamental principle by understanding them in their familiar practical workings.

He goes on to say:

On the other hand, "humanism" means at bottom being imbued with an intelligent sense of human interests. The social interest, identical in its deepest meaning with a moral interest, is necessarily supreme with man. . . . Any study so pursued that it increases concern for the values of life, any study producing greater sensitiveness to social well-being is humane study. (288)

For his next iteration of educational segregation, Dewey turns to the split between the individual and the world. Here he looks at the history of the knower, from the Greek basis in reason through medieval emphasis on religious individualism to the economic and political individualism prominent in the Enlightenment. His primary focus in this argument is on the false philosophical dichotomies between the knower and the known and between subject and object. Dewey argues that this dichotomy inappropriately separates the individual from the world. Knowledge, as a matter of fact, could have meaning only for an individual in the world, in a social medium. "Through social intercourse, through sharing in the activities embodying beliefs, he gradually acquires a mind of his own" (295). Dewey is cautious, though, not to reject the autonomy and sanctity of the individual. Dewey recognizes and even celebrates the educated "individual" as one of the goals of education. But Dewey argues that there could be no such thing as "individualness" without the primary capacity to be social and to be in the world. One becomes an individual to the extent that he is able successfully to negotiate the social world (300–3). "True individualism," according to Dewey, "is a product of the relaxation of the grip of the authority of custom and traditions as standards of belief" (305).

Dewey begins to close out his thesis by summarizing the gist of his text: "education as a social need and function"; the necessity of a "continuous reconstruction or reorganization of experience . . . to increase its recognized meaning or social content . . . to increase the capacity of individuals to act as directive guardians of this reorganization"; and the application of democratic criterion in "present social life" and the limitations in doing so (321–2). He next articulates the relationship between this thesis and the purpose of philosophy, a purpose he describes as follows:

> With respect to subject matter, philosophy is an attempt to comprehend—that is, to gather together the varied details of the world and of life into a single inclusive whole, which shall either be a unity, or, as in the dualistic systems, shall reduce the plural details to a small number of ultimate principles. On the side of the attitude of the philosopher and of those who accept his conclusions, there is the endeavor to attain as unified, consistent, and complete an outlook upon experience as is possible.

Dewey adds the caveat that philosophy in this sense cannot be separated from science in the sense that science is about our "general attitude" toward the world as much as facts about it. Dewey also adds, around the issue of science, that thinking and knowledge are different. "Knowledge, grounded knowledge, is science; it represents objects which have been settled, ordered, disposed of rationally." He continues, "Philosophy is thinking what the known demands of us, what responsive attitude it exacts" (326). Dewey connects philosophy here with thinking, not knowledge. Out of this Dewey constructs a philosophy of education whereby philosophy is the critique of "existing aims with respect to the existing state of science, pointing out values which have become obsolete with the command of new resources," and education as "the laboratory in which philosophic distinctions become concrete and are tested" (329).

Dewey treats one last issue in segregation, couching it as the dualism between empiricism and "higher rational knowing" (334). He sees the former being taken as everyday knowledge, or ordinary knowledge, and the latter as the knowledge of the intellectual. He believes the roots of this distinction lie in several places. One is the difference between the "particularness" of experiences and universality of reason. Another is in the difference between "learning" as the total of what is known in books and by men and learning as the process of studying to know. The first places authority of knowledge in external powers, whereas the second places power and authority in the ability to learn. He sees a third root of the dualism as the passive learning of one's environment making its stamp versus rational learning with an active mind. The last lies in a dichotomy between the emotions and the intellect, with the emotions an inward focus on the self and the intellect an outward—and active—focus on the world. Dewey summarizes the importance of all four as being a separation of the knower from that to be known, and the resolution as one of the knower within that to be known—the individual within the world. In his resolution, the knower is an active participant in the world, and knowledge is the means of participation. The culmination of this participation through knowledge is the scientific experimental method (335–8). Dewey broadens his point here to include the ability of the knower to connect multiple experiences, to make connections between the knowledge gained from different experiences, and to use this knowledge to learn from current and subsequent experiences. "For knowledge furnishes the means of understanding or giving meaning to what is still going on and what is to be done" (341). This culminates for Dewey in his conception of reason:

"Reason" is just the ability to bring the subject matter of prior experience to bear to perceive the significance of the subject matter of a new experience. A person is reasonable in the degree in which he is habitually open to seeing an event which immediately strikes his senses not as an isolated experience but in its connection with the common experience of mankind. (343)

He closes this argument with his definition of knowledge: "Only that which has been organized into our disposition so as to enable us to adapt the environment to our needs and to adapt our aims and desires to the situation in which we live is really knowledge" (343).

Dewey concludes *Democracy and Education* with his theory of morals, where he asserts: "It is commonplace of educational theory that the establishing of character is a comprehensive aim of school instruction and discipline" (346). His first charge here is against positions that split ideas about morals into "inner and outer" and "the spiritual and the physical" (346). This, he argues, has given us theories of morals that look at morality as either an inner state of mind or a product of outer realities to which we react, a situation, he says, that in most cases leads to a "compromise of both views" in the schoolroom (350). We have also, through the development of theories of morality, created a dichotomy between duty based in principle and action based in self-interest. Dewey finds the resolution of this dichotomy in the continuity between acting out of principle as being what one is most interested in and finding one's principles and interests in the context in which he is located and the circumstances that context presents. A final separation he presents is that between intelligence and character, highlighting the rift between morals based on rational knowledge of the right thing to do versus morals based on habits and routines—on virtue. He scorns both in isolation from each other, with the rationally based argument reducing learning morals to "catechetical instruction" (354) and routines and habits treated as if we fail to gain "knowledge" when we participate in our everyday lives.

Dewey concludes that the problem is one of having too narrow a definition of what "morals" are:

> giving them, on one side, a sentimental goody-goody turn without reference to effective ability to do what is socially needed, and, on the other side, overemphasizing convention and tradition so as to limit morals to a list of definitely state acts. (357)

Dewey claims that morals pertain to any act that affects our relationships with other people. Further, he claims that while some traits are more "central" than others—"truthfulness, honesty, chastity, amiability"—they are only a part of a much broader set of traits, and it is due in part to this connection that they are moral traits (357). Dewey argues that the moral is synonymous with the social, "identical with each other" (358). His concern, with schooling, is with those things that get in the way of "a permeating social spirit," thus restricting the possibility for "effective moral training" (358). Dewey offers the following conditions as those in which this spirit is possible: "In the first place, the school must itself be a community life in all which that implies." Second, he states, "The learning in school should be continuous with that out of school. There should be a free interplay between the two" (358). He ends with the claim: "Education is such a life. To maintain capacity for such education is the essence of morals" (360).

Our Critique of Dewey and the Philosophers

As might be evident in the comparison of the orators as represented by Adler, Bloom, and Hirsch, and the philosophers as represented in Dewey, we find in Dewey more possibilities than in the orators. But that is not to say that we have no problems with Dewey. As we have argued, our primary issue is not problems with either camp but reification of the ideas of both. On that issue we find Dewey equally guilty.

It is important to keep in mind that while Adler, Bloom, and Hirsch attack Dewey by name in their works, Dewey preceded these authors, and the problem that motivated much of the philosophical reconsiderations called for by Dewey at the turn of the century was the kind of education the orators would have us return to today. Dewey's ideas that helped spawn the progressive movement in education were a counterpoint to what he saw as overly rigid, subject- and teacher-dominated schooling.

Others have cautioned against the reified beliefs at the base of Dewey's ideas. Popkewitz (1991) saw the social conditions to which Dewey reacted as "the cultural tensions of his times," and Dewey's reaction to those tensions as one of providing society with the best elements of themselves—through education—to relieve them. Fundamental to this position is the taken-for-granted belief that, ultimately, community norms and progress, as Dewey defines them, would be beneficial for society, could be controlled, and could be vehicles to take us where we wanted to go. Dewey reifies not only rationality but its products of science and progress as well. Reification in this way denies the very democratic community that Dewey sought to create, because people become pawns of rationality, science, and progress.

Bowers (1987) critiques Dewey's ideas by focusing on what he calls the "identifiable center" of Dewey's work, "reconstructing our way of thinking":

> For Dewey, it was not modernization that was problematic, but rather the old ways of thinking and acting that prevented us from experiencing the growth that represented the promise of modernization. (31–2)

Bowers cites as a primary theme of Dewey's work that of focusing on how our understandings of the world around us and our experiences in it take us into the future, and a better future. That progress could be ensured, according to Dewey, with a dedicated focus on the promise of democracy and an equally dedicated focus on the promise of the scientific method. It was this movement to the future that Dewey holds as primary, and our ability to rationally control the nature of the movement and any given point at which we might arrive as the essence of our existence. Dewey makes that rational process, and the social progress it would supposedly generate, his source of authority and his moral end. The power of that authority would be built on the understanding that knowledge was not fixed, and that the development of individuals who were moral, rational, and progressive would lead to a society that was moral, rational, and progressive (Bowers 1987). By developing in individual students the use of the scientific method of problem solving, individuals would become better social and moral decision makers, and subsequently our democratic institutions would be socially more meaningful and morally stronger as a result. With authority properly couched in science and rational thought—our new sources of authority, according to Dewey—we would have a "better" form of authority (Bowers 1987).

One of our major differences with Dewey continuing from the above discussion of rationality, is one of his placing primacy in process. Dewey wants to place "value" and its power in the process by which we come to know what is valuable knowledge—rationality and reason. That power is not found in process, as Dewey claims, but in contexts that give process meaning. Process as an idea—scientific, rational, or otherwise—cannot transcend the context in which its meaning and value are constructed. Even Dewey's treatment of history and literature falls victim to his taken-for-granted beliefs here. Whereas Dewey attaches "moral assent" to intellectual history, our critique is that the meaning of history is partly constructed out of our moral constructions in the present. Unlike Dewey, we do not grant intellectual history the ability necessarily to determine our moral sense. Dewey necessitates and legitimates metanarratives in forms such as history and literature here and science above, whereas we see them as only one part—and not even a necessarily useful part—of moral construction.

Our problem, like Bowers's, is that in spite of Dewey's criticisms of tradition and dogma as illegitimate forms of authority, he has assigned the same power to "experience" as a taken-for-granted source of authority, and because of his nesting of morality in experience and scientific method, he robs us of our construction of the moral just as the orators do. What Dewey offers us in his philosopher's proposal is a theory of pedagogy with a theory of morality taken as the rational product of it. Dewey treats morals as if they come from knowledge (in spite of some of his protests to the contrary), and, to get to democratic society and moral construction, Dewey goes to pedagogy as a knowledge issue. As Dewey would have it, there must be a connection between pedagogy and the knowledge learned for the moral to be accomplished. For us, though, pedagogy, and much of the power we give to certain forms of knowledge—such as science and rationality—are artifacts of morality, not precursors to it.

In a general critique of what Bowers calls the liberal educational theorists (of which he considers Dewey to be one), he lays out what are his critical issues with Dewey's thought. First, he cites Dewey for his attempt to replace one set of reified beliefs with another: one form of individualism for another, one authoritative way of knowing (the premodern, irrational, nonscientific) for another (the modern, rational, scientific). Dewey failed, according to Bowers, to recognize the relativizing effects of his own beliefs by attaching the quality of social, political, and moral decisions to the ability of individuals to make them, and the quality of institutional beliefs was a function of consensus on those individual beliefs. But at the heart of this perspective, as Bowers points out, is the primary belief that historical momentum could be built toward the aligning of the individual and the social in a moral and social refinement, at least in democratic societies. Second, Bowers points out that thinkers such as Dewey failed to recognize the limiting potential of the rational tendencies they hoped to engender and the disempowering effects of the supposed move toward social and moral empowerment. Once rationality became reified in Dewey's total philosophical package, it became an unexamined belief in its meaning and in its consequences. Third, Dewey failed to consider critically the persuasive effects of tradition in the development of the individual. To the extent that traditions were problematic, Dewey's reaction was to eradicate them. He failed to acknowledge the inseparability of individuals and their traditions and that the progressive tendencies to set ideas (traditional or not) in reified terms removed those ideas from their contexts in the lives of people, in terms of both what he was reacting against in the premodern and what he was proposing as the way out of those problems in the modern. This, according to Bowers, distorted the agentic power of individuals and the false promise of rationalism, and

> as a result of separating the individual from embeddedness in context, the liberal educational theorists tended to represent tradition as the force of darkness that continually threatened to pull the individual backward. Education was to be the means for the great escape. (Bowers 1987: 51)

Finally, Bowers argues that Dewey, as a representative of the liberal theorists and the philosophical idea, isolated his thought within the reified beliefs that came to define both. The "reign of silence" (Bowers 1987: 51) resulting from this reification closed out the opportunity for Dewey to critique the set of assumptions on which his own beliefs were based. The very ideas that became closed out may have been critical to Dewey in coming to a deeper understanding of the beliefs he was developing, and would certainly have given greater critical insight to those who accepted and moved on his beliefs.

We find Dewey to be problematic on several other points as well. One is a sense of Dewey's argument being an overaccommodation to the orators. In much of his work, Dewey's quest is how we will most appropriately capitulate to the past, not whether or not we will. Though Dewey clearly does not embrace the lessons and subject matter of our heritage in the same way the orators do, neither does he offer us any sense that the *presence* of that heritage in the curriculum is negotiable. Our point is not that we should strongly consider eliminating the past from the process of education—indeed, it would be foolhardy to try, and certainly detrimental to moral construction to do so. Our problem is that Dewey has assumed the power of those great ideas, albeit with "process" as the lever of their strength. At the base of his resolution of the child with subject matter is the process by which the lessons of human history will be brought to the child, which, though something of a negotiation of the great ideas as subject matter, is hardly a rejection of its primacy in education. Dewey simply makes the location and importance of the lessons of the ages more contested, while asserting that the child will be brought to them.

We also take issue with Dewey's position that people discover truth and that what we need to do is find the process by which people are most likely to come to be educated, most likely to come to be rational, and most likely to come to be democratic. He would have all of these being accomplished by establishing processes in education whereby students come to the "best" knowledge of our society in our culture in a way that allows students to discover knowledge and truths for themselves. In this process of coming to one better truth after another, Dewey's assumption is that cultural construction is additive. At the base of this is a notion that cultural construction, as he acknowledges it, is linear and can be a rational process. If we take his ideas in their reified state, we cease to step outside those ideas, and are left to define morality, virtue, and anything else by linking it to "progress," "change," and "science." In the Deweyan sense, we are in a teleological cultural construction where one generation passes its culture on to the next generation in the quest for the "truth."

That next generation takes these "goods" and adds to their search. They then pass on their contributions to the process to the next generation, and so on and so on. Our view is that cultural construction is not linear and not additive in these ways. Though generations of cultural constructors are linked by chronology, chronology does not "fix" the process in a linear way.

We arrive at the same conclusion as Dewey as to the nature of schooling, but we get to that point in a dramatically and, we think, irreconcilably different way. For, unlike Dewey, who places primacy in knowledge such that we can have the moral, we place primacy in the moral such that we can have knowledge. We part with Dewey when virtue becomes a byproduct of knowledge and when becoming moral is linked to becoming knowledgeable. We also disagree with Dewey in his need to connect context to greater, broader meanings and ideas. We do not believe, as Dewey does, that contextual experiences have to be connected to meaning outside one's context—a metanarrative—in order to have meaning. We believe that people can construct the moral (as well as knowledge) out of the everyday realities of their lives, and these constructions have power and meaning because they are local, not because they connect to metanarratives. It is the everyday—the here and now—of moral construction that gives it meaning, and it need not be connected to anything beyond the here and now.

Dewey has us go through knowledge to get to morality and virtue. At the start of his path are science and rationality. According to Dewey, we come to knowledge and knowledge to us through our experiences, and out of that experiential base we arrive at our sense of morality. Morality and virtue are the products, in short, of an experiential epistemology. For Dewey, morality requires knowledge and knowledge requires science. In Dewey's frame, both require that we locate truth in consequences. To us, such a perspective devalues the present at the expense of the future. For us, the issue is not to disprove our latest truths; it is to decide which ones define us.

Finally, we take issue with the accumulated effect of Dewey's language and the images he invokes to cast his arguments. Dewey's language is a language of the future, and the way he constructs his thesis places meaning ultimately in a future context, in a context yet to be realized, in a pinnacle yet to come. His most consistent term—both in his own choosing and by what is attributed to him—is "progressive" and the other forms that the root "progress" takes. But that is not his only terminology that casts value and meaning into the future. He captures the process of education in terms and phrases such as "aims," "consequences of action," "anticipation of future of consequences," "prospective," "some material for some end," "in projection," and "control of new experiences." This language permeates his work and his fundamental thesis about schooling. For Dewey, the significance of the present lies in its consequences in the future, and the present has meaning only in its connection to the future. We feel that this language, and the meanings that can be constructed out of it, devalue the present and delegitimate the here and now of everyday life.

Conclusion: The Problems of Reification

Dewey is, for us, the exemplar of the philosophical position and its fundamental flaws. Our critique of Dewey and the philosophers serves to open our critique of the oratorical position as well. For us, the philosophers' flaw is in the belief that "experience" will get us to truth in the same way that the canon does for the orators. We are also troubled by the assumption by both the orators and philosophers that knowledge takes us to morality and virtue. And in both cases this knowledge is "certain," albeit in different ways. For the orators, certain knowledge means that stock of knowledge which is certain because it has stood the test of time and therefore contains the truth of our heritage. For the philosophers, we get to morality through certain knowledge being knowledge generated in a certain way (the scientific method) and used in a certain way (the reconstruction of experience).

For the orators and philosophers, the debate is about what knowledge is and how you get to it. We, on the other hand, argue that schools are fundametally about moral construction. For us, the moral questions are prerequisites to the knowledge questions. We hold that virtue is the investment in constructing the social context in which schools are located. We construct morality, and because of that we can construct knowledge. Both the orators and philosophers take it for granted that morality comes from knowledge. Both also take it for granted that schools are places where knowledge is paramount. Both are about schooling as institutions based first in knowledge and pedagogy for knowledge instruction. Both miss the point that what schools are first about is the moral construction in which knowledge can and does have meaning. What we consider to be knowledge and what we consider to be important ends of knowledge are born out of moral constructions. And as long as we believe knowledge is paramount, we will fail at reform.

Our fundamental difficulty with the orators and the philosophers is that their ideas have been reified. Their ideas act deterministically to organize our thoughts about education. Reification creates problems on at least two grounds, and in both cases because of what the great ideas fail to tell us or allow us to hear. Their reification hides the idea of multiplicity and divergence in ideas—that there are other ideas. Instead, ideas that do not work in the orators'-philosophers' framework stay occulted and outside our thoughts on education. The reification of the orators and philosophers also hides the fact that the great ideas of which they speak are only part of the cultural heritage, and only two perspectives on that one part. They are not *the* cultural heritage, and are not the only useful perspective on what ideas are and the role that ideas play in our lives. Clearly, people face issues in their everyday lives that are related to the big questions and the big ideas with which the orators and philosophers deal. Yet people also, in their everyday lives, deal with a reality that is much more immediate and much less "big" in the oratorical and philosophical sense of the term. The big ideas have become taken for granted, so people are not working from them or on them. These ideas have come to be assumed to be depictions of social reality.

We come back, then, to the problem of people being "pawns" or "participants" in the construction of their reality. Because the oratorical and philosophical ideas have become reified, people become pawns of them, and cease to exercise their human authorship over them. People become subject to the "reign of silence" (Bowers 1987) and lose sight of a "great idea" equal to that of Adler, Bloom, Hirsch, or Dewey: that virtue and knowledge are constructed out of the polyphony of everyday life. The result is that how people construct moral life is unavailable to our educational discourse. We are blinded by reified ideas.

In the perspective of Adler, Bloom, and Hirsch, ideas are great when they last, and they last because they are great. Dewey argues that true ideas will be discovered and that those ideas discovered through the process he prescribes are progressively better. The only place the oratorical and philosophical ideas have power as Adler, Bloom, Hirsch, and Dewey have defined them is in their reified states. Their debate of whether the pinnacle is past or yet to come misses—and silences—what we believe is a critical perspective and opportunity. We find the location of virtue in neither the past nor the future. Virtue is located in our present constructions and in the process of constructing our present—a point at which the orators never arrive and the philosophers never stay. In our sense, ideas are not great because of what they say about our past or our future but because of how they help us construct our present. Basing education and our lives in either set of ideas—oratorical or philosophical—without examination reifies the ideas, and results in people becoming pawns of them instead of participants in constructing their meanings and determining their use. The ideas are useful and representative of part of our cultural story, and we can show that they refer to something real. But in their isolation and reification, they miss the social construction of virtue.

These modern orators and philosophers reproduce the oratorical and philosophical ideas about education and link them indelibly in opposition. One locates truth and virtue in the past; the other, in the future. Each has a point, but the historical opposition of these ideas works against understanding the actual moral life of schools. They bind us to the historical opposition of these ideas and blind us to alternatives. This we see as a cultural trap reproduced by intellectuals and policy-makers alike. We may know both, choose one, and critique the other, but we are hard pressed to escape the hold of these ideas.

Wexler, writing about the new sociology of education, echoes our concerns:

> This form this containment takes is self-congratulatory. The exis-tence of so-called critiques and alternatives gives the aura of trans-formation and progress within society. In fact these alternatives operate as blockages to the exploration and realization of deeper differences and changes. (1987: 3)

In our case, the containment exercised by the cultural trap of these ideas and their opposition masks the moral nature of education. These ideas offer themselves as *the* explanations of education, and in doing so discredit other ideas. In the subsequent chapters, we will argue that these ideas are evident in the history of schools. It would be difficult for this not to be the case, given their reified character and historical domi-nance. Yet, as our analysis will show, they are in practice only incidental to the moral nature of schooling. In part, this is because both give knowl-edge primacy over values, and the schools we have worked with do not. In larger part, however, these ideas are only incidental, because they mislocate the arena of moral activity. For the orators, the pinnacle is past, and for the philosophers, the pinnacle is yet to be reached. For the people who went to Cedar Grove and Rougemont Schools, morality and virtue are constructed in the present. These people are not the pawns of the ideas promoted by the intellectuals in this chapter. Rather, they are participants in moral life, using relationships, narratives, each other, situ-ations, and ideas to socially construct virtue with their experiences of schooling. Virtue may be a subject of orators and philosophers, but as we will next show, people need not be either to construct virtue.

3

Cedar Grove School

In October 1987, the latest leader of Cedar Grove Elementary, the so-called graveyard of principals, invited a research team from the local state university to write a school history. With the demise of his predecessors in mind, Mr. Michaels thought that "unity through community" would be a practical slogan to draw his staff together and engender trust in students and parents. The school, built in 1916, had character and traditions. It had once been led by an American icon, a woman reputed to be the model for the formidable Miss Dove in *Good Morning, Miss Dove* (Patton 1947). The principal wanted us to discover the history of this school in a unique way. We were first to interview his entire staff to understand better the school and its traditions. These individual interviews were to be "communal" and not "divisive." He insisted that interviews would focus not on the present but on the past. Yet his stated goals were very much concerned with the present: (1) to create unity and stability in the school; (2) to relieve tensions; (3) to create a greater sense of order; (4) to change what Mr. Michaels perceived as a highly traditional way of teaching; (5) to assess the educational program at the school; and (6) to assess how the history of the school affects its future.

The staff at the school ranged from thirty-year veterans to a few teachers with only a few years of experience. All were women except for the janitor and the principal. At the second faculty meeting to be called in two years, the principal told teachers that he wanted to do an oral history project, and, for participation in the project, teachers would receive credit toward advanced certification and career-ladder merit raises. A teacher had attempted such a history two years before and had trained her students to do interviews. Mr. Michaels was depending on her to participate again in a study group composed of teachers, parents, himself, and our research team. This was to become the advisory board to the study.

As we walked into the media center—the former auditorium where "chapel" used to be held every day—for our introduction to the faculty, we felt extremely optimistic. Teachers seated themselves at round tables as far away from us as possible. They spoke very little and regarded us with the kind of teacher gaze that silences classrooms of elementary children. We began to get the uncomfortable feeling that we were not entirely welcome; that these teachers, getting ready for Halloween and attending an unaccustomed meeting at the end of a long day, were somewhat skeptical of outsiders brought in by a nearly outsider principal. It was easy to feel like heathens in this former chapel.

Under the cold, silent appraisal of the teachers, we were introduced, nervously spoke some rather banal phrases about what wonderful things we could do for the school, and sat down. One of our team had the same feelings that he had when he confronted the first high school class he ever taught: Tell 'em how clever you are, tell 'em how they'll benefit from your cleverness, and hope like hell they buy it.

The principal talked of "You Are There" P.A. announcements, Cedar Grove History trivia games, student skits, drawing and story contests, historical quilts, and visits by "oldest graduates" to newly revived elementary school graduation ceremonies. We sat, staring at hostile faces, wondering if the project would take place after all. We were trying to discover traditions; the principal was trying to reintroduce these traditions to encourage positive change. But the teachers had their own traditions which we were clearly violating.

As the faculty filed silently out of the meeting, two teachers stopped to speak with us. One stated that the project would be acceptable if we "did something good for the children." Another teacher—the one who had started a history two years before—stated that her history could be "a way of tying things together [over time]. Principals don't change; teachers don't change." She smiled as she said this, one of the few smiles we saw at Cedar Grove at that meeting.

Object Lessons

The teachers demonstrated to all of us that any efforts to render accounts of their realities would take place on their terms. They clearly communicated that we would have to build on the prior efforts of one of their own. They also communicated that history, to them, was not an academic enterprise. They understood that such a project had to have a moral result: something good for the children.

There was also a series of political lessons to be taught to Mr. Michaels and to us. The teachers used this opportunity to communicate that they held the power to kill or approve initiatives. While they later assented to participate and to facilitate our efforts, they took this opportunity to demonstrate to their new principal that their power had to be reckoned with. Indeed, Mr. Michaels considered dropping the project, but the teachers shortly let him know that they were not opposed to the project; rather, if he wished to continue with it, they wouldn't object— they simply did not see it as benefiting the children or them. In short, they taught Mr. Michaels that they were flexible but they also let him know that such projects obliged him to their interests.

The teachers also taught us that university researchers' interests were not theirs and that, ultimately, for us to do our project we were dependent on them. As a result, we redesigned the project to involve fourth- and fifth-grade students from the school's history club. We worked with the students to design an interview guide of interest to them, taught them how to do interviews and operate tape recorders, and set up a process whereby PTA parents took pairs of students to intervie- wees' houses and, after the interview, returned them either to school or their homes. As we were working with the students, a teacher signaled her acceptance of our status when she announced, "They'll be fine," and left the room and children in our charge. We had come up with some- thing sufficiently "good for children" to indicate that we had accepted the power of the teachers and our dependence on them.

There were other object lessons also, but these took us much longer to understand. The most important of these is that the teachers were also setting the stage for the fundamental moves in the social construction of reality according to Berger and Luckman (1967). We now understand that as we worked on the history project, the current and former com- munity members, former students, and parents were working to construct a moral story of the meaning of their school. They let us attend to the "facts"—dates, archives, and the like—while they began a process of negotiating an interpretive history In this way, they were creating an "object" that did not exist. This objectification of the moral lessons of Cedar Grove School and its subsequent legitimation—formally via the advisory board's acceptance and informally through reading of the documents by selected teachers and community members—created a new reality for the school. The play written and produced, based on the history, was the ultimate move in creating a new, collectively understood history.

This socially constructed history clearly silenced voices. Repeat- edly, we witnessed efforts to silence people (Weis and Fine, 1993). Two primary efforts deserve discussion, and we will return to them later. First was the effort to exclude people who were thought to be less than supportive of the school. We were repeatedly told not to bother inter- viewing so-and-so for s/he did not "know anything." When we inter- viewed such people, we learned that they challenged the view that

Cedar Grove School was idyllic. Some saw Mrs. Gregory (the "real" Miss Dove), a key character in the school's history, as an oppressive figure rather than as a moral icon. This is significant, for it reveals that the social construction of virtue is itself contested. On the other hand, these same interviews tended to confirm that Mrs. Gregory was much as she was portrayed by those who idolized her. In short, what was contested was not her behavior, but its interpretation: For some, she was virtue personified; for others, the devil.

The second effort at silencing we witnessed concerned not who should be talked with but what we could say in our document and otherwise. This effort, in turn, had a number of manifestations. First, some people were adamant that *Good Morning, Miss Dove* was not about the school or Mrs. Gregory. How this was said is important. The usual statement was: "Francis Gray Patton never said the book was about the [real Miss Dove]." This statement has two significant characteristics. First, different people repeated this almost verbatim: It was a cultural artifact as much as it was a disclaimer. It indicated that one was an insider to the debate, and a partisan of sorts. We will return later to the impact of the novel *Good Morning Miss Dove* and the person on whom the title character is supposedly based.

The statement also had a second, ironic meaning. Insiders knew that the statement did not, in fact, disclaim that the book was about Mrs. Gregory; it only acknowledged that Francis Gray Patton never acknowledged that it was about her. This put members of the research team in ironic situations. While we could not acknowledge any interest in the book, insiders could and repeatedly did. Some reread the book prior to their interview in order to be "prepared." Others opened with the above statement and proceeded to discuss the uncanny resemblance between the fictional and the real Miss Dove. The resemblance was not physical, they would point out, nor in the details of her life but in her behavior and virtues. With a full appreciation of the layers of irony, we took notes on all of this.

There were some who wished to suppress the significance of Mrs. Gregory because they believed it would undercut the contributions of the many other teachers and principals, themselves included. They understood that many saw Mrs. Gregory as larger than life, and they saw this as silencing their own voices. As a result, they attempted to silence her in order not to be silenced themselves.

Finally, as we noted in the opening paragraph of this chapter, Mr. Michaels had a vested interest in this history bringing people together rather than creating or highlighting divisiveness. His stipulations for the project limited both our efforts and the participation of community members and, especially, his staff. His stipulations certainly shaped the oral history, but less so in this book. Here his efforts are grist for analysis rather than a means of silencing.

All of the above object lessons, including the last, reveal how virtue is socially constructed. As we discussed in the first chapter, virtues are usually seen as qualities of individuals that correspond to some set of moral principles. Our argument is the direct counterpoint. In everyday life, virtues are constructed by people through discourse and relationships. They may be constructed as being qualities of individuals, and may find justification in known moral laws or tests. Ultimately, however, they are signs not of the moral rectitude of persons or of moral laws but of what an interpretive community wishes to make morally of itself. In Cedar Grove, the virtues of Miss Dove are what they wish to be their contribution of the wider moral discourse (MacIntyre 1981) through the oral history project.

In what follows, we have tried to render the narrative history as the current and former students, teachers, and parents constructed it. Of course, narrative was also socially constructed by the research team as we researched and as we wrote the numerous "cuts" on the history for professional meetings, publications, and for the consciously "celebratory" history we wrote for the school. In the narrative that follows, however, we are less celebratory than in the narrative for the school. What celebration there is comes from the study participants and is an important element in their social construction. We have also tried to be conscious of our own contributions to this social construction and to limit them in this text, but this is decidedly difficult to do. In the end, we have simply admitted they are us and we are they in all too many ways. This is yet another object lesson in sociology of knowledge. Researchers are never outside of that which they study.

The narrative has essentially two large parts. First is the history of the school and its community. This was the project all of us embarked on. As noted above, the social construction process rendered it as an "object." We will discuss the implications of this later. It provides the salient context to the second part, the narrative of virtue. The history will reveal that the ideas of the orators and of the philosophers cycle throughout the schools' lives, reflecting some of the larger societal debates. The narrative of virtue focuses on Miss Dove, this community's moral icon. Their portrayal of her is decidedly oratorical. She is the bastion of tradition, dogmatic in what and how she teaches, and culturally conservative, essentially subscribing to the classic model of cultural transmission that Hirsch, Bloom, and Adler make so much of. Seemingly everyone shares this characterization of her—the product of the book, years of discourse long before we arrived on the scene, and apparently her actual behavior. The point of disagreement regards the evaluation of her as virtuous or not.

A School for Us

Elementary education in the United States has often seemed perfunctory, a stage in which students learn to do the "basics"—read and write—so that they can get on to the serious subject-specific work of high school. It is traditionally a world of mothers, or at least of women who act like mothers. While the twentieth century has increasingly seen mothers putting children "into the hands of experts" (Tyack and Hansot 1980), these experts have tended to be other women whose roles have traditionally been devalued (see Apples 1986). Yet Cedar Grove was somehow different. Cedar Grove was more than a simple elementary school staffed by surrogate mothers; it had become a moral icon for those connected to it, one whose memory had to be protected and cherished after half a century.

The origins of Cedar Grove School date back to the post–Civil War period and the growth of urban centers in piedmont North Carolina. After the war, tobacco and textiles brought wealth, labor, and education to Treyburn. Randolph College relocated from another county in the 1890s through a combination of tobacco fortunes and Treyburn's civic pride. The college's new home was adjacent to College Dark, the section of Treyburn that was to be home to Cedar Grove Elementary School. The college, which became a major private university in time, helped insure that College Park would be home to the educational elite as well as to the upper class.

Despite its wealth, Treyburn was primarily a blue-collar, service and factory town. The College Park neighborhood was an exception. It could be described as upper-middle class, with many of its residents professors at Randolph College. Although the school board traditionally was composed largely of powerful tobacco and textile magnates, these university professionals frequently had representatives on the school board, particularly after 1910.

Although many of College Park's residents were connected with the college, the majority were merchants, businessmen, and professionals. They were part of the broader local economy produced by their families' successes in Treyburn's leading industries. These younger generations moved into modern, fashionable homes, in keeping with their own recent accomplishments, and chose not to live in the older neighborhoods where they grew up close to Treyburn's industries. In short, whether professors or other professionals, College Park residents saw themselves as being distinct in the city, as having "made it," and they wanted their part of Treyburn—and their school—to reflect this self-image.

The original settlement and growth of the College Park section of Treyburn did not include a school, and it would be well into the 1900s before the opportunity for a neighborhood school came about. Children from the area were sent to other neighborhoods to attend school until a series of events led to the creation of Cedar Grove Elementary School. On 21 May 1915, Moore School, adjacent to the College Park community, caught fire and burned. The city's board of education, reacting quickly, convened a meeting of its members that afternoon and deliberated its options.

The board was not the only group to act quickly that day. Over in the northwest corner of Treyburn, in the growing neighborhood of College Park, parents had been organizing support for a new school in their area. After a review of the idea, the board reported at the 21 May meeting that because the Cedar Grove Street area could provide an enrollment of only seventy-eight students, the option to rebuild the Moore School would be taken. Unsatisfied with the decision, representatives from the College Park community appeared before the board on 24 September 1915 with a petition requesting a school in their area. By the 9 December meeting, a committee of two (the auditor and the superintendent) had been appointed to examine all school buildings and to report measures necessary to protect the buildings from fires. Two weeks later, the board's activities indicated that the Cedar Grove group had achieved its objective. As the minutes from the 23 December meeting state:

> The committee on the site for the N.W. Treyburn school submitted a report recommending the purchase of the square bounded by Cedar Grove St., Central and Station Avenues, and Gregory St. for the sum of nine thousand dollars.

The Cedar Grove Street School was to be built on that site.

On Monday, 2 October 1916, the new Cedar Grove School held its first day of classes. The Treyburn *Morning Herald*, in the weekend edition on 1 October, compared the building favorably to its counterparts in northern cities. One month later, the school board voted to spend $10,000 in building costs and equipment at the school. By the 1917–1918 school year, Cedar Grove School faculty consisted of a principal and five teachers, and by the 2 January 1919 board meeting, a recommendation was made that the Cedar Grove School be enlarged. "The prospective growth of the Cedar Grove Street district requires that the Cedar Grove building be completed in the near future."

The school building was rectangular in shape. In the early years, segregation by gender was the rule. The left-hand side was the girls' side; the right-hand side, the boys' side. The playground was similarly split. The school consisted of six grades, with two levels of each grade. The first floor housed grades one through six. The second floor comprised rooms for civics, music, art, and geography. The auditorium (what became the media center/library) also was on the second floor; since it doubled as the chapel, often it was referred to simply as that. The cafeteria was in the basement.

Like many schools of the early part of the century, Cedar Grove School adopted a curriculum that reflected William Wirt's Gary Plan. By the late 1920s, more than one thousand American public schools had adopted this plan, which was designed to utilize school space efficiently and involved shifting students according to subject matter (Campbell et al. 1986). Classes were departmentalized so that children had different teachers for specific subjects. By the third grade, students had a different teacher for each subject area. In the two-teacher grades, students had one teacher in the morning and the other in the afternoon. In the upper grades students had some subjects three days a week and some two days a week. A former teacher reminisced that children paid attention to bells, had to be silent, and had to move without talking. According to another former teacher, students had to "learn the alphabet [and] Bible verses every morning." Teachers, who for the times were very well educated (by the 1930s many had master's degrees), attended summer workshops in New York and Boston. They returned with many "progressive" ideas inspired by Dewey. As good progressive educators, teachers employed the "project method" to get students interested in geography and civics.

Students sat at old-fashioned desks that were a seat-desk combination with an ink well on the front cover. Students wrote with steel pens. Miss Sally James, principal of Cedar Grove School, also served as the penmanship instructor for the Treyburn city schools in the 1920s. Students learned the Palmer Method of penmanship. The combination of steel pens and "using your whole arm" was, as one student remembered, "a messy experience."

The teachers during (as well as before and after) Miss James's administration were ideologically attuned to the notion that order is a prerequisite to learning and helped to ensure that the school ran smoothly and efficiently. Every subject was incorporated into the scheme planned by the homeroom teacher. In the ten periods that made up the school day, students were in homeroom with their official teacher for reading, writing, arithmetic, spelling, and English, and went outside the homeroom for extra studies. Teachers assigned projects and students kept notebooks. One geography project had students tracing their family trees back to Europe. Civics projects dealt with local government and current events. In Miss Elizabeth Ray's class, students planned a party for their parents, the object of which was to teach manners.

There was a special acceleration program offered at Cedar Grove School through what is now Randolph University. In this program, students had the chance to "attend summer school before first grade and again between first and second grade and be promoted from the upper section of the first to the lower section of the third."

By the mid-1930s, through the cooperative efforts of parents and teachers, the school and students were able to hear the Walter Damrosh Music Program. It was broadcast by NBC, and students and teachers would attend "chapel" in the auditorium for the show on Friday afternoons. "Damrosh would take a musical instrument and show what it sounded like. . . . The orchestra would play music; Damrosh would explain."

Three hundred forty-three children attended Cedar Grove School by September 1940. Yet, to them, the school seemed smaller and more intimate than these numbers suggest; it was a "neighborhood school." Going into school, the children noticed that, as usual, the place was "as neat as a pin." There were the same old wooden railings on the stairs and the same walk down the dark hallway to the newly decorated lunchroom. The upstairs hall had a new door which excited considerable comment and admiration. The classrooms were also neat and orderly. Miss Ray's classroom had musical instruments around it, while Mrs. Gregory had recently removed the white sheets of paper she always used to cover pictures on her walls during the summer. When students sat at their desks, they would find inkpots on them, as usual.

The 1940s would be characterized by shortages of books, war materials, and, later, teachers. The school would raise money, collect old keys, donate blood, and make sure that needy children at Cedar Grove had raincoats and galoshes. Parents would be instructed on health, sex education, wartime care of children, and other topics. In the late 1940s they would be urged to lead normal and healthy lives for their children's sake.

The principal "had a big desk," but perhaps it just looked big to those unfortunate enough to have to stand in front of it in disgrace or to those behind it who were to be moving on. In February 1940, Miss Sally James was informed by Superintendent Warren that she would no longer be principal at Cedar Grove after the 1939–1940 school year but would be made Director of writing for the city (School Board Minutes [SBM], 2/12/40). Miss Sally responded:

> As I had no intimation of the fact that I was not giving satisfaction from you . . . or from patrons, it came as a surprise to me. I am very sorry I did not measure up when it was necessary, and I am hurt beyond the telling when I think of leaving the children. However, I feel sure you did what you think was right and best, and I shall abide in that confidence and promise to cooperate in every way. I thoroughly appreciate the consideration I have had in the past and the fact that I may still have some work with the children here in Treyburn. . . . I will do my level best to be worth it! What ever work you and Mr. Warren see fit to assign me, I promise to undertake with the same enthusiasm I have been happy to give for the 35 years I have taught in Treyburn. (SBM 3/19/40)

The student paper, *HighLights*, welcomed Mr. Linnam as principal later in 1940. "A good impression has been given by Cedar students," the new principal said. He liked to spend time with his family, go to the movies, watch baseball, and play football. He had graduated from the University of Georgia and Randolph University, and had been transferred from Lakewood School, where he had also been principal. At the time, some kids may have thought Mr. Linnam was "mean as hell," but he was seen in retrospect as simply a good disciplinarian—not an unusual trait for principals in those days. It was no joke to be sent to the office. Other children would look down on the child who met such a fate, even though a good many shared it in the course of their elementary careers.

As always, students were expected to behave. And, in case they did not quite get the message either from their teachers or Mr. Linnam, the February 1941 Cedar Grove *HighLights* (CGH) had a full-page coloring exercise with two cartoon kittens who "sometimes forget their good manners and run through the halls and slam the doors." A question at the bottom of the page asks, "How should you walk through the halls? Write your answer here." The answer was at the top of the page: "Good manners ask you to walk quietly in the halls and rooms" (CGH 2/41). Mr. Linnam seemed to have been a highly respected principal. On 28 July 1942, the Treyburn Board of Education authorized the superintendent to increase his salary by $100 "if by doing so it would cause him to remain in the city schools" (SBM 7/28/42). Mr. Linnam stayed in the city but moved to East Treyburn Junior High to become principal. Mr. E.

L. Phips came from Mr. Linnam's old school, Lakewood, to become the new principal. According to one source, Mr. Phips was also "strict." Mr. Phips's administration seems to have been essentially one of caretaking. Few people offered anything distinctive about these years.

The Cedar Grove *HighLights* as a Symbol of Success

The Cedar Grove *HighLights*, the school newspaper, attained state and national recognition, and it represented for students one of their opportunities to live out the creation of an elite product. The *HighLights* received first prize in the Carolina Scholastic Press Competition, and ranked second in the National Scholastic Press competition during the 1930s. Cedar Grove School was duly noted as "the first school to win a blue ribbon below the Mason-Dixon Line."

A wide variety of topics were reported in the Cedar Grove *HighLights*. The reports ranged from what was being observed any particular week by the school (e.g., fire prevention, self-control, American Education Week) to trips taken by children and their families. There was a showcase each month for individual classroom news that was of note and even columns devoted to the PTA and the grade mothers. Some typical entries from October 1933:

- Damrosh Concert—Everyone Enjoys Concert—Friday, October 20, 1933, the Walter Damrosh program came to us over the radio. We especially enjoyed it because only the string instruments were used.
- First Grade News—Mumps!—Betty Campbell is sick. She was out three weeks with mumps.
- Clinton, Be Careful!—We are sorry Clinton Roach has to be out several days. He was run over by a boy on a bicycle.
- Miss Burke (at society program): "What shall we sing?"
  Leslie Christian: "Save My Teacher." (The song he meant was "Savior Teach Me")

From January 1934:

- News (Guy Andrews, 6B2)—A Beloved Teacher Resigns—The news that Miss Olive Faucette, fourth grade teacher, had resigned came as a sad blow to our entire school. Miss Faucette started her teaching career in our school, and during her five years here we have learned to love her and feel that she belongs to us. We extend to her our sincere good wishes for success and happiness in her new work. We could not forgive Miss Faucette for leaving us if she had [*sic*] left us in such good hands. We like Mrs. Carter, our new teacher, and hope she will like us.

- Rachmaninoff—Rachmaninoff, a famous pianist and composer, will appear in concert at the University of North Carolina Feb. 21. We are interested in the famous musicians who come to our towns.

From February 1934:

- Happenings in 5A1—Civics: The most interesting thing we have done this month in the civics room is to elect officers for civics society. Vernon Smith presided at the election. He certainly kept us in order.
- MUSIC: On February 22, 5A1 had a good time in the music room singing a new George Washington song. Senator Umstead sent it to Miss Reade from Washington. Miss Reade says we are very good when we sing popular songs.
- Items of interest from 6A2: Disaster Hits 6A2—A man hole [cover] fell on Jeana Davison's foot. We miss you, Jeana!

There was a news column, a sports column, literary and poetry columns, and art and joke columns. Student exchange was encouraged so that students could get a real feel for the goings-on around the world.

The Cedar Grove *HighLights* was not just a source of local and school news but a chance for children to find out how things really worked in journalism. They reported dutifully, whether it was about the school's best spellers, Miss Bray's science class, or Miss Coran's garden.

A good deal can be gleaned from the Cedar Grove *HighLights* regarding attitudes toward health and safety, play, morals, education, and the world outside the school. Physical examinations had long been a part of school routine. In addition, the trend toward mass removal of tonsils was in evidence by the number of consolation notices to afflicted classmates in *HighLights*. A fire drill in 1946 emptied the school of two hundred seventy-one children and teachers in one minute and twenty-eight seconds. There seemed to be pride in this accomplishment (CGH 10/46). Health and safety seemed to take on great importance as America emerged from World War II. Implicit in a number of announcements regarding children's injuries was the advice: If you follow the rules, you won't get hurt. A "Second Grade News" headline in October 1946 contained the following article: "We are sorry that [a student] was hit by a car. She was playing in the street at home. We are glad she was not hurt badly." In a speech in the PTA Annual Study Course entitled "The Health of Parent and Teacher as It Affects the Child," the speaker emphasized the issue of mental, physical, and moral health: "Since a child usually adopts his parents' attitudes towards life, parents should care that theirs are normal ones" (PTA scrapbook 3/48). Even in an article in September 1946 entitled "A Night of Fun," regarding "the fun, frolic, and lots of pranks" of Halloween, caution was urged against "destructible [sic] hoodlums" and "a night of destroying property, terror, and vandalism." The joke page in November 1946 contained a warning among the jests: "Cross streets carefully!"

Efficiency and orderliness were also very important in the mid-1940s. Parents were advised in the October 1946 *HighLights* (the first edition since the paper shortages of 1942–1943 and the first under Mrs. Gregory) that no visitors would be allowed in classes "without permission from the office. One mother talking to a teacher takes the time away from twenty-five children." Mrs. Gregory was referred to as "our most efficient principal," and awards were given for "efficient line monitors," "efficient librarians," "faithful shade monitors," and others who helped the school run in an orderly way. The need for rules was not lost on students, who composed poems about them:

> School isn't hard if you obey,
> And learn your lessons every day.
> But if you choose to break each rule,
> There will be no fun at school. (CGH 10/46)

Because of Mrs. Gregory's interest in natural history, "many interesting things [were] collected and preserved," such as a stuffed eagle, a stuffed owl, armadillo shells, hornets' nests, and rocks (CGH 6/48). These exhibits were set up in a school museum which classes could visit. Chapel programs included a dramatization of "Little Frog" (second grade), another play, Halloween Parade (fourth grade), choral reading, and explanation of the Lord's Prayer (third grade). As one former student noted, chapel was a time when every student had a chance to get on stage. Mrs. Gregory found a substantial number of educational films that corresponded with what children were learning in their classes, particularly social studies. Children also had many opportunities to write and get their work published in the substantial *HighLights* (one issue in the late 1940s was more than twenty pages long).

The *HighLights* contains numerous stories of classroom activities. In February 1941 the second-graders learned a song called "George Washington," in honor of his birthday. At the same time, other grades were illustrating the lives of Lincoln and Washington in the art room. Miss Ray's first grades were setting up a puppet stage and were making dolls, toy furniture, and even a blue giraffe: "Do you like to act? Do you like toys? If the answer is 'yes' then the first grade is the place for you" (CGH 2/41). The third grade had a grocery store to help students with arithmetic. Outside of Mrs. Gregory's class was a map of the United States made by several of her students. Strings led from various points on the map to pictures of different agricultural products from the states (CGH 4/41).

In addition to their classwork, children participated in a wide variety of activities, particularly during the early 1940s. There was, as always, work on the Cedar Grove *HighLights*. By the 1940s this paper had grown to more than ten pages per issue. Children also regularly participated in the Boy and Girl Scouts, the Safety Patrol, and the orchestra.

In later decades, the students of Cedar Grove School were also busy reporting on their school lives. *Cedar In the News*, the new name of the school newspaper, kept the Cedar Grove School citizenry abreast of the latest news. From the December 1965 issue:

"Boy Ruins Flack's Pop Corn String"

Friday, Dec. 10, Mrs. Flack and her class were decorating the Christmas Tree in the hall while a member of that class, whose name shall remain Mr. X, was silently eating the popcorn from the string when no one was watching; but Mrs. Cohen's sneaky class managed to see him commit this terrible crime

And for a taste of the Cedar Grove School world as it was in January 1966:

"Mrs. Monroe is Back"

The new year has begun with Mrs. Monroe back with us. No more TV and no more play. The homework is piling up and Math and English are very important subjects.

Parents as Protectors of Virtues

The Cedar Grove School PTA was created around 1920, shortly after the organization of the North Carolina Congress of Parents and Teachers. According to one community member, in North Carolina "many women's patriotic and civic groups had formed state federations before 1919 . . . but there was no concerted effort to draw these groups together until the war experience and the partial suffrage granted to women by England. . . . When the Nineteenth Amendment was well on its way to becoming a part of the U. S. Constitution, N.C. women decided to band themselves together for the welfare of the child in the home, the school and the community."

Inspired by their new expectations for women's role in society, they met in Charlotte in November 1919 and organized the State Congress as a branch of the National Congress of Mothers and Parent Teacher Association. The program that was immediately adopted makes clear that the new organization planned to act in a political and integrated way.

Several measures were taken to integrate the local groups' work across the whole state, and in such a way as also to foster men's participation. A former PTA member mentioned that "ten vice-presidents were chosen to represent geographical territory, five being men in school work." Concerning the twenty-two committees "ranging from Americanization to Thrift," she says that "they covered a vast field and were led by men and women, whose activity has been a blessing to N. C. for many years" (PTA minutes 1920).

These few observations are examples of the spirit that guided the creation of the PTAs in North Carolina. They provide the context in which the Cedar Grove School PTA developed its work for many decades. The receptivity of this school to the new organization's proposals seemed to be immediate. In the first annual session of the North Carolina PTA, which took place in Greensboro in November 1920, there were reports from many schools, including Cedar Grove (PTA minutes). From this origin came the strong links maintained by this PTA with the state congress throughout the decades as well as its commitment to the common objectives of the Parent Teacher Associations:

- To promote the welfare of children and youth in home, school, church and community.
- To raise the standards of home life.
- To secure adequate laws for the care and protection of children and youth.
- To develop a closer relationship between the home and the school so that parents and teachers may cooperate intelligently in the training of the child.
- To develop between educators and the public such united efforts as will secure for every child the highest advantages in physical, mental, social and spiritual education..

From the end of the 1920s on, the Cedar Grove School had a very active and dynamic PTA. Throughout the years it carried out a large number of projects and activities aimed at enhancing the relationships between the school and the community and improving the teaching conditions at the school. But, beyond this, it involved itself with many programs of a political-educational nature aimed at the school system's improvement, and it developed a large number of charitable activities on behalf of deprived children.

PTA meetings were usually held in the afternoon, but to encourage fathers' attendance, meetings were occasionally held in the evening. Most talks addressed the children's welfare, with greater emphasis on health (physical, psychological, mental) and preschool education. This interest of the PTA, aided by the great effort of the community, resulted in two very important events for Cedar Grove School: the installation of the health clinic, in 1928, for examinations of kindergarten children, and the opening of the cafeteria in 1929. The Cedar Grove Street Baptist Church donated the room for the clinic; the city's board of education funded the cafeteria.

During this period, Miss Sally James, the principal who was mentioned earlier, initiated activities leading to a substantial increase in the number of library books purchased and an increase in book circulation. There was some emphasis on charitable activities such as the provision of clothing and lunch for poor children. In addition, the PTA took an active role in the celebrations of Christmas and Founder's Day.

In the 1930s, the Cedar Grove PTA delegates were present at all state conventions and some national ones. The Cedar Grove PTA also took part in practically all the district and city council meetings. The PTA at Cedar Grove tried to affect the educational and moral environment of the school, dealing with political and economic issues that affected the school system. It supported, for example, the state platform of 1935, which endorsed many philosophical ideas:

> eight months school term; curriculum changes to meet the demands of the changing times; trained leadership for public schools; continuation of public health and library service; adequate support for higher institutions of learning; wise economy in government and a scientific study of North Carolina's needs. (PTA minutes)

The emphasis on attendance at meetings and full membership intensified in the 1930s. Beyond the prize for the class with the largest parental attendance, the PTA used new strategies such as visits to homes and study groups. The membership almost doubled between 1930 and 1936, rising from 136 to 252 parents.

The lectures at PTA meetings in the 1930s were quite diverse, with an emphasis on pedagogical matters ("Moral Effects of Failure," "Importance of Reading," "Remedial Reading and Reading Tests," "Homework"), values for education ("Moral Life of Children," "Character of Education," "The Importance of Mental Hygiene of the Pre-School Child," "Patriotism"), and educational politics (such as those mentioned in the 1935 state PTA platform). The PTA's efforts to aid teachers were very successful. They bought the school a radio (in 1930), a set of picture slides for visual education (1932), a microscope (1933), a piano (1937), and a loom (1938). The group's charitable activities were expanded. In 1931 the Cedar Grove School PTA began to work in connection with the Needle Work Guild in collecting clothing, shoes, coal, and money for poor children who could not attend school. Needy students at Cedar Grove were supported with funds from the PTA's regular budget.

All through the early 1940s, the PTA was busy organizing Christmas parties for the children, helping out in classrooms and on field trips (such as one that took second graders to see all the other schools in Treyburn), and presenting special programs for the parents and faculty. These programs included: "Recreation in the Home" (November 1942), "Wartime Care of Children" (January 1943), "Psychology of the Problem Child" (February 1943), and "The Platoon School" (October 1943). Because working fathers could rarely attend the three o'clock meetings, a Fathers' Night was organized in November 1943. In December 1943 a special appeal was made for workbooks for the children, and the PTA responded by requesting a small donation from every parent.

Following the suggestions of the state PTA, the Cedar Grove School PTA was guided during the 1945–1946 school year by the slogan "Together we build," which meant "an earnest effort to make the Associations a strong connecting link between home and school" (PTA scrapbook 1945–1946). The theme of building continued throughout the late 1940s and was expressed by the PTA in their continued support for school improvement projects (such as the playground fence and the purchase of ventilators for the classrooms) and their help in adding key personnel, such as a physical education director (1948). The PTA also purchased awards for the outstanding boy and girl in the sixth-grade class.

In the 1950s the Cedar Grove PTA bought duplicators, Kleenex, a portable public address system (1955), furnishings and decorations for the teachers' lounge (1957), and gifts for the faculty and principal. Money also went to the Safety Patrol, social events such as the Christmas Party, and the Children's Museum (PTA scrapbook 1951–1952,

1957–1958). The membership of the PTA hit 100 percent for the first time in the 1957–1958 school year (PTA scrapbook 1957–1958). Programs and speakers at PTA meetings reflect many of the concerns of the 1950s and the young baby boom generation: "What the Modern School Tries to Do for the Individual Child" (1951–1952), "Hobbies, Their Origin and Role in Life" (1957), "Schools and Defense," "Schools Keep Us Free," "Education for the Long Pull" (Part of the Education Week theme for 1952—"Unite for Freedom"). To keep members and children abreast of cultural activities, the music committee of the PTA published a list of upcoming events, such as a Four Freshmen concert at Randolph University or Lawrence Welk on television "for those who like good pop music" (PTA scrapbook 1957–1958). The music committee also scheduled musical entertainment for PTA meetings.

Teachers were growing scarce in the 1950s. In a lecture entitled "What We Can Do to Improve Our Schools in North Carolina," A. C. Dawson, Superintendent of Southern Pines Public Schools, said:

One of our primary responsibilities therefore is to keep our teachers (whose training ranks sixth in the nation) in North Carolina. . . . As long as we rank 34th in salaries, however, this condition [of having too few teachers or teachers leaving North Carolina] will not improve. (PTA scrapbook 1956–1957)

The PTA did not remain inactive on this issue. When a proposed 19.31 percent teacher salary increase did not receive the support of Governor Hodges, the United Forces for Education mobilized a letter-writing campaign in order to establish the "minimum program necessary to retain those teachers now teaching in North Carolina schools and to attract qualified new teachers." A leaflet distributed by the PTA went on to say:

The most effective demonstration of citizen interest has been, and will continue to be, letters from YOU. These letters will have their greatest impact if they are addressed to Representatives E. K. Powe, Cecil Hill, Jr., and Senator Claude Currie, with carbon copies to Governor Hodges.

IF the approximately 170 legislators received 50 letters AND a copy of each letter was sent to the Governor, it would mean that Mr. Hodges would receive 8,500! (PTA scrapbook 1956–57)

Clearly, the issue of teacher retention was much in the minds of parents and teachers at Cedar Grove School in the 1950s.

As in past decades, the PTA continued to influence the life and character of Cedar Grove School. Assisting needy families, fund raising, and community information sessions were just a few of the themes approached at monthly meetings in the 1964–1965 school year. In September 1964 the PTA organized an "Outgrown Clothing Drive," in which outgrown clothing was donated to the needy in both the school and the community. During the 1960s the PTA also elected it first male president, who presided for two years, from 1966 to 1968.

At different points in the year, the PTA attempted to offer sessions that could provide information for the parents and the community of Cedar Grove School. In November 1964 the theme of the monthly meeting dealt with safety, in response to a recent hit-and-run accident involving one of the school children. At the January 1965 meeting, a couple of months later, students were given an opportunity to present the results of their study of art and music at the monthly meeting on art projects. In the late 1960s the PTA emphasized the "Get Acquainted Night" (the first meeting of the year), so that parents and teachers could know each other better. On this same day, free yearbooks were distributed, showing pictures of the principal, teachers, and staff.

Rituals of Elitism, Rites of Passage

Cedar Grove School served the professional class which included university faculty. Education was valued, and excellence was expected of students and of the school. Given the consistency of these expectations, school social events took on special meaning. Celebration symbolized the elite nature of this community, and rites of passage symbolized both the success of the students and the community.

May Day and Graduation

The two biggest days of the school year for students at Cedar Grove School were May Day and Graduation Day. The May Day celebration was held on the playground, and was a fixture in the history of Cedar Grove School through the early 1970s. Each spring, as a rite of passage, the students practiced the wrapping of the pole at Cedar Grove, and then had the honor of actually wrapping the pole in the May Day ceremony. A student recalled:

The celebration was a big event at Cedar Grove School. . . . The dancers wore crepe paper dresses, with each grade level in a different color. The Maypole never seemed to be wound correctly. The grassy north side of the school was the ideal place for the dancers then.

And about graduation she recalled:

> I will always remember that auditorium upstairs at the front of. the school with its stage at one end and its wooden chairs riveted to the floor. I'll never forget, too, that I was sent to the cloakroom for talking during graduation practice.

According to a student who attended the school in the late 1920s, graduation was an event, especially for the boys, since they got to wear long pants for the first time—white ones at that—instead of knickers. It was a another rite of passage complete with a valedictorian and salutatorian. The salutatory address began: "We welcome you this glad day our parents, friends and teachers of Cedar Street School"

At the 1947 commencement exercises, Jimmy Vaughan made a speech in which he fashioned an "acrostic" of F.A.R.E.W.E.L.L. (friends, appreciation, remembrance, experience, wishes, earnestness, love, loyalty). His description of love for that event was as follows:

> The first grader feels it the moment he enters Miss Ray's room—so much that he soon forgets he has left mother for the first time. Each teacher continues to show her love, and soon a great chain of love binds all the pupils and teachers, firmly clasped together by the great love of our beloved principal. (CGH 6/47)

A teacher who was at the school from the late 1940s through the late 1970s remembered graduation this way:

> Have you ever been to a Randolph University commencement or any college commencement? We had one too at Cedar Grove School. The girls wore white and the boys wore their ties and we had a valedictorian and we went through the whole deal with sixth grade marching in, and flags and speeches and had camellias flown in from Florida.

Safety Patrol

The Safety Patrol was a singular honor for upperclassmen—boys in fifth and sixth grades. The patrol members were hand picked at the end of the fourth grade by their teachers. One student remembers, "It was some question what authority you had to stop a car, but the chance to do it was pretty big for a ten year old."

Participation in the Cedar Grove School Safety Patrol offered one of the more demanding extracurricular activities for fifth- and sixth-grade boys. Over the years this award-winning team of Cedar Grove School's finest had seen to the safe travel of community children. The patrol made sure that students crossed streets on the corners, and as part of their duty reported crosswalk deviants to the principal for punitive action. Members of the patrol were expected to keep brass on their uniforms buffed, keep their pants pressed, and wear white gloves. Each year the Treyburn City Schools selected the best Safety Patrol team from among its elementary schools, an award Cedar Grove School won on many occasions.

Voice of the Elite: A Self Study

During the 1973–1974 school year, the professionals working at Cedar Grove School had an opportunity to describe their school to themselves and a group of educators outside the school who would be there to assess in detail the quality of education going on. In that year Cedar Grove School underwent Southern Association Accreditation. All schools that undergo the accreditation process follow the same plan and must carry out the evaluation in the same amount of time. The accreditation process, whereby committees of teachers and administrators evaluated all aspects of their school, included not only academic programs (e.g., social studies, math, and science), but also the following analysis of the self-study based on six areas covered in the document: (1) "The School Community," (2) "the Children Served By the School," (3) "Philosophy," (4) "Language Arts," (5) "Emergency School Assistance Aid" (ESAA), (6) "The Teaching–Learning Process."

At the time of the 1973–1974 accreditation study, Cedar Grove School had one principal, a faculty of fifteen, and a staff of ten. Cedar Grove had undergone its last full accreditation self-study in 1963, and dramatic changes had occurred since then. The faculty at Cedar Grove School gave this description of their school in the foreword to their self-study:

At that time [1963] the membership consisted of 378 all white students. Most of these students came from upper-class business and professional families. Today the school is completely integrated and has a membership of 233. Of these, 124 are white and 109 non-white.

For the most part, the building had not changed since 1963, however bathrooms for both boys and girls had been built on the second floor. The library had been renovated to make it more usable.

Cedar Grove School drew most of its students from the College Park community, and, as the self-study suggests, a majority of the students were healthy, clean, and articulate. Even at the early stage of elementary school, according to the study, Cedar Grove children had visions of college and technical school. During the year students were treated to performances by the State Symphony, dance groups, and plays, both on and off the Cedar Grove campus. For the boys, it was deemed an honor to be able to serve on the Cedar Grove School Safety Patrol. Select students also put in extra time at Cedar Grove as library assistants. Outside school, students could participate in YMCA/YWCA activities, Boy Scouts, Girl Scouts, and lessons in music, dance, and art. Civic clubs and churches sponsored football and basketball leagues for Cedar Grove School boys as part of a community effort.

The community that lived around Cedar Grove School was led by an active PTA. The school kept contact with the community through bulletins, conferences with parents, and open house. The community was a ready source of guests to speak or demonstrate in classes and assembly programs. PTA activities included fund raisers for clothing, Safety Patrol trips, and instructional supplies.

Following is a sample of the text from the report on the school. Our comments about each section follow. These selections of text give some insight into what was held to be important about the education of children at Cedar Grove school.

Community

Integration was no big problem here. Most parents were interested in the welfare of children. This current year we have a Black an president of the PTA, the first, but an excellent choice.

Many of our parents are business and professional people. They hold high aspirations for their children. Others want their children to finish high school and attend a trade school. Most of them realize that education must go beyond high school.

The Children Served

The majority of children attending Cedar Grove School are in good health, clean, and able to communicate well with their teachers and peers.

Most of the students are cooperative and polite. A very few, due to poor home environment, use language that is not up to our standards. Constant efforts are exerted to improve this.

Most of the children who attend Cedar Grove School are eager to achieve. Quite a number plan to go to college and some plan to go to technical schools. The children like Cedar Grove and are loyal to it. There are no dropouts here in elementary school.

Teachers encourage pupils to have things to do in their spare time.

Philosophy

The faculty at Cedar Grove School believes that the elementary school should aid in the development and adjustment of the child for the assumption of his personal role in American society. Our philosophy is that each child is an individual who should be helped toward a self realization of his potential as a member of his community.

To promote a better understanding and appreciation for children from all social, economic, cultural and ethnic backgrounds.

Language Arts

Oral Expression: The goal is for each child to communicate through the use of clear diction, correct grammar, and a good vocabulary in both formal and informal situations.

Emergency School Assistance Aid

The slow learning child is the focus of this special program involving pupils in grades 4, 5, and 6.

The program is aimed at preventing a gradual regression of a pupil's achievement level in the math and/or reading area.

The Teaching–Learning Process

The faculty of Cedar Grove School believes that the teacher is the key to the learning process. Thus the teacher should be trained in effective teaching procedures, have a wide educational background, have wide interests and a stimulating personality, have an understanding of and love for children, and serve as a leader in all learning activities. Other conditions conducive to learning include pupil–teacher planning, teacher motivation, good teacher–pupil–parent relationships, a relaxed classroom atmosphere, a variety of learning experiences and media, effective evaluation procedures, and an attractive and stimulating physical environment.

Through the years, the parents of Cedar Grove children had shown a great deal of interest in the school. Most parents were interested in the children's welfare. The parents of Cedar Grove School were mainly business and professional people with high aspirations for their children. The Cedar Grove faculty drew a distinction between these parents and "others" who "want their children to finish high school and attend a trade school." These parents were not included in the "aspiration group." While most realized education had to go on beyond high school, the nature of that education was different depending on who your parents were. It is also interesting, keeping in mind the social and political climate in 1974, that integration anywhere was without its problems. Yet the Cedar Grove self-study states, "Integration was no big problem here."

The faculty at Cedar Grove School believed that the elementary school should aid in the development and adjustment of the child for the assumption of his personal role in American society. The philosophy of the faculty was that each child was an individual who should be helped toward a self-realization of his potential as a member of his community. The school sought to design an environment where the child could develop responsible interpersonal relationships, opportunity for self-expression, and the means for using a child's natural curiosity to promote learning. The "purpose" of Cedar Grove School was to teach "the art of living" in a fast and ever-changing world and society. Teachers believed each child was an individual and should be treated as such. Their job was to encourage each child to experience his potential and to achieve success. Physical and mental health, proper use of leisure time, and the ability to get along with others, in addition to academics, were essential.

The Cedar Grove study, referring to "dropouts," states, "The children like Cedar Grove as a school are loyal to it. There are no dropouts here in elementary school." The self-study for Cedar Grove implies that "dropouts" are nonachievers, uninterested in college, and disloyal to the school. It is also interesting that the children at Cedar Grove—kindergarten through sixth grade—"plan to go to college and . . . technical schools." Children at elementary schools planned their futures in such a way, and with such distinctions. This attribution tells more about the assumptions made about the children than whether the children actually believed or said this. Cedar Grove also draws a distinction between those who use proper language and those who don't, and associates poor language with a particular group: "A very few, due to poor home environments use language not up to our standards."

The Cedar Grove philosophy treats school as a prerequisite to "assumption of [the student's] personal role in American society " The student has a role he will assume rather than an already-existing community role as a student. Education is preparing to be, not being. In this process the teacher was the key. There is no mention of the student's place in the process, other than "pupil–teacher planning," and "teacher–pupil–parent relationships." The teacher had to be trained in effective teaching procedures, have a wide educational background, have wide interests and a stimulating personality, have an understanding of and a love for children, and serve as a leader in *all* learning activities. In the subject of language arts as one area of this process at Cedar Grove, the goal was "clear diction, correct grammar, and a good vocabulary." The standard was the socially accepted way children were supposed to express themselves. The standard was competence and excellence—a strong preference for the oratorical idea.

Emergency School Assistance Aid provided grants to school districts in the early 1970s to help alleviate problems brought on by desegregation. Cedar Grove used ESAA funds to attempt to improve math and reading performance among students. Cedar Grove states as its goal for the program "preventing a gradual regression of a pupil's achievement level in the math and/or reading area." Its target is "the slow learning child." The slow-learning child came to Cedar Grove School with desegregation. Instead of integrating the children into the regular curricula, the school responded with special educational programs which resegregated them.

The Self-Study Revisited

The Cedar Grove story has a "this is who we want you to think we are" nature; the Cedar Grove authors have done the interpreting for the reader. There is little description; the story is built. The Cedar Grove story is a managed story, one in which the image has been created for the audience (and maybe for the authors). When the Cedar Grove story becomes specific, it is to displace blame. Cedar Grove tells what parents are; it tells what children will be.

The Cedar Grove story in the self-study is about two communities, and thus tells two stories whenever the difference between the two needs to be recognized. There is at Cedar Grove one group that achieves and has always achieved; There is another that does not and has not, the interlopers. Cedar Grove School's self-study reveals the legacy of elitism. As the student population diversified, the school responded with stratification. While differentiated curricula is a philosophical idea, the stratification of Cedar Grove reserved the more oratorical approach for the elites and allowed the non-elites a more philosophical approach. In accommodation, the oratorical idea remained superior.

The Ultimate Symbol of Virtue: The Real Miss Dove

When we first arrived at Cedar Grove School in the Fall of 1987, we were presented with what would become one of the most intriguing and controversial issues of the oral history project. The principal of the school gave us a copy of the book *Good Morning, Miss Dove* written by Francis Gray Patton and first published in 1947 The offer was made on the supposition that the central figure of the book—Miss Dove—was based on a person who had long been associated with Cedar Grove School— Mrs. Dorothy Gregory. We soon found that the similarity between Miss Dove and Mrs. Gregory was more than literary—the two shared almost inseparable stories.

As stated earlier in this chapter, a person's place at Cedar Grove school could in part be discerned by his or her view—acceptance or denial—of *Good Morning, Miss Dove*. Mr. Michaels quickly learned this when it became known that he had given copies of the book to the research team. Powerful teachers and community members led him to demand that we distance ourselves from the book, avoiding reference to it and, if pressed, disclaiming any interest in it.

The shared identities of Miss Dove and Mrs. Gregory, and *Good Morning, Miss Dove* and Cedar Grove School, were not all positive. In many cases we were confronted, as researchers, with situations in which people adamantly opposed linking the two stories together. One such situation was an interview early in the study where we talked with two former teachers and a former principal of the school. One teacher had been a student of Mrs. Gregory's as well as a teacher under her; the other teacher had worked at Cedar Grove while Gregory served as principal. The principal who talked with us in the interview knew Mrs. Gregory only through stories passed down in the school's lore, of which *Good Morning, Miss Dove* and Mrs. Gregory had become a part. During that interview we were challenged directly on the relationship between Mrs. Gregory, Miss Dove, the book, and the real-life Cedar Grove School. During the interview, one of the teachers asked, "Have you read *Good Morning, Miss Dove?*" The other teacher quickly followed with, "Have you read that?" The former principal (who had also been principal over these two teachers for part of their careers but had never met Mrs. Gregory) broke in rather demonstratively, "Allright, keep that book out of it, though, because Frannie Patton has never said that was accurate." The second teacher qualified the conversation with, "No, I didn't mean that, but I meant it was so similar." And the first teacher finished the qualification with, "You would see a lot about Mrs. Gregory if you read that book." In another similar incident, a secretary with whom we scheduled an interview talked with a former principal to see if she had any information as to whether we were writing a sequel to *Good Morning, Miss Dove*, a fear that both people had after our initial contacts.

We found over the course of that interview, as well as during the rest of the oral history study, that Miss Dove and Mrs. Gregory were practically inseparable in people's memories of the school. A former student of the school, and at the time of the study a teacher at the school, thought that Mrs. Gregory had written *Good Morning, Miss Dove*. This interviewee referred to Mrs. Gregory as "kind of the legend of Cedar Grove." On many occasions, we were warned in conversations setting up interviews that the book had nothing to do with Mrs. Gregory or Cedar Grove School, only to have the book brought up in the interview by the people who had warned us in the first place. Separating *Good Morning, Miss Dove* from the school and Mrs. Gregory was not an option left open for us.

In a chronological sense, Mrs. Gregory had been synonymous with Cedar Grove School. She first arrived as a teacher in 1924, a position she held until 1946, when she became principal and held that post until her retirement in 1964. By the time she retired, Cedar Grove School had existed for forty-eight years; Mrs. Gregory had been there for all but eight.

The impact of Mrs. Gregory on the identity of Cedar Grove School was unquestionable, if not always desirable. One teacher, who had been a former student of and teacher under Mrs. Gregory, commented of Cedar Grove School, "That was her baby." Another commented, "She ran it like a private school." Her influence on the lives of those who had known her personally as a teacher, principal, and colleague was woven throughout the narratives constructed for us in the interviews where she was remembered. Our conversations with the people who still carried her legacy in their memories were held almost a quarter-century after she left the school, but the descriptions of her were vivid, the emotions behind those memories open, and at times intense, as witnessed in a conversation between two former teachers who had taught under her:

Van:	How much of an atmosphere did [Mrs. Gregory] establish?
Mrs. Hart:	She isn't going to read this [interview transcript], is she?
Van:	She's not.
Mrs. Dell:	Well, don't put our names on it.
Van:	I'm not.
Mrs. Dell:	You start, Jane Ellen.
Mrs. Hart:	No, you start it.

They then went on to a discussion of some of the characteristics of Mrs. Gregory (which we will present later). But, clearly, such a conversation was not taken lightly, even after both teachers had been retired for more than ten years and Mrs. Gregory for twenty-five. A person who had been a student of Mrs. Gregory's sixty-five years prior to our interview with him asked that the tape recorder be turned off when he discussed her, further testimonial to the influence that Mrs. Gregory had over people's lives, long after she had ceased to have contact with them.

Hawley (1982), although discussing the book and not Mrs. Gregory, pointed out that at mid-century the image of excellence in teaching was not what it is today. Being a stickler for rules and details, being strict in their enforcement, and being morally beyond reproach were all seen as appropriate and idealized in a teacher. In response to papers we have presented at professional meetings, many audiences have interpreted the characterizations of Mrs. Gregory that follow in decidedly negative ways. She was seen by these audiences as a battle-axe, as unreasonable, and even as evil incarnate. We cannot force readers to change their historical context and to see her as the moral icon she was to College Park and Cedar Grove. Many of our interviewees spoke of her with reverence, for she achieved that to which many aspired but which few were able to achieve. Clearly she was feared by many, but, for many, fear and reverence were coupled. For some she was simply fearsome and lacking virtue. For others, she was feared and revered because she had virtues beyond those of most mortals. In either case, Mrs. Gregory was constructed as the moral (or amoral) icon for people from Cedar Grove. With this understanding, let us consider the social construction of virtue that people from Cedar Grove School and College Park offered us in Mrs. Gregory.

A former teacher remembered her in this way:

You didn't speak. The children didn't speak. Even in the cafeteria the children ate and they didn't talk. The teachers didn't get to sit together. And you didn't converse. And you held your breath when you were in the hall that a child wouldn't talk because . . . [Mrs. Gregory] could look at them and it would cut. It would scare them to death.

Another teacher recalled that the location of Mrs. Gregory's office provided her with optimum surveillance of the hallways through which children and teachers passed daily. "And you walk out of your room, she'd be standing right there in that door like this [crosses her arms across her chest]."

And she would be standing just like that. And you did not speak and you just held your breath that the children didn't speak.

This same teacher wished that, in order to avoid the scrutiny, she could have found a way to "get out of a window, or something, or take my children out without walking by." When teachers and students had no option but to pass through the hall, they were subjected to Mrs. Gregory's scrutiny even when she wasn't there herself. Mrs. Gregory's portrait, which hung in the hall, caused teachers to "jerk to attention" as they walked underneath, a practice that continued after her retirement and after the portrait was removed.

Teachers commented on Mrs. Gregory's punctuality, recounting her morning walks to her office just a couple of blocks from her home. Her walks were always at the same time, unaffected by weather. "People could set their clocks in the morning [by] when she walked by going to school, rain or shine. She was so punctual in everything she did."

The most visible symbol of Mrs. Gregory's presence at Cedar Grove School was the universal possession of a handkerchief by the students of the elementary school. One teacher traced this back to a bout of tuberculosis Mrs. Gregory suffered through. In the event of a sneeze, the handkerchief had better be visible. Her former students would even pull out a handkerchief in interviews in way of recounting her long-term effects on them. An even more inexcusable sin was for students to become sick in class, as a former teacher told us:

> She had had tuberculosis and had been in a sanitarium, and if you sneezed in front of her or had any problem with your nose or your mouth, you better have a handkerchief. Oh, she would just go into a frenzy when children would spit up sometimes; little ones, not knowing it was coming. And she would make us get the children out of the room and raise the windows, freezing cold, and have the janitor to come clean it up. That was just the worst thing that could happen because germs go in everything.

Two teachers relished the memories of children becoming ill in Mrs. Gregory's office. Such events proved that despite what Mrs. Gregory wanted to believe about teachers' ability to ward off such disasters, students were as prone to become sick in her presence as anyone's.

If Mrs. Gregory was a stickler for time and hygiene; she was equally mindful of teachers' clerical duties, according to teachers we interviewed. The faculty at Cedar Grove dared not turn in reports to her with inaccurate figures, misspelled words, or improper punctuation. In a group interview of retired teachers, one said that

> Mrs. Gregory always got everything, reports and everything, in . . . before she was supposed to.

Another former colleague in the group broke in:

And if you sent a report to her and one little figure was supposed to be a two and it was a one, she would bring it down the hall for you to change. She wanted to show you.

The two went back and forth: "She would go over and over those monthly reports," which was followed by "That's the way she kept up with us." One teacher remembered the embarrassment of being called back to school two days into summer recess to change an incorrect number on a report that Mrs. Gregory easily could have changed herself.

In like manner, Mrs. Gregory kept an eagle eye on supplies:

Mrs. Gregory kept up with the book room. She kept up with every single last book and you were in trouble if you lost one. She charged you.

In the event that a book was lost, teachers sometimes went to the book warehouse in the state capital, about thirty miles away, to replace a book rather than face the wrath of Mrs. Gregory. Teachers would even make such a trip for children who had lost books, rather than report the infraction to the principal: "Yes sir, 'cause you kept up with those books like they were gold."

Nor did Mrs. Gregory tolerate students coming to school without their school books, ill-prepared for the learning she had in store for her students. One student of Mrs. Gregory's in the 1920s recalled a time when he realized on the way to school that he had forgotten his geography book. He was then faced with what was to him an epic decision. Should he return home to retrieve his book and face the penalty for arriving late in Mrs. Gregory's class? Or should he go on to school and accept his punishment for not remembering to bring it? In the renewed anguish of recalling the event, he didn't remember which of the two evils was the lesser.

Teachers who had been at Cedar Grove under Mrs. Gregory's watch described her mission there as being "to make those children behave and make those teachers teach." In 1964 Mrs. Gregory retired, and teachers described her retirement as "the biggest bash you have ever seen." What made her retirement even more memorable for her faculty was that she planned her own retirement party.

She had everybody in that school district working on her retirement and they fixed a book for her, and had many of the men and women who had been to school there and outstanding business people there. They got letters. They took up money. . . . That was one of the biggest things.

She continued, "She told everybody what she wanted." Another teacher added, "And it was decorated. It looked like a reception for a bride."

Only on one occasion did we hear of a person who directly challenged Mrs. Gregory. This teacher was not from the College Park area, had never been a student at the school, and had worked for Mrs. Gregory for only five years. Mrs. Gregory was less an icon for her. She relayed to us a story of a day when she was working as a hall monitor, watching a girl tossing another girl's cap into the air, and Mrs. Gregory's reaction to this activity:

I was on duty right at the front steps. You didn't allow a child in the hall. . . . This little girl, Ellie, [whose] grandmother walked her to school every day, [and] little Lisa, who was an outgoing child . . . were in my room. Well, Lisa had Ellie's cap and she was throwing it up. They were just kind of playing and Mrs. Gregory saw it. She says, "Lisa, what are you doing with that child's cap? Give it to her!" And she did. Well, Lisa started crying. That's the effect it had on her, and she was wiping her eyes and everything. And . . . of course I did exactly what she didn't want me to do. [I said,] "Come here, Lisa . . . Let's go wash your face." . . . And you know, Mrs. Gregory didn't speak to me for two days. No. And later she [said,] "Well, Mrs. Dell, I found out you have a temper." [I said,] "Mrs. Gregory, when you do something, say something that hurts one of my children, I have. . . . Now say anything you want to me, [but] . . . Lisa is the only friend that Ellie has, 'cause her grandmother keeps her lately." [Mrs. Gregory said,] "Well, I didn't know that."

Mrs. Gregory was not portrayed as always the stickler. Some maintained that in her later years as principal, she began to loosen her control over the teachers, allowing them to sit together at lunch, or even leave the lunch room altogether while she watched over the children. More important, however, was how the meaning attached to relationships with Mrs. Gregory changed with time. It was common for people to argue that, after some period of time, they came to see that she was trying to teach them significant lessons that would be important to them in later life. One teacher described to us how she began to send Christmas cards to Mrs. Gregory a tradition she continued up, to the time of our interview in 1988. This particular teacher had been a student of Mrs. Gregory's in the 1920s, and had then gone on to teach at Cedar Grove herself from 1946 through 1979. She told us about the last card she had sent to her former teacher and colleague at Christmas in 1987. In an emotional and tear-filled voice, she said she had written to Mrs. Gregory, "You have no idea what an impact you had on my life."

One interviewee commented that, as a former student and later as a colleague, she admired Mrs. Gregory, and, "children did, too, after a while." This same sentiment was expressed by other former students of Mrs. Gregory who had gone into other walks of life. One group of men with whom we talked, who had been in Mrs. Gregory's class and were now successful businessmen, remembered the fear that the teacher could and had struck in them; but, upon maturing into adults, that fear had grown into respect. Students remembered the lessons learned from her not only about geography but also about rigor, standards, and performance. Other students remembered that "she was a wonderful geography teacher. She was thorough." Mrs. Gregory had written, according to some accounts, a "Geography Song," which she used in her instruction. A student highlighted the point that geography lessons were more than recital. "Now she pushed us on place names and river names and geography that was taught, period. Now she tried to work the understanding of the culture in with it. It wasn't just place names, state names, and so forth."

In the eyes of her former students, Mrs. Gregory "was almost as stern as a bear, and everybody was intimidated by her." Students remembered few of their friends going to the principal's office to stand in judgment before her, because that fate was to be avoided at all costs. Students remembered her posture as "kind of imposing" and her general physical presence in this way:

> She was rather tall, kind of big. I mean not fat big. Big structured. And I never remember her smiling. Or ever showing a loving attitude toward the children. I mean, it's not in my memory of it. She might have, but I was so much in awe of her power.

The student just quoted was the daughter of the teacher and former student who had sent the Christmas card mentioned earlier. The daughter recalled her mother's admonition, "Be sure you're quiet in that hall. Mrs. Gregory might be there." She also recalled, tellingly, "I don't ever remember her speaking specifically to students."

But ultimately, like the teachers who had worked under and with Mrs. Gregory, students remembered most the lessons of her demeanor and how those translated into lessons about their lives. One person recalled of her former teacher:

The only teacher that I remember that people really disliked was Mrs. Gregory. She was a quite strict disciplinarian, and quite, sometimes, almost harsh.

She later continued her description of Mrs. Gregory's class:

It involved being totally disciplined. Just a narrow focus. If these are the subjects, then these are just what we are going to learn. Just walking her narrow line. That way you will be able to learn what you were supposed to learn while you're here. That was the Gregory thing.

Many former students recalled standing at the blackboards that pivoted from the closet doors. Opening one door caused several to turn at once, leaving each student in line with an individual board, and a solitary place to exhibit her or his excellence through the mastery of states by geographic region, capitals by states, and other geography rituals. A student described those classroom experiences:

She would put one of us in each one of those and we'd have to write on them the western states or whatever. . . . I would go to school deathly afraid that I would make a mistake. And then at the end of the day she gave us a test on it.

Succinctly and descriptively, students recollected, "People did things because Gregory told them to." "You had to be dependable." "She wasn't a bugaboo if you did what she said."

What were the people constructing as virtue in their representations of Mrs. Gregory? Clearly, virtue for the people of College Park was something exceptional. The narratives of Mrs. Gregory make it clear that virtuous behavior is not associated with everyday actions and people. It takes someone with a special strength of will, someone who is willing to go beyond the norms of everyday behavior. Cedar Grove's Mrs. Gregory was not tempted by normal human wants and needs. She could put virtue before any immediate need she may have had to be accepted or loved. She could also make others live up to her standards, because her adherence to virtues could not be challenged. Clearly, she had the authority as principal to order compliance, but in these accounts it is more that she was given the authority because she was so exceedingly virtuous. Moreover, because of her virtue, her authority was unchallenged and unchallengeable. You could fear her and hate her, but you could not deny her right to ask you to live according to her rules, as the teacher and the two little girls on the front steps of the school reveal. You accepted your punishment.

The group of businessmen we quoted earlier could see her importance to them as adults, and we think this is no accident. The virtues exemplified by Mrs. Gregory serve elites quite well. These men could see that individual success and virtue were indeed connected in College Park's construction. She became principal because she was virtuous. Her right to her status was based in moral right, not just material good fortune. Virtue separated her from the everyday person, and, indeed, she was beyond the everyday mores that govern life. She could enforce abstract rules over human wishes and desires in herself and made those who did not act accordingly feel somehow inadequate. Her representation of virtue justifies elites and their right to demand that people submit to the rules of bureaucratic organization, industrial efficiency, and capital accumulation. For those from College Park who retained their elite heritages, this construction of virtue serves them well. It also meant that those students who did not do well in school and in later life would also feel somehow base and undeserving. In College Park, virtue is not for everyday people.

This narrative construction of Mrs. Gregory also has some specific virtues associated with it. In many ways, these virtues are essentially oratorical, requiring adherence to established and known standards. Clearly, the central virtue is just this—upholding standards. As above, though, the standards in question are essentially abstract and somewhat mechanistic in their service of systems over human desires. The precise standards seem to be respect for authority, efficiency, obedience, and punctiliousness. Let us discuss each of these in turn.

Respect for Authority. In these accounts of Mrs. Gregory and Cedar Grove School, it is clear that a key virtue is respect for authority. People believed they should do what a person in a position of authority asked, even if they disliked that person. This virtue allows a hierarchical social order, but there is more to it than simply this. In this construction, authority is legitimated by more than law and rationality as in Weber's classic model of bureaucratic organization (Weber 1947). Mrs. Gregory's authority was justified by her moral status as well as by legal structure of schools. In this, authority became unimpeachable in that it comes from adherence to virtues beyond normal humans

Efficiency. These accounts show how people attributed efficiency to Mrs. Gregory. She gave awards for efficiency, was cited in the school newspaper as the most efficient principal, and so on. The virtue of efficiency gives the needs and goals of the organization first priority. Therefore, even elite parents could be required to get permission from the office to go into a class, because it interfered with the system of instruction in classrooms, The virtue of efficiency gives authority the grounds for acting in the interests of the school, an impersonal organization and system.

Obedience. Clearly, a corollary virtue to respect for authority is obedience. In the account constructed of Mrs. Gregory we see obedience to the virtuous repeatedly emphasized. However, there is another side of obedience in these accounts. Mrs. Gregory herself was obedient to virtue. She assiduously acted in accordance with her virtues; only in her later years do we see her relaxing this obedience. The virtue of obedience binds both the less virtuous to the virtuous and the virtuous to their virtues.

Punctiliousness. In many ways, this construction of virtues is typically modernist. They justify the modern world of organization, system, and progress through organization and denial of human emotions. Yet, in the accounts above, there is something exceptional at work, something more than the usual values of modernity. As noted above, there was something about Mrs. Gregory, as portrayed to us, that made virtue extraordinary. That something seems to be punctiliousness. The people in Cedar Grove saw her as emblematic of their values but beyond them as well in her attendance to the detail of all these virtues. Everyone was in favor of punctuality, but they could set their clocks only by Mrs. Gregory. Everyone was in favor of obedience, but only Mrs. Gregory could be obedient in both ways discussed above, and so on. College Park made a virtue of her punctiliousness.

Conclusions

We did not realize except in hindsight how telling our entree into the College Park community had been. When we tried to gain access to people in College Park and were looking for symbolic support for our study, we received it from one of the "leaders" of the community who was also a key parent in the school. She lived on the same street as the school, which was considered the choice place to live in College Park. She was one of the three most powerful parents in the school, and clearly represented the elite and authority, both inside the school and in the community. At one point, when we were not sure the study would take place, we had scheduled an interview with her to find out what she knew about the school and community. She gave our work her blessing and communicated that to Mr. Michaels, and that translated into support from others in the school and community. Respecting elites pays off in College Park and Cedar Grove School.

As closely as we came to work with the teachers at Cedar Grove School on the creation of the school history, it is hard to remember how coldly we were received on our first visit to the school. Our work in the school brought us in weekly contact with the principal, faculty, and several community members over the course of three years and more sporadically for another year. We found that even after Mrs. Gregory had been retired from the school for twenty-five years and the school had been desegregated for nearly twenty, vestiges of the virtues constructed over the earlier history of the school were still present. This was at no time more evident than during one of our visits to Cedar Grove when an African-American member of our study team commented that it felt like a white school—even though the school had been predominantly African-American for a decade. To us, this was testimony of the power of the virtues that had been constructed in the school over most of its history, and how they dominated the identity of the place even after 70 percent of its student population and more than half its teacher population came in from other communities.

We also came to realize the power of the central figure in the school's narrative. Not only did Mrs. Gregory dominate the character of the school; she also dominated the process of our data collection as well as conversations about our work and about people's memories of the school. Mrs. Gregory, and the school she influenced for forty years, reinforced the virtues of authority, efficiency, obedience, and punctiliousness long after the personalities who inhabited it had changed.

We also learned that, historically, virtues at Cedar Grove School did not belong to children or to other teachers but to Mrs. Gregory and, as became evident during our work there, Miss Dove. People (the current elites), in telling their story, did not see themselves as virtuous when under her tutelage; but after becoming elite themselves, they saw her virtues as the source of their own status, and only as adults did they claim her virtues as their own. At Cedar Grove, students and adults alike were exposed to authority and the virtues of the elite, but Mrs. Gregory was unlike everyone else, and held a symbolic position no one else held. The other teachers emulated her, and her students were molded through a set of expectations, rituals, and activities through which they would come to embrace the virtues she represented. As children, they may have fit their lives into the world as Mrs. Gregory saw it; As adults, they fit the world as Mrs. Gregory saw it into their lives. Mrs. Gregory had set the context of their lives. To protect virtue, that could not be compromised.

When we first became involved in the oral history project at Cedar Grove School, we were unaware that our attention to the school would ultimately include a school that had at one time operated in an African-

American neighborhood adjacent to College Park. We learned early on that in order to do justice to the identity of Cedar Grove School and the history of all the students who attended it, we needed to come to an understanding of this African-American community and what had been its school. In that decision we were introduced to the Rougemont community and school, and it is their story to which we now turn.

4

Rougemont School

We first learned that Rougemont School had been the heart of the community by how we were introduced to the Rougemont community. On the night of Sunday, 29 January 1989, we attended an interdenominational church service in Rougemont. We were there to introduce ourselves and to have our history project sanctioned by the community. We had already done some interviews with people from Rougemont, but in general had had a luke warm response. We learned a telling lesson. The remaining vestige of a formerly close-knit community with strong and visible leadership and a powerful sense of identity was the churches. There was no other way for us to be introduced to the community than to go to the one gathering that cross-cut the community: the interdenominational service that incorporated all the churches that served Rougemont whenever there was a fifth Sunday in the month.

The "fifth Sunday" service rotated through the five Rougemont churches and this night met in a church that was in the geographic center of the community. The church would seat about two hundred people. Some one hundred attended, including six of us representing the school history project. As we waited for the service to begin, an elderly woman inquired why we were there, and, having learned of our intent, launched into a description of how the community had changed during her lifetime. "We didn't have to shut our doors," she began, in a portrayal similar to one many Americans nostalgically recall about their own—a community without crime in its boundaries, homes that could be left open without fear of robbery or assault, neighbors that were life-long friends—free to go into each other's houses at will and encouraged to supervise and discipline each other's children. She said her feeling of safety ended about fifteen years before, when her husband died, just as the community began to change. Fifteen years before, Rougemont School was closed as the city desegregated its schools.

"I bought a pistol about that long," she said holding up her hand and laying a finger across her wrist. She went on to explain that she came to realize that, while things had changed in Rougemont, the pistol was an excessive response. A well-dressed gentleman going into the chapel interjected, "The Holy Spirit told you that you didn't need that pistol and that's why you're safe." This faith was not sufficient for her, however. She retorted as she went into the chapel that if anything happened, "I won't need a pistol . . . all I need is this [shakes her fist in the air]!"

The diminished sense of safety was part and parcel of the changes in the Rougemont community since the school was closed in 1975. There were other related changes. Home ownership had decreased, meaning that there were more people living in the community for shorter periods of time renting houses. The children of the community no longer saw the neighborhood as the idyllic community their parents were raised in, and now move to other neighborhoods to raise their families. There were no longer visible communitywide cooperative efforts to help those in need, aged, or infirm, as was the case in the past. Yet the church service was evidence of the remaining sense of community. Like services in many African-American churches, the "fifth-Sunday" service was based on considerable shared knowledge and understanding. Getting seated was a long process, as people stopped to speak with each other, sharing information about families and friends and inquiring about one another's wellbeing. Ushers would only have interfered with this activity.

As people began to get settled, a man and woman walked to the front of the chapel and sat at a small table. The man tapped his foot a few times and began singing. The congregation picked up the song and sang heartily. We were the only people who needed hymnals—everyone else knew this song and, as it turned out, all the songs. As the hymn ended, the man stood and haltingly read a passage from the Bible. This culminated in his asking the congregation if anyone wished to speak or lead a song. Testimonies followed to the grace of God and individuals initiated hymns that the congregation would then join. To us, it was a testament to a community that was struggling to survive and using the only remaining institution it had that served the community broadly.

The pastors of all the Rougemont churches assembled and sat behind the altar. A young pastor was to preach, asking the congregation to read along with him from Exodus 14:13:

When Pharaoh drew near, the people of Israel lifted up their eyes, and behold, the Egyptians were marching after them; and they were in great fear. And the people of Israel cried out to the Lord; and they said to Moses, "Is it because there are no graves in Egypt that you have taken us away to die in the wilderness? What have you done to us, in bringing us out of Egypt? Is not this what we said to you in Egypt, 'Let us alone and let us serve the Egyptians'? For it would have been better for us to serve the Egyptians than to die in the wilderness." And Moses said to the people, "Fear not, stand firm, and see the salvation of the Lord, which he will work for you today; for the Egyptians whom you see today, you shall never see again. The Lord will fight for you, and you have only to be still." (Revised Standard Version)

"Stand firm" became the theme of his sermon, confronting the impatience of people today, people who want answers "right now." We did not know then that it was through standing still and firm, and having faith in others, that Rougemont lost its "heart."

After the sermon, an offering, and a series of testimonials, the pastors introduced us and our task to the congregation. They encouraged people to help us, then the service was brought to a close by having everyone stand in a large circle and hold hands. Together we sang "We Shall Overcome" and prayed.

This was the most moving introduction to a community any of us had ever witnessed. It came when we were afraid that we would fail to be able to write a history of Rougemont School. We had searched widely for archival materials such as those available for Cedar Grove. We found little, testifying to the effects of school closings and denigration of the value of the records from an African-American school. We were having difficulty identifying people who had worked at and had attended the school, and even when we could identify them, few were willing to talk with us. On the night of fifth-Sunday service, one of the church elders took it upon himself to arrange a Saturday meeting at the church where people could come and talk with us. Another woman offered to share a history she had assembled about the community that focused on the churches. Others recounted how central the school had been to the community and how much they wished it were still in operation. People repeated that the closing of Rougemont School marked the beginning of decline in the community. We were well on our way to learning what Rougemont School could have taught us about education had its voice not been silenced.

In retrospect, we learned on that night that Rougemont and its churches embodied the oratorical idea. They had memorized passages of the Bible and many hymns to recount as moral lessons and to be emulated in everyday life. The truth was known and definable. The challenge was to live up to it, especially in a world full of trials of one's faith. Rougemont was not a community of progressive thought. Dewey's ideas were neither reflected in their lives nor known to the residents, as best we could determine. Rather, Rougemont was trying to stand still and hold fast to its traditions, even as outside forces rent the boundaries and soul of the community.

As Relph argues in his *Place and Placelessness*:

> People are their place and a place its people, and however readily these may be separated in conceptual terms, in experience they are not easily differentiated. In this context places are public—they are created and known through common experiences and involvement in common symbols and meanings. (1976: 34)

Rougemont had been created as a pocket of opportunity for African-Americans. Employment, largely at the nearby university, and home ownership formed its material base. But what made Rougemont a community was its churches, its school, its political organization, and its park. All of these provided for common experiences, symbols, and meanings. And importantly, they were all constructed by the community as essential to their social and cultural lives. With only the churches left, it was becoming harder and harder to find people who identified themselves as "from Rougemont." Even place was dissolving, as we soon learned.

Subject Lessons

In College Park we were treated to a series of object lessons. In Rougemont subject lessons were the rule. The difference is significant. Cedar Grove School was clearly constructing its image for the future, objectifying it, and legitimating it through a series of processes. Their picture of virtue was to be permanent, and we were part of the process for insuring that it would be inscribed (Clifford and Marcus 1986) and then legitimated both by the community and by our status as university researchers. Our status, once we were put into our place, was an asset in their construction of their story.

In Rougemont, being an object had a long, ugly history. The legacy of slavery was a constant reminder of being an object of the directives and whims of white masters. However, the end of slavery had not terminated being an object to others. Whites continued to treat African-Americans as less than full citizens. The post-Reconstruction efforts to deny African-Americans full citizenship rights, including literacy tests as prerequisites for voting and outright intimidation by whites, continually threatened to return African-Americans to their object status. Segregation, while it allowed the creation of African-American social institutions, also certified that African-Americans were still determined by the laws and whims of whites. Their identities and rights were objectified and dependent on white legal structures.

"Subject," of course, has two meanings in its common usage. On the one hand, it refers to having the capability of thought and reason as in being "subjective." This is how we use the term in the first paragraph of this section. Slavery and segregation (and ongoing racism) denied that African-Americans were capable of thought and reason, denied that they had a legitimate contribution to human discourse, and denied them the opportunity to demonstrate their capacity for reason and their contribution to human discourse. The debate between Booker T. Washington (1965) and W. E. B. Du Bois (1965) can be framed in this understanding. Booker T. Washington was in many ways working to get African-Americans a place in American society so they would have the opportunity to demonstrate reason and contribute to society. Du Bois recognized that white definitions of reason and discourse had a distinctive Western cultural content, and he was concerned with ensuring that African-Americans receive this valued cultural content. Both were working to give African-Americans the status of subjects in American society, but each focused strategically on different elements of the issue.

The second common usage of "subject" refers to being in the dominion of others. The classic image is being a subject of a king. In our above discussion, we highlighted this meaning as being determined by, or "subject to," the laws of white America. This definition of "subject" has two meanings. On the one hand, it renders a person an object to more powerful others. On the other hand, it can be seen as indicating that one is part of a larger system and can legitimately claim the benefits (and limitations) that ensue from that system. For African-Americans, it seems clear that few benefits accrued from being subject to the laws and practices of white America. Rather, their object status consistently was used to benefit the system over those serving it.

The legacy of slavery and segregation was alive in 1989 as we negotiated our study, even though slavery ended some 125 years earlier and school segregation effectively ended in 1974, when the Treyburn schools were finally desegregated under court supervision. The people we wished to talk with had personal stories of being objectified. The Rougemont community, moreover, was a direct result of segregation. It existed because African-Americans could not live in the same neighborhoods as whites. White neighborhoods expanded around this once rural neighborhood and made it an enclave, restricting Rougemont residents, their movements, and their housing options. Rougemont School also was a product of this segregation, as we will discuss. The Rougemont community existed to provide low-paid labor to Treyburn, enabling it to develop into an industrial center that was relatively rare for its time in the South. Segregation benefited white Treyburn, once again teaching Rougemont residents that they were subject to white society. Rougemont did get some benefits, as we will discuss, but most of what was valuable was the result of African-Americans' construction of their own community within the context of segregation. As will become evident, even school desegregation proved the object status of Rougemont and other African-American schools and community, even though the manifest result was supposed to benefit African-Americans.

Our arrival revealed the legacy of objectification. We knew that all too often, white researchers invaded African-American communities with resulting information being used as objective "facts" that could be acted upon without consultation with the residents of the communities. We, of course, believed our intents were different. We were doing a history of their schools, the now-closed Rougemont and the desegregated Cedar Grove School, sponsored by a PTA president from their community and a number of African-American teachers. This written history would be reviewed by an advisory board that included African-Americans (including the PTA president). We were there explicitly to tell their story.

However, Rougemont knew better. They knew better than uncritically to embrace a university research team, racially mixed or not. They required that we become subject to their community. The church attendance was a dramatic demonstration of this, making us dependent on them for cues as to how to act and which hymns to sing out of the hymnals, and requiring us to join with them in the traditional demonstration of unity at the end of the service. However, Rougemont did not do to us what had been done to them. They never used our being subject to their practices to make us objects. Rather, they employed the meaning of "subject" all too often denied to them: We became part of their system, gaining both benefits and limitations. We do not wish to be misunderstood on this point. We did not become part of their community. Rather, they gave us a place and a status in their system. We were outsiders, but we were, in the end, sponsored and given access to considerable information about their story and struggle.

They sought to be treated as subjects with thought, reason, and a meaningful contribution to a wider discourse. Being a subject in this sense means, of course, retaining the right to refuse to be interviewed, as one person did when he inquired if this information would be used in a dissertation and was informed it could be. Subjects often declined to be tape recorded, so their own words could not be used against them. Subjects tested interviewers to see who they were and how they treated information. Subjects were skeptical as well as trusting. Subjects read the school history and wrote corrections for it.

These were some of the subject lessons we were taught in Rougemont; they also have implications for this book. In the same way Cedar Grove School was pursuing objectification, Rougemont was pursuing subjectification. The social reality they wished to construct was one that gave them heart, substance, and humanity. Clearly, we could not write this chapter in the objective voice of Cedar Grove. We had to attempt a subjective voice. This was helped, ironically, by the lack of records, but hurt by the reluctance of some to be tape recorded, thus reducing the possibility of relying on verbatim quotes. Further, it seemed inappropriate to use the device of telling the story of Rougemont through the eyes of one person's life, real or fictional. This violates what we believe was being taught us as part of our subject lessons. White researchers should not be making African-American people into objects, even in the service of rendering the narratives of African-Americans.

We have experimented with the voice of this chapter in a couple of related publications (Dempsey and Noblit 1993a, 1993b). Reviewers considering these articles complained that our treatment was "romantic," and suggested that we had "gone native" and taken Rougemont's story uncritically. Their solutions ranged from simply recommending rejection of the articles to getting some distance from the story and taking a skeptical stance toward it. That is, the reviewers—who were experienced qualitative researchers—wanted us to objectify the account of Rougemont. We knew then we were on to something good. We rejected the reviewers' advice and now understand that the best we can do is to tell a "romantic" story of Rougemont. Such a story, while it may not be what Rougemont would write of themselves, responds to our subject lessons. It comes as close to maintaining the heart and soul of Rougemont as we can, and treats their story as a mean-ingful contribution to human discourse (even if a "romantic" contribu-tion). It does not reveal the thought or reason that went into the story they constructed with us, for they withheld that as subjects in their own right, but it does attempt to respect the residents of Rougemont as reasonable and thoughtful human beings.

The story that follows is both romantic and tragic. One of the subject lessons of Rougemont we will discuss is that their social construction of virtue embraces suffering and tragedy with an ultimate faith in redemption. This chapter will follow the general logic of chapter 3: We will first present the history of Rougemont and Rougemont

School, follow this with Rougemont School's moral icons as constructed by Rougemont's residents, and end by identifying the virtues that people socially constructed as part of their emblematic narratives of their moral icons.

A Place for Us

Rougemont was settled in the late nineteenth century when Randolph College moved from Trinity County to the outskirts of Treyburn. Charles Walters, an employee of the college, decided to move with the college, and built a home on nearby farmland. He cleared a path to allow him to walk to work. The path would eventually become the main thoroughfare of Rougemont. Other African-Americans also found employment at the college and built small homes. The path became a dirt street, and eventually the farmland became a neighborhood. The neighborhood had definite boundaries. In the era of enforced segregation, Rougemont was bounded in part by neighborhoods, including College Park, being built by white employees of the college and eventually by other white professionals and businesspeople of Treyburn. It was also bounded by the college itself on the south and a notorious district of gambling and bootleg houses on the north. The boundaries were so rigid that people recalled the special meaning of Mr. Ted Drew's hay rides for the children. They were billed as a "trip around the world,' for Mr. Drew took his horsedrawn hay wagon full of children beyond the reaches of Rougemont, circling the entire city.

It is important to understand that Rougemont was not then a community of poor African-Americans, but neither was it the neighborhood of higher-status African-Americans. The latter community was across the city surrounding Treyburn State College, an African-American institution. Rougemont, rather, was a community of stably employed people, originally at Randolph College and later in the local mills and as maids and servants in the adjacent white neighborhoods. The vestiges of this are still evident, but these residents lament the influx of unemployed people and transients and the decline in home ownership.

Rougemont was a "close-knit" community; "everyone was one big family," according to residents. Friends visited, and neighbors helped each other out. If someone was sick, neighbors pitched in and took food to the home. The elderly were looked in on, and the elderly looked out for the children. A long-time Rougemont resident described it this way:

I used to joke, especially when I started driving, . . . "I wish I had a third hand." Because knowing everyone in Rougemont when [I] went down the street, I would have liked to have two hands just to wave as I went by and have my third hand on the wheel. But walking or riding or whatever, you knew everybody. Everybody would speak, would carry on a conversation with you, would want to know how things were going and whatnot.

Child rearing was also seen as a community venture. If an adult saw a child misbehaving, generally the adult would punish the child and then report the infraction and the punishment to the parent:

It would not bother your parents at the time if someone took you in their house and gave you a spanking if they saw you doing something wrong. And when you got home you got another one. There was that kind of closeness.

Another resident remembered the epitome of the close-knit discipline network, a woman called "Ma Franklin":

All the families were close, close-knit families. There was a lady there all the kids called Ma Franklin. She's still living, she's about ninety years old now. We still call her Ma Franklin. She was everybody's mama. If she caught you doing something wrong or fighting, she might spank you and then take you home. . . . She was everybody's mom.

Rougemont was a community of strong and shared values. They valued hard work, religious faith, discipline, and individual and collective responsibility. They took care of their own and expected each to look to the others' welfare. The neighborhood was their place and they shared the responsibility for it.

The neighborhood included all the amenities of a separate small town: grocery and clothing stores, barbershops and beauty salons, churches, scout troops, and recreation centers. They even reclaimed a garbage dump to create a park for the residents. It became a place for children to play, adults to stroll and visit, and families to picnic. It was also the site of community celebrations. It symbolized just how much Rougemont was a place especially for and of them.

Rougemont was not an incorporated town and was not active in the wider political world of the city or of the African-American population of Treyburn. It got few community services and had no representative in the city's political structure. Neither of these was or is unusual for African-American neighborhoods in cities, especially in the South.

Isolated from the wider political apparatus, Rougemont created its own. The "Bronze Mayor" of Rougemont and his "Board of Directors" took care of everything from voter registration to helping people in trouble. These positions were honorary, going to the men with the "most money" and "know-how " In Rougemont, material success and knowledge were to be not hoarded but shared. Success engendered an obligation to the collectivity.

The directors organized community projects, lobbied with the local political structure for needed public services, and had a special responsibility to help residents in financial difficulty. Taxation and tithing were linked, as the churches took responsibility for special collections for the projects and people in need. The Bronze Mayor's wife traditionally carried the heavy burden of door-to-door soliciting when needed. Probably the most significant community project in the history of Rougemont was to become its key symbol: Rougemont School.

A School of Our Own

In the South, education of African-Americans was first outlawed, then suppressed, and, in a great step forward, ignored. In African-American communities, getting an education is equated with struggle. We often speak of the struggle to achieve civil rights, but we tend to forget that for African-Americans, education and civil rights are historically linked. Education is a civil right in itself, and it prepares leaders for the struggle for civil rights. Education also provides the knowledge and credentials for better employment, and is a prime source of employment for educated African-Americans.

Residents of Rougemont were daily reminded of the significance of high-quality education in their work at the college, but were denied access to existing schools. Most likely, the first efforts to educate Rougemont's children were church-sponsored and volunteer efforts, although the details are lost to history. The county began sponsoring schools for African-Americans by the late 1800s, and the children of Rougemont first attended Bricktown School. To get to Bricktown School, the children had to walk through white neighborhoods and were regularly harassed by white children. Fights ensued, and, after a particularly violent fight, local citizens pressured the county school board to fund a temporary school in the Walters Street Church in Rougemont. This was an obvious expression of community spirit, and signaled one of the key values of the Rougemont community—to take care of their own. The parents did this collectively when they disciplined each other's children, and the collective press for a school was another manifestation of it. The community repeatedly rallied around this value. It was also connected to the value termed "stand firm." Taking care of your own and standing firm, sure in your faith that you are morally correct, are much like the oratorical idea. The focus is on preserving traditional values which, in turn, create a cultural ingroup, insular unto itself and distinct from other communities.

Following the establishment of the temporary school, Rougemont residents took it upon themselves to procure funds for a permanent school. They raised local funds and arranged a grant from northern philanthropist and Sears executive Julius Rosenwald. By 1919, Rougemont had its own school, housed in a wood-frame building at the edge of the neighborhood and across the street from the park that the neighborhood had established. According to one former student, it was "a white building with long, low tables and a wood stove." In 1921–1922, the first year for which attendance records are available, there were 104 students enrolled in the school, while the daily attendance averaged 78. The school was poorly funded, and the teacher-to-student ratio was abominable by today's standards. There were only two teachers listed for this academic year: Laura Pursell and Celia Truman. Records indicate that Mrs. Pursell had twenty-two years of experience and was paid $93.50 for the school year. Mrs. Truman was less experienced (only four years) but was listed as the principal as well as a teacher, for $85.00 per annum. Large, multiple-grade classes were the rule.

The school was originally part of the segregated county system. The city grew around Rougemont in the 1920s, and in 1926 the school was redistricted into the city school system. Throughout this period enrollment grew steadily, and the demand for more teachers grew. Laura Pursell remained with the school throughout this period and was joined by her daughter, Lena, and three other teachers through the early 1930s. Salaries grew substantially, even if still not at parity with the white schools, ranging from $810 to $1,000 per year. In the 1931–1932 school year, the first grade at Rougemont School went to a two half-day attendance schedule (called "double sessions") to try to deal with overcrowding in the city schools. This plan continued for two and a half years, and expanded across the grade levels.

It became evident that public officials were not going to act to alleviate this and other insufficiencies in the African-American schools in the city, and by 1933 the African-American citizens of Treyburn were organizing for the struggle to improve their schools against an unresponsive white school board. At the 21 August 1933 meeting of the city board of education, a committee of African-American citizens made their feelings known to the members of the board. Their requests included the following:

1. that an advisory committee be created to confer with the board of education on matters concerning "Negro" schools;
2. that the board of education use one-third of the supplement money to upgrade Negro teacher salaries;
3. that a Negro attendance officer be hired;
4. that twenty-five necessary teachers not provided by the state be provided;
5. that telephones be put in all Negro schools.

With the exception of the first request, these were designed to bring African-American schools up to the standards of the white schools. The board responded to the requests by putting phones in two of the city's Negro schools, but Rougemont was not one of them. The board members stated that Negro representation was not a matter for the board. The board did decide to create the position of a full-time attendance officer as requested. Apparently, the board felt it was more important to enforce attendance than to bring the African-American schools up to the standards of the white schools. It would be a long and difficult struggle for the African-American citizens of the city to achieve parity with the white schools, and, as we will see, when parity seemed to be approached, Rougemont and other African-American schools would be closed and others desegregated, ending their identity with the African-American struggle for civil rights.

The African-American school-age population grew rapidly during the 1940s, and Rougemont School was distinguished as being particularly overcrowded, again having to resort to "double sessions." By August 1940, the Treyburn Committee on Negro Affairs reported that African-Americans represented 41.4 percent of the city schools' enrollment and that African-American teachers constituted 35.8 percent of the city schools' total population of teachers. This was a remarkable improvement but still left African-American schools with larger classes and without other resources common in the white schools. There was only one art teacher for the eight African-American schools to share, and no African-American schools had gymnasiums or indoor playrooms.

The struggle continued. The Negro Affairs Committee wrote long letters to the city school board concerning the state of their education and schools. These letters detailed exhaustive studies that examined the differences between the white and African-American schools in Treyburn. The head of the committee urged that African-American schools needed equal facilities and educational opportunities in order to be in concert with Treyburn's reputation as a friendly and fair city and to bolster the African-American community's contribution to the defense effort in the war. "Defense Education" not only would be good for the country but also would reaffirm that African-Americans were loyal Americans, too.

Through the 1940s, the faculty at Rougemont School grew to eight, including three teachers who had been there since 1926. By the end of the decade, the Superintendent of the City Schools was authorized by the board to employ an architect to draw up plans for an addition to Rougemont School, more than fifteen years after the request. In 1952, the Bronze Mayor led the push to renovate the now aging building. The result was a brick structure with a new cafeteria and a new wing.

However, Rougemont School did not need these facilities for it to be a symbol of the community. It achieved that by exclusive service to students from Rougemont, by its presence in the neighborhood, by its longstanding faculty, by its reinforcing community values, and by its identity as "a school of our own." As we noted earlier, this insularity was one of the characteristics of Rougemont. It was a community unto itself, with boundaries, churches, stores, and a political system. Families were large, with many of the mothers staying home to raise their children. It was solidly working class, even if such employment was limited to domestic and service employment. The traditional employment patterns continued. Treyburn University employed Rougemont residents as custodians, cooks, and dormitory workers. Some were employed in the local mills and tobacco companies, but, in general, Rougemont people had little exposure to the wider African-American and white communities. Connections with the other African-American communities in the city were largely through the teachers at Rougemont School, most of whom were said to have come from the African-American middle-class neighborhoods around Treyburn State College, where they also studied. In this community structure, Rougemont was one step down from the influential African-American community and another step down from the white communities. All this contributed even more to Rougemont's insularity and to the value expressed in the first church service we attended in the neighborhood: Stand firm and have faith. Their struggle was defined by being stalwart and hardworking and by investing in education, religion, and their community. They struggled to improve their lives, their churches, and their school, but engaged little in the wider struggles for civil rights in the community.

This is nowhere more evident than in the 1960s, when civil rights was a major issue in many African-American communities. While Rougemont was no exception to this, the community was active only in a limited way in support of integration efforts in the community, and this was in support of integration at a local high school, not in their own neighborhood. The Bronze Mayor did not push it for Rougemont School. Further, Rougemont kept a "very low profile" in civil rights protests, according to one resident. "Our first lady," one person commented, knew how to deal with people, and Rougemont adopted the posture: "Just let Connie do it." Connie Dunn, the Bronze Mayor's wife, would go to meetings and talk with people. The community saw her as effective in getting the things the community desired, but there came a point where Rougemont recognized the need for collective action. In 1964, African-American leaders from other areas of the city came to Rougemont and held a meeting at St. John's Church to plan and elicit support for a boycott of downtown stores. The community voted at that meeting to boycott. However, it was also recognized that it would be necessary for African-Americans to become more active in the electoral process if they wished to have a voice on the local political scene. The Bronze Mayor and the Board of Directors organized voter registration drives in Rougemont and campaigned to get out the vote. Negro college students and faculty actively supported these efforts, in direct contrast to the active resistance of the nearby white neighborhoods, including College Park. Rougemont, however, was a minor actor in the local civil rights movement inasmuch as the leadership came from other neighborhoods. Equally important, however, was Rougemont's basic insularity and its belief that their role was to stand firm in the face of adversity and have faith that destiny was on their side. They continued to invest in their community and their school, never realizing that their values would contribute to the demise of their school and eventually their community.

Rougemont School, Community, and Virtue

Rougemont School was the community's ultimate cultural symbol, and reflected the basic patterns and beliefs of the neighborhood. As we heard earlier, Rougemont was characterized as a "family," and this was also true of the characterizations of the school. As we were told, Rougemont expected its school teachers to "educate the children and to be involved in the community," even though most of the teachers lived outside of Rougemont. The teachers at Rougemont fulfilled an educational and ideological role in the community. Beyond the usual responsibilities of teaching, they were expected to be present "every time there was something at the school" whether or not the "something" was educational or student related. They had to attend all picnics, celebrations, community meetings, and similar events that happened at the school. Clearly the teachers were to be role models for the children. They were to dress well, comport themselves as respected and exemplary citizens, and foster close relationships between the school and community. They were, for example, expected to attend church services in Rougemont periodically. The community reciprocated by treating them with deference and respect equal to that accorded to the ministers of the churches they would attend. In the church services, their presence would be publicly announced and ministers would take time as part of the service to thank them for attending. One resident told us this:

> You have to remember, too, that for many years . . . and this was certainly true when I was a child . . . for many black people, for most black people, the teacher was the person in the community. . . . That was because primarily [teaching] was the profession that most blacks went in if they wanted to get ahead and so forth. So, when the teachers came to church, then everybody took a back seat and they were always allowed to speak. . . . It was really a big thing when they would come [to church].

A former Rougemont school student recalled, "There was prestige. My parents thought preachers were good, but teachers were great!"

Rougemont teachers had expectations of their own, mostly directed at their students. Teachers attempted to instill in children a sense of the importance of success in school. A former principal explained:

> They expected kids to learn. They expected high performance and the kids gave it. Kids responded like that. Rougemont School wasn't somewhere to run and hide and be lazy.

Another former principal elaborated:

> The teachers wanted their kids to be proud of themselves. They wanted their kids to have an understanding of their culture and history, and what they were doing . . . what they were needing to do.

Teachers expected students to approach school with purpose. Teachers wanted their students to "want" to learn and to do well. Rougemont teachers were of one mind. According to a former student,

> You knew when you went to school that morning that you will be doing whatever you were told to do and you were going to stay there until you finished it. That was another thing—you didn't finish your work, you didn't go home when the other kids went home.

She continued to explain what the teachers communicated to the students:

You're going to learn. You're going to do well. You're going to excel and you're going to compete with anyone. They didn't take excuses lightly.

The importance of this closeness was not lost on those who taught at Rougemont School and who came into this neighborhood from other parts of Treyburn. One former teacher remembered:

I have heard every teacher and principal say who has been at Rougemont that there was really something special about that community, but I think the relationship was because of the parents really taking interest in the children and really working together.

Students, teachers, principals, and community members all expressed feelings similar to this about the relationship between Rougemont School and the community: "It was a community school and everybody seemed like they loved it."

It was a wonderful community that people stick together, that cared about each other, that loved each other. It was just great. They were fully involved in the school. Whatever went on, they were there.

While Rougemont School in its later years had a cafeteria, many students were too poor to buy their lunch on a daily basis. They brought lunches from home except for a few days a year. Thanksgiving, Christmas, and other holidays were special celebrations at lunchtime. Parents and teachers made a special effort to see that children had money for these meals. Teachers would pay for students when parents could not, so that all could be included in the celebration.

Religion was an integral part of Rougemont School's routine. The more restrictive legal decisions came late in its history, and, in any case, the rather homogeneous community agreed that religion was vital to the upbringing of their youth. The school day opened with morning prayer. Lunch was preceded by saying grace. At least one teacher had "devotion" on Monday morning to review the Sunday School lessons from the day before. The Bible was a "Great Book" for this school and community. In ways envied by Adler and Bloom, this book was a part of the basic curriculum of both the Rougemont School and community.

Assemblies were held each month. They were designed largely to show the students to the community. These assemblies were celebrations of the capabilities of the students, the role of the school in the community, and the community itself. Unlike many school assemblies, which were and are solely for the large mass of students, assemblies at Rougemont invited families to attend.

The close bond between Rougemont School and the community was best expressed in a description of the spring carnival in Rougemont Park across the street from the school.

> I remember the parents there, they always planned the social gathering in the spring over at the park. . . . It reminded you of a family type of situation. . . . This is where the parents would (like in the olden days, I guess—I'm from the country where people would pack picnic lunches) go to church and spread. Well, they would do these things in the park for the kids. They would grill food and things of that sort. That was a very good relationship. It was other things. . . . You could just feel the warmth.

One student remembered the carnival as the "biggest event at our school," something everyone looked forward to. Students would play games such as "Go Fish" for prizes.

> You might pull up a baby doll on a fishing pole, or some spectacular gift, not a little spider or things like we do now. But the parents in the neighborhood went way out, because that was the main event of the year at our school. Like people have baby dolls and stuff they clean it up at home, and make new clothes for it. And if you were lucky you'd pull up a baby doll or a yo-yo, which was a big thing then, or a bat and ball. . . . And you might pull up a booby prize, but you know, you're lucky to pull a good prize.

The school and community also came together at school fund raisers. Grade-mothers would work with the teachers in planning events such as movies, hot dog stands, and sock hops. All of the materials were donated to the school by the community, and the profits were used to buy instructional materials. A former student said, "I remember that well when I was a little girl. It was a closeness, a sense of family, because of some of the projects like that."

The Rougemont parents were integrally involved with Rougemont School on a daily basis, not just at special events. One teacher described the parents' effect on the school:

> They were special. They would come to the school. You didn't particularly have to go to them. They would come to you to want

to help to do. For parents that is good, you know. . . . If you had a problem at school, or maybe if you needed something, . . . they would try to get it for you. If there was a problem with a child they would [take care of] that.

A former principal said:

The parents liked the school. The community enjoyed their school. The community would come in to visit and to eat with the kids. It wasn't like pulling eye teeth to get people in.

Another principal said:

The PTA was there one hundred percent. They always had a large crowd. Any principal or leader would call and they would help out. The attitude toward the teacher was different. The parents wouldn't say anything negative. It was a family school, like being a member of a family.

As mentioned earlier, the family atmosphere of the community made disciplining children a shared responsibility. Teachers were allowed to make full use of that network. One principal stated:

I knew it was a tight-knit community that had always been tight knit. Folks helped each other. Relatives lived a couple of blocks away, so there was extended family in the area. There was a grand-mother or uncle nearby. I was just as free to talk to them as to the parents. Whatever you said would get back to the parents verbatim, and in some instances the relatives would just handle it.

Students were fully aware of the parental support teachers received as disciplinarians:

Well, in those days we got a spanking. Your teachers spanked you and called your mom, and then you went home and knew what you were going to get when you go home—the same thing!

Another student recalled:

If your were disobedient, oh yeah, the call was made that very day and you didn't want your parents to know that you had misbe-haved, because the rule was if you got it at school, you got it again when you got home.

Many teachers and principals discussed school–community interaction in terms of problems brought into Rougemont School by students
from home. Children would at times bring in problems first thing in the
morning to which the teacher lent an understanding ear. Though students
generally got along well in the school, sometimes problems were brought
in from the previous evening or weekend, and teachers would attempt to
defuse the problem early.

When necessary, and sometimes for social reasons, teachers would
visit the children and their families in the homes. One teacher commented:

> The parents [were] right there whenever there was a problem. I
> had a little thing where I would walk home. . . . If I had a problem
> with a kid that day then they knew "I'll walk home with you
> today." And I guess this was one thing that kept the children from
> having so many problems.

As stated in this teacher's comment, having a parent so available to the
school reduced discipline problems. With parents so close to the school, in
many cases walking children to school, they had ample opportunity to
converse with teachers. Required home visits by the teacher, as well as
voluntary ones, helped to build a great deal of rapport between the school
and the teachers, strengthening the connection between home and school.

> Primarily if [teachers] would visit in the afternoon after school it
> was because of a problem that was going on and they would try to
> get with the parents before it got out of hand which, again, I think
> is really important. And I think that personal touch really showed
> the concern, the interest.

One teacher remembered a particularly poignant example of
teachers going into the community to deal with a problem.

> I remember one year, [another teacher] and I were involved with a
> family . . . one of the kids was in her room and one was in mine.
> We noticed that the children needed assistance, and they were not
> getting it from Social Services. . . . It was cold this particular day,
> and very rainy. We went by to see the parents, and this was a little
> old lady. The little fella, he and his sister [were] living with the
> grandmama. She was too old to care for the children. So after going
> in there we found that they didn't have any heat, and at that time
> we came across [the city] to Scott Coal Company, got coal, went
> home, got blankets and things of this sort.

Self-Study as a Collective Voice

Like Cedar Grove School, Rougemont School conducted a self-study for accreditation in 1974. In that year, Rougemont had one principal, a faculty of thirteen, and a staff of seven. The faculty's experience in education ranged from three teachers with one full year of experience each to three with thirty-two or more years of experience. The recently desegregated student body totalled 209: 105 black, 103 white, and one Native American. In 1973 Rougemont continued a gradual decline in enrollment from a 1971 high of 245.

The Rougemont faculty described their school in these excerpts from the section "The School Community":

This school formerly housed all elementary children living in this section, but since desegregation only the majority of them attend.

The change in district lines brought to this school children who had previously attended all white schools.

Following are samples of the text from the Rougemont self-study. Our interpretations follow. The language used in the selections gives some insight into the attitudes of the Rougemont faculty about the education of the children in their school.

Community

The people in this community live in privately owned homes, rented homes, or apartments. A home improvement project has recently been completed which brought all sub-standard homes up to standard. Paved streets and sidewalks were also included in the project.

Family Income

$ 1000 or less	5%
2000	6%
3000	4%
4000	4%
5000	5%
6000	16%
7000	7%
8000	8%
9000	3%
10,000	10%
12,000 or over	26%

Educational Level of Parents

Did Not Reach High School	13%
Incomplete High School	17%
Completed High School	46%
Some College Education	14%
College Degrees and Above	10%

Most parents express a desire for their children to attain the highest education level possible, or at least some type of training which will enable them to achieve an acceptable standard of living.

Parental Employment

Skilled	19%
Semi-skilled	28%
Unskilled	32%
Service Occupations or Housewives	21%

The Children Served

The general health of the students at Rougemont School is good and a high rate of absenteeism is not a problem.

The manners and language usage of the students are fair, but some improvement is needed in this area.

Family Size

Number of Children	Students from a Family This Size
One	26
Two	46
Three	56
Four	35
Five	17
Six or more	29

Family Status

Working Mothers	144
Father at home or parent and step-parent at home	139
Broken homes	43
One parent at home	20
Guardians	5
Parent deceased	2

What Do You Do after School?

Play	107
Work at home, then play	16
Do home work	33

Watch TV	47
Read	2
Work at a job	4

Number of Students Who Have Been to the Following Places

Movies	190
YM/YWCA	54
Children's Museum	182
Randolph University	118
Treyburn State University	14
Tour of a tobacco factory	26

Do you want to go to high school?

Yes	91
No	1

What would you like to be when you grow up?

Teacher	1
Doctor	4
Dentist	1
Nurse	13
Athlete	8
Artist	8
Veterinarian	4
Secretary	5
Policeman	6
Pilot	4
Oceanographer	2
Janitor	1

Philosophy

We at Rougemont Elementary School believe that the challenges of speed, complexity, and impersonality of modern day living in today's changing world, are frightening experiences for many of our elementary school children. Therefore, an atmosphere must be obtained in which a child's social, emotional, intellectual, physical and moral needs can be meet on an individual basis.

The child is the focal point in the teaching-learning process.

We believe that the school is an integral and vital part of the community. Therefore the school should strive to serve the needs of the community.

The community shares in the task of defining educational goals.

Only when both the School and the community acknowledge their responsibility to and develop each other can the needs of children be met.

Language Arts

Oral Language: Since children enter school with different levels of development, the first task of the teacher is to accept the child as he is. The teacher should not impose her own concepts of correct speech and her own concepts on the student. Rather, the teacher should guide each child and help him develop the style of oral expression best suited to his needs. At the same time he must be encouraged to broaden his vocabulary and cultivate a more fluent, correct usage of the English language.

Emergency School Assistance Aid

While racial tension still exists in our community and probably will for a number of years it was felt this was not our greatest need.

The fine work of professional groups, student groups and several community groups has given the community a relatively good base for human relations.

Our school administration stresses human relations at every opportunity and will continue to do so during all activities of the project as it is funded.

Many [students] come from homes which are economically, educationally and socially disadvantaged and many have 1) poor attendance records, 2) low self concepts, 3) low aspirations, and 4) lack of motivation in home environment.

Children are born with intellectual curiosity as proven by the thousands of questions they ask from the time they start talking until they are turned off by some who ridicule, laugh at, or belittle them. We feel that the project teachers and aides with the help of the central office staff will rekindle this curiosity. They will work with the parents to help students 1) experience some success, 2) improve their self image, 3) aspire to higher goals, 4) become better citizens in their school community.

The Teaching–Learning Process

A sound approach to the learning process will recognize that learning is the interaction of the learners with a situation which includes, among other things, a problem, material to help solve the problem and, in the case of the child, an adult to help and guide. Thus, factual knowledge, instead of being important in its relation to its possible usefulness in the remote future, has value because it contributes to the improved quality of present living of the learner, which is the best preparation for living in the future.

A child is not always clear about his purposes or sufficiently mature to define them. It is the teacher's privilege to help the child establish goals and clarify hazy purposes. By using their interests, arousing their curiosity, and expanding their horizons, the teacher can bring the goals of the children and the objectives of the school into closer harmony.

The 209 children who attended Rougemont School in 1973 had, as reported in the self-study, a multitude of personalities and interests, as varied as school kids could be. Outside school, the Rougemont youngsters had equally multiple and varied interests. In constructing the self-study, the teachers included these varying interests as provided by the children on a number of issues and questions. This variety of information was also gathered about the community itself, its context, and the parents and families in it.

The motto prefacing the Southern Association Self-Study Report read, "Let each become all that he has within him to be." This motto had new meaning in the desegregated Rougemont School. The school was no longer just for their own. At Rougemont School the concern was with creating an atmosphere in which a child's social, emotional, intellectual, physical, and moral needs could be met on an individual basis—a decidedly philosophical idea. This was, of course, a bit of a change for the rather oratorical heritage of Rougemont School. The presence of an outsider group (to Rougemont) meant that the school's identity with community was undercut. There was now a varied clientele. Somewhat like Cedar Grove School, Rougemont School began to differentiate its instruction. The lesson for both schools is that when difference was introduced, each school increased stratification, and accommodated more to the philosophical idea. The self-study of Rougemont is different from Cedar Grove's in the regard accorded the students and the communities. The faculty based their concern on the challenges of modern-day living and the experiences it created for elementary school children. Emphasis in the school's philosophy was put on child-centered learning, allowing students to work at their own levels, being sensitive to the needs, values, and developmental levels of each child. The basic aim was to help children meet the challenges of the day's world. It was to be accomplished with a staff of imaginative teachers, alert to research findings and possessing love, warmth, and an understanding of children. Each teacher was to investigate and attempt to understand special problems or difficulties demonstrated by individual students in their classrooms.

Rougemont School was not to accomplish that task alone. In order to meet its goals, the school had to work with students and the community so that the learning process of the individual would be enhanced. School was an integral and vital part of the community. Rougemont School served the community and needed to be sensitive to social and moral issues of the Rougemont community and to the new members of the school. The communities could provide personal and financial support, work for and with the school, and share in the task of defining educational goals. Rougemont School could share responsibility for development of the school and involve community members in the challenges and solutions of school problems. Once both the school and the community acknowledged their responsibility to support and develop each other, then the needs of the children in the school could be met.

As represented here, the Rougemont self-study gave a detailed description of its community and a specific accounting of the social and economic nature of the community. The Rougemont teachers, without resorting to labeling, express a desire for their children to attain the highest education level possible.

Rougemont's self-study referred to attendance by associating it with their health. The Rougemont document made a general reference to the state of manners and language, describing it as "fair, but some improvement is needed in this area." To describe what children wanted to be when they grow up, the teachers asked the children, and then presented their answers, a process they similarly followed with children's use of leisure time.

The Rougemont philosophy was concerned with helping children cope with the world in the present. At issue was how the child's understanding of the world affected the fulfillment of his or her needs as a student. The Rougemont philosophy viewed the school as part of the community; school and community are part of the education of children. The community was a participant in the educational process, not just a beneficiary of it.

Rougemont recognized variance in ability levels and attempted to "accept the child as he is." Oral expression was developed according to student needs, with encouragement to "broaden his vocabulary and cultivate a more fluent, correct usage of the English language." The standard was the student.

Like Cedar Grove School, Rougemont used ESAA funds to attempt to improve math and reading performance among students. Rougemont's self study presents an involved description of the project's nature and goals. The Rougemont self-study gave background to the problem, describing the "intellectual curiosity" of children, how it is stunted, and how, as a goal of ESAA, it can be enhanced by working with parents and participants to help students.

In the desegregated Rougemont, factual knowledge was valuable because of its present utility, not its potential utility. The teacher's purpose was to help the child find value in knowledge by taking advantage of the personality of the student.

The Teachers as Paragons of Virtue

Growing from a faculty of two in 1921 to eighteen by 1974 had little effect on the stance of the teachers nor how they were regarded by the community. One mother whose children attended the school across three decades (the 1950s, 1960, and 1970s) recalled: "They had a good group of teachers, some of the best. They were extra good." One former principal who worked at the school during the early 1970s said it succinctly: "I found a lot of good teaching going on." Another explained how the teachers got the children to believe they were able to live up to the high expectations:

There was a lot of praise, there was a lot of boosting. But not illegitimate praise, not a facade, not a false sense of pride trying to be instilled.

These recollections, however, do not convey the true significance attached to the teachers by the Rougemont community. The above social constructions were offered us to convey the history and general significance of the school to the community of Rougemont. Yet, in our interviews, the tales of virtue inhered in stories of particular teachers whose lives were offered as emblematic narratives of the values of Rougemont School. Values and virtue in Rougemont School were not located in knowledge or in abstract thought; they were located in people and the relationships these people had with the children and adults of Rougemont. While many teachers were discussed in this light, three will suffice for our purposes here: Laura Pursell, Lena Pursell, and Billie Jackson.

Laura Pursell

Much of the beginning and history of Rougemont School was told as revolving around Laura Pursell. She appears in the Treyburn County

Board of Education records as far back as 1920, and her teaching spans the decades into 1950. While this in itself would be a long teaching career, especially for the early part of this century, the board records from 1921 to 1922 show she had then already accumulated twenty-two years of teaching experience. While she is remembered to have first taught at Bricktown School, for Rougemont residents the story of Rougemont School and Laura Pursell are synonymous for almost half of this century.

Except for brief periods when other women were principal, Laura Pursell was the principal and the main teacher. When there were enough teachers for each grade level, Mrs. Pursell took over the sixth grade with the express purpose of ensuring that students were ready for secondary school. Her self-defined job was "to get them out of Rougemont School's sixth grade and send them on to high school."

Mrs. Pursell was well educated for her time, having attended Howard University and numerous teacher-training seminars throughout the years. Laura Pursell was described by former students as a tough teacher, but a "good tough." As her students recall,

We didn't leave Rougemont School to go to high school unless we knew something. She kept you there until you were ready.

Mrs. Laura Pursell would keep somebody in the sixth grade until they were twenty years old before she'd let them go down to Lincoln High School and not know [anything] in the seventh grade and say they've come from Rougemont School.

A parent recalled a breakdown in the oratorical common curricula of Mrs. Pursell:

One year a class graduated and a girl was in the class, and Mrs. Winston, who was at the junior high school in the seventh grade, she got this girl and she said "Goull—you know, instead of "girl"— "Goull, where you from?" She said she was from Rougemont. Mrs. Winston said, "Did Laura Pursell teach you?" And she said yes. Mrs. Winston said, "I've got to talk to talk to her. I've got to tell her she's slipping because she ain't never sent nobody from Rougemont like you."

Mrs. Pursell was clearly legendary in Rougemont. She was reputed to be able to write on a blackboard as easily as others could write with paper and pencil. This clearly amazed those who studied with her. Mrs. Pursell approached omniscience. Children believed "she had eyes behind her head." She did not have to witness a disruption to know invariably who was responsible.

As tough as she was, Mrs. Pursell did not embarrass children, and was characterized as seeing mistakes as opportunities to learn. She would go to the children having difficulty, sit with them, and work out the problem, according to her former students. As a result, students were not afraid to ask questions or to seek help.

For most of her career, being principal was a title and responsibility that was added to her teaching a regular load of classes. Even with this situation, other teachers regarded her as a good principal and liked her as well. She was their role model: a good teacher, a pleasant personality, and good, fair, and honest with her faculty. Equally significant, Laura Pursell was a symbol for the entire community of Rougemont. Her virtues were evident, and children were admonished to emulate them.

Lena Pursell

It must have been a burden as well as a blessing to have followed your mother into a teaching career and into the same school, especially when your mother was Laura Pursell. Lena Pursell reinforced her mother's powerful presence in Rougemont School by joining the faculty in 1926 as a first-grade teacher. Her day-to-day support of her mother continued until her mother quit teaching in 1950. Lena Pursell continued teaching until 1966, giving the school some forty years of continuity in style and beliefs.

One of Lena Pursell's favorite methods of teaching was to get down on the floor with the children first thing in the morning and ask, "What are we going to do today?" The children, who were well imbued with the routines of her classroom, would then recite what would normally be part of their day—except reading. The children would leave out reading because reading was hard for them, and because of that, it was Lena Pursell's priority, as math was her mother's. Lena Pursell taught reading from charts and pictures she placed on the wall or on a frame. The first-graders were expected to complete a pre-primer, a primer, and two readers. *Dick and Jane* was always the last reader. Although the children tended to like everything about first grade but reading, Lena Pursell got the job done, according to former students; her children learned to read. It was more than her job; it was a moral responsibility to the children, Rougemont, and African-Americans. It was also a commitment to her mother who would later teach these children.

The first-grade children preferred physical education. Like so many children, they liked to play outdoors. They also liked to sing, especially to the accompaniment of Lena Pursell, who had a piano in her classroom. Some of the standards were "My Country, 'Tis of Thee," "Lullaby Baby," "Way down upon the Swanee River," and "Weep No More, My Lady."

In Lena Pursell's class, some subjects were taught with the children and her on the floor. Drawing was one such subject. She would say, "We're going to draw. I'm going to draw my apple, and I want yours to be prettier than mine!" (This, of course, is more "progressive" and Dewey-like than the image of the real Miss Dove.) She wanted the children to do the best they could in all the subjects, and worked hard to "get it out of them." This was a consistent message of Rougemont School. For more than forty-five years, getting it out of the students was the message championed by the Pursells. And for almost a quarter of a century, the message would be taught first in the first grade and last in the sixth grade by a Pursell.

Billie Jackson

Billie Jackson came to Rougemont School in the 1940s and remained there until her retirement in 1973. Like the Pursells, she was a most respected figure in the school and community. A principal who served with her, and on more than one occasion sought advice from her, recounts her effect on Rougemont School:

She was a very special lady in the building and in the community. She was very supportive, and she was much respected in that community.

She was a third grade teacher. She was a consummate actor in terms of getting points across in a variety of ways. Sometimes she'd put on a "dog and pony" show, but not to that extent. But she stressed discipline, she stressed attention, and she maintained decorum for her students and made sure the classroom functioned as it should. But in the process of that, there was a friendly, open, relaxed atmosphere. She was unafraid to use different approaches—other kinds of resources and media—to try to get skills and concepts across to students.

Her classroom was very vivid. She used a lot of color in there. She had a lot of displays, and that was the time when the bulletin board was the big thing in terms of classroom context. She took advantage of it. She had student work on display, her work on display, commercial stuff on display, and it was a constant change thing. Whatever went up in September wouldn't be there at the end of September. There were a lot of different activities going on in there.

She was willing to work with students in any capacity, and would work with the families to help that student. School would be out at 3:00, and she would be over there [in the homes of her students] at 3:15—this kind of communication back and forth.

She had been teaching quite a few years. She was very open and very flexible. That was one thing that led to a lot of appreciation and respect for her by her students and teachers. She was very good with kids.

She wanted those students to be able to walk out of that classroom saying that they did the very best they could do, and carry that concept into anything else they did. She was able to instill that. She was able to instill that feeling that "I am able to do certain things regardless of the status I'm in or the situation I find myself in."

Billie Jackson was as close to a progressive teacher as Rougemont School had. She was an innovative teacher and concerned about a student's self-concept. Yet she also had a good dose of the orator in her. She wished to instill virtues in the students and bind them to their cultural histories as Americans and as African-Americans. While the orators would wish it away, Miss Jackson recognized that not all Americans are Westerners. Nonetheless, she recognized that one's status was determined in part by how close one was to being Westerner. To this end, she and the Pursells taught the curricula that were being taught in white schools, even if the materials they had to teach with were old or hand-me-downs from the white schools. In this they supported Du Bois more than Booker T. Washington. Yet they also taught with the purpose of trying to help all African-Americans improve their status in American society. This effort at collective mobility meant that African-American students also had to know their own heritage and understand that individual best efforts were necessary for collective mobility but less likely to alter their personal status or situation. This inured the students against the devastating effects of individualism. Individualism, according to the orators, undercuts virtue and the notion of a common culture. Rougemont teachers understood this in a slightly different version. A people subject to segregation, prejudice, and discrimination cannot afford to judge themselves by the attainment of individual success, because the consistent denial of opportunities for success would leave the individual alone and in despair. Placing success in the context of collective mobility meant that the meanest efforts have value, for each is part of a larger struggle. Billie Jackson poignantly reinforced this virtue when she, upon reading narratives about herself in the celebratory history we prepared for the (current) Cedar Grove PTA, called for its removal. She felt it was unfair to former colleagues to highlight her above the other teachers who had worked at Rougemont.

Virtue was still important—people should be taught to do their best, for, without that, collective mobility was morally hollow. Yet unlike the white Protestants who brought Africans to America, one's material success should not be a measure of one's moral value. There was no external measure for the people of Rougemont—one simply did his or her best, regardless of circumstances. The oratorical idea was well in place in Rougemont School, but fashioned to the real cultural heritage of its people, not to just the heritage that Bloom, Hirsch, and Adler wish.

Rougemont invested its virtues in these emblematic narratives of these and other teachers. It is probably no accident that Cedar Grove School had one primary narrative of virtue and Rougemont had many. Cedar Grove's construction of virtue is highly individualistic and vested in their own assured status as elites. In Rougemont, individualism was tempered by a collective responsibility. For them, one was part of a larger struggle. In Cedar Grove, this conception of struggle was absent, except possibly to maintain one's elite status—and virtues were connected to this elitism. Virtues in Rougemont were more widely distributed; seemingly all the teachers had some status as moral icons. They were all contributing to the struggle in the way that Rougemont constructed its tale of virtue.

Rougemont residents constructed a set of virtues that allowed both wide participation of and benefit for the community as a whole. The teacher narratives above reveal a large set of virtues: respect for others, responsibility for others, discipline as a community endeavor, struggle and suffering, excellence for its own sake, and standing firm with faith.

Respect for Others. In the preceding history and teacher narratives, we see that Rougemont was creating in its images of its teachers a virtue of respecting others. The teachers were strong disciplinarians but did not embarrass students. They were convinced the children were academically capable. They respected parents as partners in educational endeavors, and worked to include them. The principals respected the teachers, and teachers respected each other. Respect for others was characteristic of the wider community: Parents respected the teachers, the young respected the old, and so on. The research team experienced such respect, too, in the church service and in the interviews.

Responsibility for Others. Rougemont's construction of virtue had respect for others as central but insufficient in itself. Respect for others could imply that one would let them be. This was not a virtue

Rougemont wanted. They instead coupled respect with taking responsibility for others. We can see this in the portrayals of the teachers who did not simply teach students and accept whatever student performances resulted. Laura Pursell was portrayed as taking responsibility for the performances of her students in math, and Lena in reading, and Billie Jackson tried various instructional approaches to ensure the students did their best. Again we see this virtue throughout the community. Spanking others' children was conceived of not as potential abuse but rather as being morally responsible as a community member. Again, the research team experienced this virtue of corporate responsibility when those at the fifth-Sunday service took on the responsibility of setting up interviews for us.

Discipline as a Community Endeavor. All the portrayals of the teachers recount the strictness of the teachers. Yet the historical account and the teacher narratives also reveal that discipline was not simply to make students behave in class; rather, discipline was a community endeavor and a virtue in its own right. The construction of strict teachers was coupled with parents and community members being correspondingly strict. When a teacher spanked a child, the parent would also. The portrait of this virtue being constructed is one of community members sharing a set of beliefs and sharing the view that they must be enforced universally. Indeed, discipline is seen not as imposed but as agentic, a moral choice made and acted upon.

Struggle and Suffering. Lena Pursell's students recounted what their lessons for the day would be, but regularly left out reading. Reading was a struggle for them, they struggled to avoid it, and Lena Pursell struggled with them to ensure that they learned to read. Math was the struggle for her mother. The struggle for civil rights characterized their efforts and those of the entire community. This account creates struggle as a virtue in its own right. Note, however, that struggle is not coupled with achievement or success. In a segregated community and school, economic success was controlled by those against whom you were struggling. Coupling struggle with success would likely result in the virtue being transformed into struggle and failure. Instead, the virtue as constructed in Rougemont is struggle coupled with suffering. The teachers and children were seen as struggling together, suffering together much as the community struggled and suffered under segregation. Suffering was part of what it meant to be an African-American. In this construction, suffering is not fatalistic but redemptive, especially when coupled with the last two virtues.

Excellence for Its Own Sake. As we have discussed, segregation meant that the value placed on excellence was different than in Cedar Grove, where excellence was coupled with individualism and elitism. Excellence in the narratives constructed of Rougemont's teachers did less to distinguish an individual than to bind one to one's community. Doing one's best was the virtue. It contributed not to the individual's economic success as a member of the elite but rather to the uplifting of African-Americans as a whole. It was part of the struggle for civil rights and for collective mobility. In this account, teachers did their best, as did the students and the parents, even when segregation meant that excellence could only be a virtue and not a vehicle for an individual's success in the wider society. Doing one's best could lead to higher status in the Rougemont community. Note, however, that in Rougemont material well-being incurred the obligation that one support those less fortunate.

Standing Firm with Faith. Returning to the sermon we discussed in the chapter's opening, one of the virtues in Rougemont's account of its school and teachers is stalwartness. Oppression and segregation helped create a community that was stable, insular, and largely self-sufficient. They had for over seventy years created a way of life that they valued and for which they had little alternative. The community had simply little need for adaptive strategies. In the accounts of the teachers and the school history people constructed, it was a virtue to know what the community stood for and to be stalwart in reproducing that. There were, of course, situations that challenged the community's sense of itself and its assuredness that they were doing right. Yet they had taken Moses' injunction to heart. They stood firm and had faith in ultimate salvation.

These are virtues that Rougemont constructed with us and that were ever present in their accounts of the teachers and the school. These virtues are in distinct contrast to those constructed with the Cedar Grove School.

Conclusions

We did not realize upon our introduction to Cedar Grove School that we would be doing the parallel histories of two schools instead of one school history. Only after we had been involved with Cedar Grove for about six months did we realize that to fully embrace the history of Cedar Grove School as it stood in 1987, we would have to pay special attention to a school that had formerly served students in an adjoining neighborhood who had been redistricted into Cedar Grove during desegregation. We felt that, without the Rougemont story, our work would be incomplete and we would have misrepresented the histories of the students, parents, and professionals who were associated with Cedar Grove.

Our entree into Rougemont proved to be as telling as our entree into Cedar Grove had been. Our initial attempts at access to the Rougemont community were through what we and those at Cedar Grove School considered to be key individuals for the community. When we pursued that avenue in Rougemont, we found that it gained us nothing and that our access would come in the form of a community gathering, not from the blessing of an individual. To get to College Park and Cedar Grove School, we went through one of the elite. To get to Rougemont community and its memories of its school, we went through the community itself. This was the first among many lessons of the importance of community and the collective in Rougemont.

Rougemont also was where we learned that while the oratorical and philosophical ideas were present in schools, they were disconnected from morality and virtue in fundamental ways. This insight forced us to look more closely at Cedar Grove School and ultimately to understand that the ideas that have guided educational reform throughout Western history have little to do with how people construct morality and virtue in, and with, schools.

We learned that virtue and community in Rougemont were inextricably linked, and to understand how virtues were constructed there, we had to understand what had once been the community. Virtue was constructed in the contribution to the collective. We also learned, as we sought voices in Rougemont to give us its narrative, that a collective can have a voice only as a collective and that the individual or elite voice in such a context is not virtuous.

We learned that in the Rougemont community, the school may not have been the sole location of construction of virtues, but it was the primary place within the community where all virtues constructed came together. As we will see in chapter 6, taking away the place where the virtues came together for the community "de-moralized" what had historically been a community where virtues were constructed and where the nature of the moral was clear and easy to comprehend.

5

Books and the Power of Narrative

> Books are to be call'd for, and supplied, on the assumption that the process of reading is not half-asleep, but, in the highest sense, an exercise, a gymnast's struggle; that the reader is to do something for himself, must be on the alert, must himself or herself construct indeed the poem, argument, history, metaphysical essay—the text furnishing the hints, the clue, the start or framework. Not the book needs so much to be the complete thing, but the reader of the book does. That were to make a nation of supple and athletic minds, well-train'd, intuitive, used to depend on themselves, and not on a few coteries of writers.
>
> —Whitman (1964 [1892])

As we have seen, both Rougemont and College Park have constructed virtue in largely, but not exclusively, oratorical fashion. Yet it is the orators who argue that philosophers have dominated education and are responsible for its ruin. Clearly these schools are not fully oratorical, and this may be Adler's fundamental complaint. This also demonstrates that Adler is guilty of a selective reading of history. Anyone who puts such faith in the great works of the past should realize that the orator and philosophical ideas are locked in a seemingly timeless opposition, an opposition that, we argue, is essentially institutionalized in Western society.

Adler, Bloom, and even Hirsch would no doubt argue that the fundamental flaw with Rougemont and Cedar Grove Schools is that they do not have a curriculum organized around great books, ideas, or works of Western culture. However, we will argue in this chapter that the orators have misunderstood what makes a "Great Book."

In part, we believe this is because the orators overvalue tradition. Thus, they are likely to invest in works that represent their notions of Western tradition and ignore those works and ideas that on first reading speak to a person's beliefs, values, and ways of living that are taken for granted; those yet to be reasoned about. Works that speak to people on first reading may or may not change taken-for-granted's and, more importantly for the orators, may not replace these assumptions with reason, as they define it. Great Books accomplish this, but only with concerted study, continued rereading, and much dialogue led by an appropriately trained leader. Reason is seemingly something that requires leaders and followers. The books most of us read, which call to our taken-for granted's in all the ways possible, are not eligible to be Great Books, according to the orators. These books are too particularistic—too concerned with *our* everyday lives and *its* meaning, too bound to single times and places, too idiosyncratic to belong to the Western tradition, at least to the orators' way of thinking.

The philosophers share the orators' valuing of knowledge and reason. They look to books and to curricula as media for the search for truth. Indeed, Dewey's critique of the progressives is that they abdicated knowledge as part of being what he considered excessively child centered. This indicates that the philosophers share with the orators a view of knowledge as existing independently of the knowers. Moreover, the philosophers have no objection to students reading the Great Books. Their objections are with claims that such content should dominate the curriculum and with how these Great Books are read. The philosophers see such books as important in developing the critical faculties necessary to the pursuit of truth, but as only one way to accomplish this. In short, there are some important parallels among orators and philosophers, and philosophers often have deferred the creation of canons to the orators. For these reasons, our focus in this chapter is primarily on the orators' use of books, even though we will discuss implications for both the oratorical and philosophical ideas. The important point, however, is that orators and philosophers wish for knowledge to have a unique status in human life, one distinct from the meanings of everyday lives. In this they devalue narrative. Yet narrative has much to recommend itself, especially for its power in moral discourse. As Witherell and Noddings write:

> Stories and narrative, whether personal or fictional, provide meaning and belonging in our lives. They attach us to others and to our own histories by providing a tapestry rich with threads of time, place, character and even advice in what we might do with our lives. (1991: 1).

Thus, part of our purpose in this chapter is to redefine Great Books as narratives with the power to evoke social construction of virtue.

In the preceding two chapters, school curricula played a peripheral role in how people constructed virtue. The content of curricula was not used to create the substance of morality in any direct sense. The moral lessons of schools have little to do with the content of these subjects. The moral lessons, rather, are those that people invest in social and cultural acts of schooling, instruction, and learning. People remember not the moral lessons of *The Odyssey* but rather the moral lessons they give to the teaching of *The Odyssey* in the classrooms and schools they inhabit and construct.

Nonetheless, in Cedar Grove School there was a book that was read, remembered, and directly implicated in the common culture of the school. This book was *not* part of the explicit curricula, either oratorical or philosophical, and leads us to reconsider the role of books in creating values. Since the orators have a well-developed concept about this, we will contrast their notion of Great Books with what these schools teach us about books that count in the construction of morality. Yet we will also learn that books that are important for moral construction teach not about the philosophical pursuit of truth or virtue but about creating continuities between pasts and futures. That is to say, the books we discuss in this chapter teach us that rather than choose between the oratorical and philosophical ideas, we must develop ways to connect the oratorical and philosophical ideas in our everyday, present lives. Moreover, this is the power of narrative.

The Good and the Great

In 1921 Mortimer Adler was a student in the first Great Books seminar offered in the United States. It was taught by John Erskine at Columbia University. Erskine had developed a list of about sixty books, most of which have survived the revision and expansion of the list at Columbia, the University of Chicago, St. John's College, the University of Notre Dame, St. Mary's College, and other institutions of higher education (Adler 1990). Adler sees the Great Books program as involving the seminar format and a dialectical teaching method. As noted in chapter 2, this seems to mark him as a philosopher, but his oratorical foundation is in his assurance that there are prescriptive, objective, universal, and absolute truths (1990: xxix). His faith in Great Books is simply that they are "good for the mind" (1990: 326). He argues that there is universal agreement that these are the best materials for the mind to work on to gain wisdom, insight, and understanding:

By everyone's admission they are the repository of whatever insight, understanding, and wisdom Western man has so far accumulated. By everyone's admission they set forth the ideas, the problems, the principles, and the subject matters of the arts and sciences, which make our culture what it is. . . . Certainly there can be no better books. (1990: 327)

In his epilogue to a collection of his essays on education that span his career, Adler tries to address what he sees as misunderstandings people have about the Great Books approach. In doing this he specifies what he and his coworkers do not claim. They do not claim that the Great Books contain all worthy knowledge; do not claim that they will develop all possible virtues of humanity, especially the moral virtues; do not claim that reading these books will necessarily make better people or citizens; do not claim that they will save the world or safeguard democracy. All they do is provide "the best opportunity for the improvement of the mind" (328) which, if taken, *can* lead to all of the above.

He also claims the ideas explored in the Great Books are in some sense universal: They are the ideas with which any individual must think about his own life and the world in which he lives. They are the problems which any society must face. They are the subject matters which represent the things worth inquiring into and learning about, certainly for anyone who wishes to understand a little about the nature of the world, of society, and of himself. (328–9)

It is not that any work is error free or complete. Rather, it is that each work must be read for its basic truths, basic errors, or mistakes and be read in the context of other works that refute and contradict these truths and errors. This prepares the mind, according to Adler, for critical thinking and reflective thought.

Adler proposes a number of criteria for determining the greatness of a book. He is quick to note that probably no book can meet all of these, but the Great Books come closest. He starts with the five suggested by Scott Buchanan in 1937:

1. It is a book that has been read by the largest number of people . . . that have, over the centuries, had more readers than other books, and that have "stood the test of time."
2. It is a book that has the greatest number of alternative, independent, and consistent interpretations. . . .
3. It raises the persistent unanswerable questions. . . .
4. It must be a fine work of art. . . .
5. It must be a masterpiece of the liberal arts. (Quoted in Adler 1990: 333)

To these he adds some criteria of his own. First, the books must deal with basic ideas and issues in a variety of ways, making the book eminently discussable. Second, they have to be read many times before they are fully understood (if, indeed, they ever can be fully understood). This is related to Adler's admonition that books should be chosen for students which are over their heads at least enough for them to have to struggle and seek the meaning of the texts. Third, they must be written by a generalist for the intelligent reader. Fourth, they must be drawn from all types of literature and from all arenas of learning. Finally, a negative restriction is that author influence should not be a basis for inclusion if the other criteria are not met. To this last, he notes "The fact that, in the Western tradition until the nineteenth century, there simply were no Great Books written by women, blacks, or non-Europeans, does not make those that were written by white males in earlier centuries any less great" (1990: 334). Adler also has another criteria, possibly better understood as a decision rule: that the works must be Western and not, for example, Asian—only because we understand so little about our own heritage that this is first priority. He attributes to Carl Van Doren the best summary definition: These are books that are so good at what they do that they never need be written again.

Adler, consistent with the orators' interest in intellectual communities, defends his approach as different from others, especially Bloom's. His argument with Bloom is manifold, as we discussed in chapter 2. Of interest to the themes of this chapter is Adler's accusation that Bloom errs on the side of focusing on the truths contained in the Great Books to the exclusion of errors—what he sees as a doctrinaire approach to the Great Books.

Bloom, to be sure, is less concerned with an immediate and pragmatic solution to the orators' problems with education than is Adler. His critique of Adler might be that the problem is so fundamental that Adler's practical program is likely to play to the opposition rather than resolve the issue in an appropriate manner: "It is hopeless to attempt universal reform" (Bloom 1987: 65). Nevertheless, Bloom shares with Adler the belief that only the great works can speak to the perennial issues of humanity. Bloom's lament that students no longer find the classics (Bloom uses this term unashamedly while Adler eschews it) instructive is coupled with his belief that without classic lessons and heroes to guide them, today's students are left simply to play out their culture, to conform rather than to lead or to dare to be great. He writes of the Bible as but one example of what Great Books permit: "I mean . . . that a life based on the Book is closer to the truth, that it provides the material for deeper research in and access to the real nature of things" (60). The real nature of things, for Bloom, involves a rational understanding of the whole of humanity, of the continuity between feelings and what humanity can and should be. He sees all else as a surface understanding in which immediate interests are treated as significant to the deeper, real nature of things: "The folk mind takes the place of reason" (192). Only the study of the Great Books can prevent this for Bloom.

Bloom also shares Adler's belief that it is only through the study of Great Books that our nation can be experienced as a common project, though Adler sees Bloom's emphasis on elite education as compromising this project. Bloom sees the study of the works of the nation's founders as well as those of Western civilization as the basis of shared understanding of what our nation is and ought to be about. Moreover, it is a remedy for the rampant individualism and self-centeredness he sees in America's young and which undercut social solidarity (to paraphrase him). The Great Books allow a way to reestablish virtue as a product of reason and to destroy value relativism. In Bloom's arcane view, vision is a product of the study of the past and involves holding to traditions.

The Great Books, for Bloom, are generally recognized classics, and are rarely found only in the separate disciplines such as science singularly. The sciences, guided by positivism and an open-ended search for the truth, are more interested in incremental progress than in Great Books. Bloom argues that even when Great Books are read for university courses, they are read as history and not as the center of the scientific idea. The social sciences are little better, given their goal of becoming scientific. In any case, Bloom believes there are no social science books that are truly classics. Even the humanities are split over their use and their meaning. They may teach classics but they do so with modern, leftist, or revisionist tendencies. The issue, as Bloom sees it, is that all the disciplines have lost contact with the content of classic works, devaluing both the meaning of a text and the reason for studying it.

Bloom has little to say about the criteria that determine Great Books, but he does describe what they give students. He agrees with a number of critiques of the Great Books approach including complaints of its cult nature, evangelistic tone, amateurishness, the inability to read all the Great Books, its exclusion of a range of books (making it difficult to understand what makes a book great), the indeterminacy of what a Great Book is, the books being treated as ends and not means, and so on (344). Yet he assures us that these are not truly important. For when the Great Books are the curriculum, students are excited, fulfilled, and satisfied:

> The advantage they (the students) get is an awareness of the classic—particularly important for our innocents; an acquaintance

with what big questions were when there were still big questions; models, at the very least, of how to go about answering them; and, perhaps most important of all, a fund of shared experiences and thoughts on which to ground their friendships with one another. (344)

His assurance is supreme: "Men may live more truly and fully in reading Plato and Shakespeare than at any other time, because they are participating in essential being and are forgetting their accidental lives" (380).

Although his approach differs from Adler's, Bloom agrees with Adler that it is the method of reading and teaching that makes the difference. Adler's critique of Bloom's seeking only the truths in a Great Book is belied by the latter's critique of his own teacher who was silent about Plato's "embarrassing disagreements with current views" (Bloom 1987: 375). In any case, the classics should not be read from today's perspectives, according to Bloom. These are all too grounded in the accidental, the particular, and the surface meanings of human life. The texts must first be simply read, not interpreted. The books should be allowed to dictate the questions and the methods of approaching the questions. This is accomplished by trying to read the books as the authors wanted them to be read; therefore, they should be read not as historical products but as books speaking about issues that remain central to humanity.

The above, of course, is what we have meant all along by the oratorical idea. Great Books are key to this idea, as, in referring to a student, Bloom confirms:

This student did not have Socrates, but he had Plato's book about him, which might even be better. (381)

E. D. Hirsch, as we discussed in chapter 2, has a rather different approach to the Great Books. He is after a "universal public discourse" (1987: 109) in much the same vein as was Cicero, and he argues that this was the goal of the nation's founders. He sees cultural literacy as the modern version of rhetoric. In this the Great Books are a means to an end, apparently sharing with Bloom the critique of Great Books as ends in themselves. Again, Hirsch does not share the full perspective of either Bloom or Adler. He has some respect for relativism, for science, and for anthropology. There is no doubt, however, that he would agree with Adler that it is the misuse of science, not the idea of science itself that is the issue—for this is how he critiques the research on reading skills and educational formalism. Hirsch shares the oratorical belief that the redemption of our democracy lies in a shared understanding of the great works and ideas, even if he wishes to intervene more between the books themselves and a student's understanding of them. This he justifies as being in service of society, as it creates a national vocabulary and culture, even though Adler is worried about the possibility of a "thin veneer of cultural literacy" in Hirsch's approach (Adler 1990: xxxi).

While both Adler and Bloom advocate a junior Great Books program, Hirsch is working more directly on the issue of having a wide variety of content shared by the youngest students in a politically decentralized educational system. His focus is on giving students the variety of associations that words, phrases, and names are intended to invoke in a literate member of our society. Given Adler's extensive work with *Encyclopaedia Britannica* and his *Synopticon* and *Propaedia* (Adler 1990), it would seem that Hirsch's approach is consistent with even the most ardent Great Books proponent. Moreover, Hirsch's approach, given that it emphasizes both factual information and the development of schema, would easily fit in one of the "three columns" in Adler's *Paideia Proposal* (1982). This seems to be consistent with both the didactic instruction and the coaching "columns." Hirsch is intent on getting the specific content of important works identified (as are Bloom and Adler) and put into useful form.

There are fundamental differences between Hirsch and the other two orators. Hirsch wants to teach directly the associations that go with words, phrases, and names so a reader can understand the meaning of sentences and not just the definitions of the words themselves. There is an impatience in his approach, implying that, while it would be nice for all children to read the Great Books, there will not be enough time in their young lives to read all of them and to read the more mundane works that are always putting new meanings and associations to words. His solution is to identify and list the core contents of literate culture so they can be studied directly. We see him as being about "Great Ideas."

In working out his approach, Hirsch has had to face some of the same issues Adler faced in identifying what should be included as items to be learned. Hirsch's effort at a *Dictionary of Cultural Literacy* (1993) required first the identification of the goal: creating a "common reader" sufficiently literate to read and understand what is contained in the newspapers and other basic media of societal communication. For this initial effort, he and his colleagues defined sufficient literacy as that equivalent to high school graduation. Second, they had to face the issue of who is qualified to decide what is essential to be included in the dictionary. They decided on a two-tiered system. He and his colleagues, drawn from the humanities, history, and the sciences, generated a list of candidate items from a wide range of sources. In this process Hirsch and his colleagues made two decisions. First, the list should represent the existing literate culture; and second, it should attempt to alter it by enhancing the knowledge of science and technology that should be common in our culture. In the judging of what would be finally included, however, Hirsch eschewed academic expertise for the advice of a large number of consultants outside the university. The difficult decisions of what items to include and when to add or delete associations with single items were referred to the panel of advisors. This process was sufficiently effective to produce the *Dictionary*.

Hirsch, however, does not see the dictionary as the end in itself. He sees it as an intermediate step: a listing that can then be used to devise his notion of an "extensive" curriculum, a guide to textbook writers and publishers as to what ought to be included in a new generation of textbooks, a basis for general knowledge examinations to replace existing standardized tests, and a guide for educators' decision making about what content should be emphasized. In the last, he suggests some criteria for texts to be used, emphasizing "factual narratives" and "traditional lore" (1993: 140). For him, these are the bases for the Great Ideas in that they provide the schemata through which students can accumulate facts and participate in our national, common culture. Great Ideas, and not Great Books, are the basis of cultural literacy.

The orators may have a number of disagreements among themselves, but they also share fundamental premises. When it comes to Great Books or what counts as Great Ideas, there are five key points of agreement. First, that which is important is in the past. Our heritage is what makes us what we are. These works and ideas have withstood "the test of time" in that they have continued to be included in our reading and our writing. Second, these works and ideas are universalistic. They speak of, and to, the perennial issues salient to Western culture. For Hirsch, these are the meanings, the associations, and the context that give our modern language its depth and its capability to express our culture. Third, these works are to be beyond the current understanding of the student at least initially and, in some sense, always; therefore, they always lead the student. The challenge is to improve and enlighten the literacy and the minds of those who are in the process of being socialized. Fourth, these works are basic to understanding and promoting a "common" culture. They are both the origins of our culture that we need to share and an enduring part of our cultural lexicon that give us continuity and a shared system of meaning. Fifth and finally, they are the basis of national greatness. When they are known and shared by all, we will regain our past status.

Each of these points can be argued, of course. In promoting the test of time, the orators violate their own assumption that humanity is responsible for knowledge and virtue. There is no test of time independent of people who actively read, select, and promote these works and ideas, as, indeed, the recent works of our three orators attest. Universalism is never complete. To claim it requires a selective ignoring of instances where it does not apply. For example, the orators' complaint against the philosophers is testimony to a lack of universalism. Selecting items that are beyond the readers may challenge them, but it is also an indication that these works are not about their lives. The notion of a "common" culture may be argued to be a gross abstraction in our diverse society. It may also be the basis of a stagnating sameness that would impede innovation. Further, national greatness for the United States has long been tied to the diversity of the population, the mix of cultural ideas, and a pioneer spirit. These arguments are, of course, rather cursory and need much more development before they can be fully justified.

The remainder of this chapter develops our thesis that the Great Books and Ideas of the orators may not be all they are proposed to be. We will demonstrate that they are better considered *good* books and ideas than great ones.

Great Books Reconsidered

We have already discussed the position of philosophers on Great Books. They have no reasoned objection to their use, and, in fact, are often satisfied that such a curriculum is a good vehicle for developing intellectual ability and, therefore, intellectual and scientific skills. However, the philosophers are also guarded in the endorsement of any book, author, or idea. In their way of thinking, books capture what was known at one point in time. Since knowledge evolves, any book or idea is better understood as a historical landmark in scientific progress. Nevertheless, there are books that inspire new ideas and that remind philosophers of things to be perennially careful about. Thomas Kuhn's *The Structure of Scientific Revolutions* (1962) is one such work, and in each field there are others. In education, the works of Dewey clearly fit this bill, even with the vociferous objections of the orators. Nevertheless, the philosophers look ahead and invest little in the past or in the present except as it informs their search for the truth yet to be found. Greatness is always yet to be obtained, for any accomplishment is quickly eclipsed by what it inspires.

The conflict between the philosophical and oratorical ideas about the greatness of works and ideas need not immobilize us or force us to choose sides (as Adler would wish). As we discussed in chapter 1, both ideas have distinguished histories that are linked in controversy with the other. It may be that together they can lead us to a way to revisit the idea of the greatness of books. The orators see the greatness in the idea, and the philosophers see the greatness in what the idea inspires. It is likely that both are true, and what we need is some understanding of how this could be. Moreover, it is also likely that what is required is not a new idea but simply an idea that has existed outside, or alongside, the prominence of, and controversy between, these two. Our epigraph by Whitman is but one marker of a centuries-old idea that only recently has been recognized as an important idea in its own right: that the greatness of a work is better understood as being in the reading of it than in the work itself or the things it inspires. The reading alone is to be valued. This idea, of course, rejects the orators' thesis that a Great Book must be beyond the reader. Whatever the sophistication of a work, the reader is actively deciding its worth as she or he reads it. The idea contradicts the philosopher's thesis that the value of a work is in what it inspires. The value of the work is invested by the reader as she or he reads, and inspiration may or may not result. As Ralph Waldo Emerson put it, "'Tis the great reader that makes a good book" (1876: 264–5).

This idea is being heralded as new in both deconstructionism and in reader-response literary criticism, but, in reality, what is new is the championing of the idea. The idea is newly seen as a way to put democracy into education in a way rather different from either the orators' or the philosophers'. We should be clear that deconstructionism and reader-response criticism are quite distinct enterprises. Yet both are about participative reading. Deconstructionism liberates the literary critic, whereas reader-response liberates the reader.

A contrast may help us understand this idea. Adler sees the job of the reader as understanding the work itself:

> To understand a book, you must approach it, first, as a whole, having a unity and a structure of parts; and, second, in terms of its elements, its units of language and thought. (1940: 124)

Pater puts it rather differently:

> What is this song or picture . . . to me? What effect does it really produce on me? and if so, what sort or degree or pleasure? The answers to these questions are the original facts with which the aesthetic critic has to do; and, as in the study of light, of morals, of number, one must realize such primary data for one's self, or not at all. (1910: viii)

Pater is framing reading not as passive but as involving both aesthetic appreciation and critical appraisal. In this view, reading is not the understanding of the unity of the work as the author intended it but participating in the work as an active and qualified reader—making of it what you will.

Rosenblatt (1978) distinguishes efferent reading and aesthetic reading. Efferent reading involves the search for, and identification of, concepts, ideas, and facts. This is what most of us experienced in high school literature classes. These items are to be learned and retained. Efferent reading can also be evocative in that one can read to learn what actions are to be performed as the result of the reading. In this we can see both the orators and the philosophers. Clearly, the focus on facts is what the orators seek at least initially. Their emphasis on virtue can be seen in the evocation of action. The study of Great Books and Ideas for the orators prompt moral action consistent with these works. Rosenblatt argues efferent reading to be what most educators want students to do, but her critique is that this kind of reading makes the reader an "invisible eavesdropper" (2) rather than an active participant in the event of reading. Even with his critique of formalism and skill emphasis in reading, Hirsch clearly conceives of reading as efferent reading. More generally, the oratorical idea is based on this orientation to reading. The oratorical idea treats the reader's ideas as surface or accidental, to echo Bloom, and ineligible to engage with the Great Ideas while a person is in the process of reading. The philosophical idea shares much of this, given its reliance on oratorical study to determine eligibility for the search for truth. They, too, emphasize facts and what should be done with them. The philosophers themselves do not read solely in this manner, but their students do.

Aesthetic reading, for Pater and for Rosenblatt, is quite different from efferent reading. It is not about finding the truths in a work as much as it is about a reader putting the truth, the beauty, into the work. The focus is on what happens during the reading. Rosenblatt explains that "the reader's attention is centered directly on what he is living through with that particular text" (25). In this type of reading, the reader is eligible to engage the author and the ideas but is also eligible to make something new. The reader can engage in cultural and moral construction.

Stanley Fish, one of the United States's most prominent advocates of reader response, sees reading in a more anthropological manner than does Hirsch, for all the latter's claim to an anthropological theory of education. Fish points out that, in a book, "what is noticeable has been made noticeable . . . by an interpretive strategy" (1980: 347). Reader response, for Fish, is not an "anything goes" proposition, regardless of the fears of the orators. Rather it is, on the one hand, an expression of the reader's experience, beliefs, and ways of interpreting life's events—that is, an expression of one's culture. On the other hand, it is also the creation of new meaning. Reading allows people to use their cultural backgrounds to create something new, an interpretation that is not just what they had before they read the book but something they construct as they read. They begin reading with an interpretive strategy, to be sure, but the meaning they construct is more than the strategy they start with. This gives reading the focus on content that the orators so desire, but the content is not located only in the work itself.

The orators' objection (shared by many philosophers also) can be seen in Bloom's critique of deconstructionism. He writes:

The school is called Deconstructionism, and it is the last, predictable stage in the suppression of reason and the denial of the possibility of truth in the name of philosophy. The interpreter's creative activity is more important than the text; there is no text, only interpretation. Thus the one thing most necessary for us, the knowledge of what these texts have to tell us, is turned over to the subjective, creative selves of these interpreters, who say that there is both no text and no reality to which the texts refer. (1987: 379)

Here Bloom is attacking a straw argument. Both deconstruction and reader-response approaches to participative reading claim that there is plenty of reality here. For the writer it is a reality she or he wishes to construct through writing; for the reader, it is that which is constructed in interaction with the work. The problem for Bloom is that there are multiple realities that undercut the orators' claim to universal values.

In Rosenblatt's language, a book becomes a text only when it is read. A book exists as "a stimulus activating elements of the reader's past experience" and as a blueprint, "a guide for selecting, rejecting, and ordering of what is being called forth" (11). Yet it becomes a text only when the symbols on the pages are given meaning by the reader. The aesthetic reader works hard to make the book great. Reading does not have to be aesthetic, but the orators—even Hirsch, with all his knowledge of reading—have poorly captured all that reading is. Rosenblatt elaborates:

In the broadest terms, then, the basic paradigm of the reading process consists in the response to cues; the adoption of an efferent or aesthetic stance; the development of a tentative framework or guiding principle of organization; the arousal of expectations that influence the selection and synthesis of further responses; the fulfillment or reinforcement of expectations, or their frustration, sometimes leading to a revision of the framework, and sometimes, if necessary, to rereading; the arousal of further expectations; until, if all goes well, with the completed decoding of the text, the final synthesis or organization is achieved. (1978: 54)

Reality, as best it can be found in a piece of writing, is transaction between a book and a reader, not some independently existing thing, either in the revered past of the orators or in the future to be discovered by the philosophers. Greatness is not a judgment made by panels of experts or by popularity, currently or historically, or by prevalent usage as an association or referent in the media. Greatness must be constructed by readers in interaction with a work that allows readers to make meaning out of what the writer provides. Great Books are made by those who read greatness into them.

How are we to judge books then? Probably not all that differently from how we judge them now. We let people read them and see what they make of them. Of course, we now rely on people who are identified as critics or reviewers, a status conferred on them that gives their judgment special weight. Even with this, we know that readers find some books worthy about which reviewers are skeptical. Of course, people read reviews just like they read books, and most are free to read reviews aesthetically. Great reviews and Great Books are those the reader can do something with.

Readers may find that a book speaks to what they believe already. They use the book to confirm their current assumptions, to justify their beliefs, or simply to reaffirm the lives they lead. This type of reading makes the reader's life "efferent." One's life becomes reified as a fact, not as a human construction, and one then becomes "subject to" his or her culture rather than a participant in it. Books read like this are good books, for they do speak to us, if only in this way. Following our argument in chapter 2, Bloom's book is a good book, as are those of Hirsch and Adler, for they speak to what we already believe: The nation is declining and education is to blame. A reader can also find that reading a book challenges his or her assumptions, beliefs, and life or invites the reader's participation in constructing meaning from the book. These are difficult books, however. The reader must choose to be challenged and invited or must choose to read the author's cues as challenging and inviting. Otherwise the book can confirm by negative example. The reader must choose to create a new idea, to construct a new belief, to see a new life. A reader cannot do this if he or she believes that all the ideas are already thought, that the pinnacle is past, as does Adler. If readers believe that all ideas have been already thought and are unwilling to consider other beliefs, then all reading is efferent, all humanity is about recapitulating the ideas others have thought, and virtue is to be found in tradition.

The difference here is between a Great Book and a good book. Good books strike a chord we recognize. Great Books are opportunities for cultural and moral construction. The reader finds in them something that prompts a desire, a belief, a value, or an idea that was not there before. Plato may have written Great Books, but he maintained that you could not discover greatness by reading them. You had to work on ideas yourself. If in reading Plato's books people engage in using their beliefs to construct other beliefs, then Plato's books are great, as are those of Cicero and as are those of the meanest author.

As we will show in what follows, books may be good and great at the same time, depending on who reads them and what meaning they invest in them. This is even true of books that the orators would disdain. The books we will discuss are narratives—particularistic about specific people, times, and places rather than about universal truths. These are not sophisticated books. They were written for a general audience, and the ideas in them can be understood readily on first reading. These books help us understand more about the schools and communities we discussed in chapters 3 and 4 and about what might have been had these communities not been "efferent" in reading and in life. They are both good and great books, as are so many narratives that are written about the lives we have lived or might live.

In our work on Cedar Grove and Rougemont Schools, we have found books that would not fit the orators' definition of great but that are nonetheless important. One book is clearly a good book by our definition. It speaks to readers about their existing lives and beliefs. It is a book Cedar Grove School and College Park residents took to narrate the story of their school and themselves. No such book exists for Rougemont School and community. The school was closed and the community has waned. There is no narrative for readers to chance upon, to consider, and to make something of: no book to be made good or great. There is a book, however, that is about a nearby community. Like the story of Rougemont, it allows a reader to construct an interpretation of possibilities, always remembering that the work itself is only the cue. The interpretive community that was Rougemont is almost gone. What they would have done with such a narrative cannot be known, only speculated. The same is true with how the discourse about education might have been affected had Rougemont's narrative, and all the narratives of African-American schools that were lost to desegregation, been available for readers to interact with.

The discussion that follows is inadequate to remedy this. What we will give is *our* reading of what these texts say to us about education, ideas, intellectuals, and our culture. We encourage you to read for yourself the books we discuss. Our reading is not to substitute for yours but to start a dialogue about what these books, and what narrative in general, might mean for our culture, education, and nation.

Good Morning, Miss Dove

Liberty Hill was a small freshwater town—not a hill, really, but just a modest rise in the land—where streets were named for trees and for heroes, and a sense of life's continuity ran in the air. It was like a hundred American towns, smug and cozy, and it put its special stamp upon its own. . . . They had all, for the space of a whole generation, been exposed at a tender and malleable age to the impartial justice, the adamantine regulations, and the gray, calm, neutral eyes of the same teacher—the terrible Miss Dove. (Patton 1947: 1)

So begins Francis Gray Patton's best-selling book, *Good Morning, Miss Dove*. The orators would find this book unworthy of being considered a great book. It is relatively recent, post–World War II, and, while popular, it has not even survived the test of recent time. It is not a learned book, even though well written. It makes few pretenses, and certainly it is not over the head of many readers. Today copies of the book are hard to find, but this was not always the case.

Francis Gray Patton first wrote a couple of short stories for popular magazines. These were well received and led to the encouragement to write a book based on these stories. The book was first published in 1947, and went through two more editions in 1952 and 1954. It was a best seller. Reviewers found it an interesting bit of Americana, and it fit well the mood of the postwar period. More importantly, however, it was read by a wide range of people. In many schools, at least in the South, it was required reading for students and was assigned reading in many programs for prospective teachers. It was a book that spoke to values and traditions, albeit in a contemporary vein. As the epigraph above testifies, it also spoke of a shared experience of almost all Americans, the experience of being subjected to schoolteachers.

The success of the novel led to it being more popularized in an off-Broadway play of modest success and a more successful movie, starring Jennifer Jones in the title role and Robert Stack and Chuck Conners. The reviewers found the movie a morally uplifting tale, if of mixed cinematic quality. The movie is still shown occasionally on cable television. Clearly the book and its offshoots struck a chord with Americans. As we argued above, it certainly was a good book. Readers (and viewers) responded with enthusiasm, for here was a story with which they could identify.

The more important history to this book, in our way of thinking, is not about this universal appeal but about its particularistic appeal. We discovered this book not as a result of library research or by suggestions of experts but by being invited to work on the history of Cedar Grove School. The principal who initiated our collaboration first drew our attention to the book. At the time we saw it as interesting but, at best, marginally related to the task of writing the schools' histories.

We found out very quickly how wrong we were. This book is personal, for the people of College Park take this book to be about themselves. They see themselves, their school, and their community in it. To them, the fictional Miss Dove (whom we discussed as the "real Miss Dove," Mrs. Gregory, in chapter 3) is the most prominent historical actor in their school and, given the centrality of the school in their community, in their shared lives. The people of the community are not of one mind, however, about the *meaning* attached to the book and the real Miss Dove. Some promote the association; some deny it. Some find it to have captured the essence of the school, Mrs. Gregory, and the community. Some point to its flaws in detail. Some who promote the association revere Mrs. Gregory and what she stood for, and others do not. Some who deny the association of the book with this community agree that it is an accurate portrayal of the school, Mrs. Gregory, and the community. And so on. Furthermore, this is complicated by people saying one thing in public and another in private. The conclusion that is undeniable is that a lot of the dialogue about education in this community is about this book, in one way or another. Dismaying as it was for our factual intentions of writing the history of the school, we have since been heartened to find that books can have a significance that the orators have not even imagined. Here fact and fiction are hopelessly and wondrously intertwined. Fiction is history, and fact often meaningless. The point is that the meanings College Park people assign to their own history are in many ways a reflection of the book. The community used the book to create a shared set of beliefs that even the shared experience of the school and the real Miss Dove could not create. For them it is a very good book.

Synopses

Adler's advice would be to look first to the unity and the structure of the work and then to its elements. While clearly this is *not* what the people of College Park have done, it may help someone who has not read the book, especially if combined with a second synopsis based on our more aesthetic reading of the book. The whole of the book is the story of a feared and revered schoolteacher who is caused to reconsider her approach to teaching and to students by her own sudden onset of disease and the role reversal it causes. No longer is it her duty to dominate; her duty is to submit to the orders of her doctor and the routines of the hospital. The book is structured into a series of flashbacks that enable parallels between these two duties and reveals the morally uplifting effects of her duty-bound behavior on the students, the parents (who were also her students), the other educators in the school, and the wider community. The book opens with the quote with which we started this section. This leads into a classroom scene that shows her sternness and emphasis on rules but also her unwavering impartiality. This scene establishes the key theme of the book: The "complete suspension of will" (Patton 1947: 12) is a comfort in the structured and impartial setting of her classroom. It is in the classroom that Miss Dove first has her pain and becomes aware that this is one thing she cannot control. The flashbacks reveal that her duty-bound behavior is due to a father who did not live up to his duty. Her entry into teaching enabled her to extinguish his failing and to provide for her mother and sisters. She compares herself to other teachers who, unlike her, will not or cannot control their classes. When the pain strikes, she sends a student to get her doctor, but he is not available. Instead, a young doctor, one of her former students, is brought to her in her classroom. She is carried by the young doctor and the Reverend (also a former student) through the neighborhood to the hospital. This scene is also comic in that the neighborhood is shaken by the possibility that its pillar is mortal. This is also occasion for more flashbacks revealing more of Miss Dove's character, the other characters, their relationships, and the powerful effect this woman has had on the people of Liberty Hill. Here we find she stood for what so many people desired to stand for: "certitude, principle, authority" (86).

Arriving at the hospital, Miss Dove finds that even though her role is now similar to that of her students, she approves of the formality, the order, and the determination of the hospital. The hospital occasions more flashbacks, giving greater depth to our understanding of her character and her sense of responsibility. It also affords the usual occasion of visitors to the sick that both set the stage for the flashbacks and show her relationships with others and her morally inspiring effects on them. These reveal the reverence that both the highly successful and the morally suspect share for her. She inspires a common virtue, even if few can approach hers. We learn about her secret gradebook in which S for "satisfactory" is the highest grade; T for "tractable," the most common grade for those amenable to reason and with leadership capable of being good citizens; and *O* for "original," referring to the unregulated. We learn of her equality with other moral professions such as the clergy and the devotion of the children to her.

Miss Dove has a tumor that may be fatal. The doctor decides to operate, and she entrusts herself to her former student. Under ether, Miss Dove has bizarre dreams that revisit her life as it could have been had she not been bound by duty. She toys with changing how she would teach, exchanging her devotion to duty for the joy of children's exuberance and freedom from rules, but she awakens to her duty as a patient to wait for the doctor's verdict. She is cured, revealing both the virtue of her willing acceptance of responsibility as a teacher and the appropriateness of suspension of will to persons of authority in the hospital.

This synopsis emerges from an efferent reading of the novel. This is not what the reader experiences when she or he simply opens the book and begins reading. The reader must interact with the words and imagery as they develop, and Francis Gray Patton is quite explicit about the cues she wishes the reader to find, repeating them in numerous ways as the book progresses. Yet the meaning of these cues will be different to people from different interpretive communities. Our reading of the novel is no doubt informed by our interests in, and knowledge of, the real community, our backgrounds as academics, and our interest in writing our book. The text we create from our reading is about a set of virtues that the book promotes and the mechanism through which these virtues come to be. To our way of thinking, this novel is a classic oratorical product with one major exception. There is little in this book about knowledge conceived as great works or classic ideas. Knowledge is portrayed as facts to be learned that are imbued with moral value (more like Hirsch than Bloom or Adler), drill and practice is shown to produce virtue, a community is established by a common curriculum, and the virtues of Miss Dove are beyond question.

One set of cues Francis Gray Patton gave us referred to duty and sacrifice. Miss Dove's life is about these linked themes. Her first duty was to clear her father's name and to provide for her mother and sisters. For this she sacrificed marriage and committed herself to a career of teaching that would have been below her status had not her father succumbed both morally to defrauding the bank and mortally on the night of her debut to Liberty Hill's people of well-to-do status. Her second duty, which became the banner of her existence, was to the children in her charge. In service of them, she was "Woman Bereft" (62)—"a position of her own choosing" (65). She surrendered not to impulse nor to temptation, but she always put before her own needs those that were necessary to fulfill her obligation as a teacher. Because of this, Miss Dove considered herself superior to mothers, who were dependent on men and had "lost the power of reason" (64), and to other teachers, those who had "more soul than sense" (40), who eschewed their responsibility for discipline, "who encouraged self-expression" (41), who let the young "reason things out" (117), or *"whose heart was not in her work!"* (41, emphasis in the original). There is a cue to the reader that duty is binding not only to those with authority but also to those who follow. When she is a patient of one of her students, even Miss Dove has the duty to obey the doctor, and in this duty she was not to respond to impulse or to fear, for in restraint all find dignity. Her now-adult students reflect this same theme of duty and sacrifice with its consequential claim to a higher moral ground.

The second set of cues involves the relationship of knowledge and values. Francis Gray Patton gives Miss Dove an unusual purchase on the fact–value distinction that the orators despise. Miss Dove took it upon herself to introduce "moral value into factual matter" (32), giving both a certainty that is usually reserved for the latter. She rejected letting children reason things out, because "it encouraged agnosticism" (117). Not that she was promoting religion, but she was promoting the relationship of knowledge and virtue. For her students, *"she* drew the conclusions" (118) and they wrote them down. Like a good orator, Miss Dove saw that *how* things were learned was linked to *what* was learned. If one wanted to value exactness, then one both required students to be exact and modeled that exactness for them. Her students copied a robin exactly as Miss Dove drew it. She knew what one looked like and there was no need for artistic variance. They did the same with the sentences they copied from the board. The children lived by her rules, just as she did. Patton also shows these rules to be relevant to life beyond Miss Dove's classroom. Her students were the best in the state on the proficiency tests, and her students attribute their success to her (and any failures to their own weaknesses); even the wartime survival of her surgeon was due to her lessons of restraint as strength.

Miss Dove had dramatic effects on the children. In her classroom, they experienced "a complete suspension of will" (12) that was comforting and reassuring to them. Miss Dove was called "terrible" not because of any nastiness—for she would never reduce herself to this—but because she was aloof and objective. Even in her rulebound classroom, "she had no rule relating to prevarication" (11). She took the child's word at face value, trusting that the lie is more disturbing to the child than being found out. She was terrible because she was all-knowing. Nothing missed her eye, and a child's thoughts were believed to be open books to her. The children obeyed her, and they respected her as they obeyed and respected no one else. They even learned her morality was correct:

And just as a teacher with genuine love for poetry will awaken that passion in her pupils, so Miss Dove imbued her charges with her philosophy. By her insistence upon even margins and correct posture and punctuality and industriousness, she told them, in effect, that though life was not easy, neither was it puzzling. You learned its unalterable laws. You respected them. You became equal to your task. Thus, you controlled your destiny. (34)

These lessons were largely permanent, even though Miss Dove admitted she had only six years with the students (she taught geography to all grades) and worried that she could have done something more. Those who were moral failures attributed their failings to anything other than Miss Dove. She had tried to teach them correctly, they avowed, but they lacked the upbringing or temperament to follow her lessons. The former student playwright who paid Miss Dove's way to New York to see the opening night of his first play attributed this success to her, even while bemoaning that he had much to do to be the moral man she expected of him. She had even given the surgeon the traits he needed to do well at his work: "It was she who, day after unremitting day, had drilled into him respect for industry, desire for exactitude, and the civilizing grace of inhibition" (43). She taught them, and they learned morality and virtue—possibly more than they learned geography, the subject she taught.

Miss Dove taught all the grades and all the children for over a generation: This community of experience was absorbed, of course, into the stream of consciousness. It was so settled, so accustomed, that it seemed a manifestation of natural law. (1–2)

Miss Dove's presence reduced all adults to children and negated all "progressive" (11) assaults on her classroom, not by aggression but by her imposing morality. She was "the town's perfectionist," and, as a result, "everyone, from the superintendent down, rose to the challenge" (90). She represented the "old, comfortable conviction that if you obeyed the law—if you sneezed in your handkerchief and raised your hand for permission to speak and kept your margins neat—that globe and all it represented was certain to be your oyster" (66). She stood for what so many of the community wished they could stand for: exactness and moral authority. When she became ill and the community witnessed her being carried to the hospital,

> they felt betrayed as people feel when they first glimpse the outrageous fact that their parents are not immune to change but have been touched, as by frost in the night, with an intimation of mortality. If Miss Dove's strength could crumble, what of their own? (57)

Francis Gray Patton is careful not to let this happen. Her book is about redeeming Miss Dove. Miss Dove reconsiders her lifelong role and flirts with freeing the children, only to see the "amorality" (216) of this. She is born again, after surgery, to "Good Morning, Miss Dove" (218).

The College Park community read something quite different from what we read or what Adler would have read. College Park read the book at the time it was published (whereas we read it forty years later). For them, it confirmed the beliefs that World War II, the postwar recession, and the start of the cold war were all justified. Duty and sacrifice were necessary if the United States was to be the pinnacle of civilization, the highest moral ground in the world. In this College Park saw themselves. While the effects attributed to Mrs. Gregory were socially constructed, the narrative in many ways created the belief that they were immutable truths. It created a cultural reality, a history-in-use by the real residents of College Park. Even today, they believe their virtue is tied to this historical actor, for better or worse. They point to her and her values as what is important in education, and largely believe this is what has made their community successfully survive threats of decline, such as immigration of the lower classes. This, of course, makes the narrative have many of the effects that Mrs. Gregory is said to have had. It negates all contrary evidence and even reason. This reading of the narrative holds College Park to its beliefs as they were when it was written, and has inhibited change. In confirming and reaffirming the community's postwar beliefs, it does not allow moral constructions based on current conditions or on a vision of the future. The pinnacle is past for College Park.

Of course, this book had a different effect on us. We read the book as strangers and outsiders. For us, as our book attests, it was an opportunity for cultural and moral construction, and, as we will discuss in the next chapter, our construction has had some effects on Cedar Grove School. What would be just *a* book for the orators was a *good* book in terms of the community and a great book for us. The narrative we read spoke to the prevailing images of education in the College Park we were studying and in the society at large. As we talked to people who had read this novel or seen the movie, we realized that here was a cultural icon for schooling in America. On the one hand, people read it as the caricature it was; on the other, the distortions in scale made little difference to the readers. To many, this narrative was teaching as it was, is, and should be (Hawley 1982). There was one noticeable exception to this. Teachers were more mixed in their assessments. They compared Miss Dove not to their experience as students (as did the other readers) but to themselves. In this the caricature was too extreme. Teachers agreed that many teachers existed like this, especially in the past, and that even they were like her in some ways. Teachers, however, were not as taken by the morality play the book offered. They saw children as too complex and teaching as more active and responsive. Miss Dove was too fixed in her ways to deal with all this. In our language, these teachers were talking about their work as cultural and moral construction: They had to make classrooms anew each day. Unwavering duty helped but would not deliver what *Good Morning, Miss Dove* promised.

Of Discourses Lost

In some sense, *Good Morning, Miss Dove* froze the discourse about education in College Park much like the orators wish to freeze the wider discourse about pedagogy. School desegregation did little to alter this, for, as we will show in chapter 6, Rougemont School's prevailing beliefs about African-American education were also essentially oratorical. The negotiation of what education would be like in the postdesegregation Cedar Grove School found this common ground. White and African-American teachers could agree on strong discipline, a focus on content, and their authority over educational matters. History, a novel, and negotiated unity made these topics sacred, and, although they are continuing topics of concern, the oratorical idea was fixed as the image of good education. There was little reason to challenge, and great risk in challenging, this idea.

This tragedy of fixed beliefs is minor compared to what happened to educational discourse in Rougemont. Their teachers were scattered, reassigned in order to bring the school district into compliance with the court order to desegregate. The profession of education ceased within Rougemont and with it the opportunity for the parents to talk about education with teachers they saw as their own. The fact that the teachers were usually from outside the community also meant that the main vehicle for Rougemont's ideas to be disseminated more widely in the African-American community was lost, as was the opportunity to have other ideas enter the community. The students were sent to other schools. Probably most damaging to the educational discourse in Rougemont was the fact that, at first, different grades were assigned to different schools. In the first few years after desegregation, Rougemont could not have a unity based in a single school for all of their children. Talking about education became dissentious rather than unifying for the community. This, of course, was also true at College Park, but they at least had constancy in the school, their children, their principal, and some of the teachers. The community institution that was shared by all in Rougemont was no longer there for participation or discussion. The churches were the second major institution, but they were separated into five congregations. Rougemont now even looked outside for leadership. The political structure of Rougemont's "Board of Directors" had waned with incorporation into the city and with increasing political power of the middle-class African-American civil rights community. Without the school, there was little left to hold the community together. Home ownership patterns changed, fear of crime increased, and pride in their accomplishments of some sixty years now seemed hollow. There was little to talk about in a community that was disintegrating, other than to bemoan the deterioration. Rougemont's pinnacle was past.

A book written about Rougemont School may have enabled a discourse that would have survived desegregation. This we cannot know, for no such book was written. No doubt there are many reasons. Rougemont was a working-class community, and fewer books are written of such communities than middle- and upper-class ones. Rougemont was African-American and heir to an oral tradition of story-telling. Rougemont was isolated from both the white and the middle-class African-American communities. The people there had little experience with participating in a discourse beyond their own community. Whatever the reasons, there was no book written that would enable us to see what books would do for the community, what they would contribute to the postdesegregation Cedar Grove School, or what they would offer to a wider discourse about education.

It is likely that had a book been written it would not have been a novel. African-Americans, in this century, have been more likely to write autobiographies than novels (Johnson 1986). Autobiography, of course, is a genre that is well suited to demonstrating the lessons of a people struggling to overcome injustice and exclusion. The genre enables the message that real people have struggled with some success, and reveals the strategies that they employed to overcome the obstacles they experienced. Autobiography can inspire others to continue the struggle and educate as to what might be needed if the struggle is to be successful. In comparison with *Good Morning, Miss Dove*, an autobiography of an African-American would likely emphasize a steadfastness to the cause (as did Miss Dove) but through a more strategic process, revealing how one must act when faced with circumstances beyond one's control. W. E. B. Du Bois (1965) chose to champion the oratorical idea not because the idea was an end in itself (as the orators believe) but because it was a strategy that enabled African-Americans to compete with whites on equal ground (thus accommodating the philosophical idea). In part anyway, the medium is the message.

What might have been the contribution of Rougemont School to our discourse about education? Any answer to this question is speculative. Yet it is possible to suggest what might have been by looking to books that come from nearby communities, that are about African-Americans, that discuss education, that are drawn from the time period we have been discussing here, and that are in the genre of autobiography. As one might guess, these are stringent criteria to fulfill, and, in fact, there are only a couple of books that even come close. *Proud Shoes* by Pauli Murray (1956) is an intriguing history of her African-American family and discusses education, but it is located in a smaller town and devotes little space to this century. In short, while it could suggest much, it is not close enough for even our speculative attempts. A better fit is *Mary* (1981) by Mary E. Mebane, the autobiography of an African-American woman's youth. It discusses education, covers the years 1933 through the mid-1950s, and is about a community geographically near Rougemont (to discuss the details of this would compromise our promise of confidentiality to the people in our study). It is well written and, we think, sufficient for our speculative task. Again we encourage you to read it. Your reading may well be different from ours.

Mary was a successful autobiography. Its origin was a series of pieces in the *New York Times*. It was published first in hardback in 1981 and was quickly issued in paperback for use in courses in higher education. The book was well received by reviewers and is still used in English courses today, especially in those courses outside the oratorical canon so favored by the orators. It is an inspiring narrative of struggle and ascension. She describes her humble origins and her youth, from which she went on to receive a Ph.D. and become a university professor. As we did with *Good Morning, Miss Dove*, we will offer two synopses of the book: one efferent and one aesthetic.

Struggle and Ascension: Mary's Story

> I was in the center of life and I didn't miss a thing: nothing slipped by unobserved or unnoted. My problems started when I began to comment

on what I saw. I insisted on being accurate. But the world I was born into didn't want that. Indeed, its very survival depended on not knowing, not seeing—and, certainly, not saying anything at all about what it was really like. (Mebane 1981: 11)

Mary Mebane begins her story with the recollections of her early childhood, and this excerpt presages both what she was up against and her resolve. Mary lived in a segregated, rural community that bordered a Southern city. Her father farmed and her mother worked in the tobacco mills in the city. She had two brothers, one older and one younger, and for several years her father's sister, Aunt Jo, lived with them.

First, let's see how Adler might have read *Mary*. The book's unity is achieved via the focus on her life and the obstacles she faced and over-came. The structure is essentially chronological. Dramatic tension is achieved by two sets of contending forces. First is the contention between her mother, who wants Mary to accept her lot in life, and her Aunt Jo, who inspires her to make something else of her life. Second is Mary's dual oppression by, on the one hand, whites and segregation and, on the other hand, the more direct oppression by African-Americans, especially the middle class, who controlled her education and thus her ascension. There is a mysterious event that lingers but is not revealed except in its consequences for the withdrawal of love by her mother. The elements of the book are basically time periods and various arenas of life and relation-ships. The first three chapters are devoted to her early life at home on their small farm and her interactions with nature. This is broken by the loss of her mother's love and the violence that was evident in life around her. Into this enters Aunt Jo, who inspires her. The following chapters begin her schooling and all the perplexities and fears it caused. This is paralleled with her emerging consciousness of the threat white society poses for African-Americans. A third-grade teacher inspires her, and Mary begins to win awards for her ability and to dream of doing great things, further alienating her mother. Religion and music are discussed, as are their role in the community and her family. Her understanding about her family and her understanding of race relations emerge together. She is successful in school in spite of the bias of educated African-Americans against the darker skinned. Her educational success and college attendance at an African-American college is paralleled with the disintegration of her family and increasing loneliness. The book ends with her resolve both to find someone to share her life with and to face white society, now that she had successfully completed the educational system controlled by African-American society.

Our reading of the book was not at all like this. We read the book to find what it might suggest to us about what our society lost when it closed so many African-American schools in the process of desegregation. We found a romantic image of her childhood: "Life had a natural, inexorable rhythm" (18). Her community shared more than a school and a teacher, as with College Park. They shared the necessities of life and the rhythm of the seasons. She discusses the women and children going every year to pick blackberries. Here are poor people trying to gather food to preserve for the winter and in it a sense of natural community:

> We didn't know whose berries they were; nobody had heard of the idea of private property. Besides, the berries grew wild—free for everyone. (26)

Yet Mary Mebane did not write a testimony to the romanticism of Rousseau or to the pragmatism of Dewey. As romantic as the book's opening is, she and her siblings' lives were little like Rousseau's Emile. Her portrayals of her own learning describe little discovery method but her own stubbornness. Mary Mebane gives the reader cues that her will was wrought from the interplay of denial and encouragement.

Denial was everywhere in her life. The most prominent, of course, was that of her mother: "The chill was my growing knowledge that my mother, Nonnie, had no warmth, no love, no human feeling for me" (29). At first this prompted Mary to ever-increasing efforts to please her mother. Mary found she had talents in music and reading, and she spent much of her time in these pursuits. Almost inevitably, these began to conflict with her household duties. Her mother's reaction was another denial, this time of the prospect of Mary having a different life than that lived by her family. Mary learned to deal with these by denial also. She stopped listening:

> I knew that I didn't listen. I had learned the practical use of the "tune-out." When the stimuli from the outside world came in too strongly critical of what I was interested in, I tuned out. (112)

There was an escalation of the conflict until Mary ran to the aid of her Aunt Jo, who now lived in the city. Aunt Jo advised Mary to focus on getting an education. Mary returned home to a new relationship with her mother:

> Nonnie was angry and I was defiant. She got her switches to whip me, but I started yelling that I was going to leave again and I

wasn't coming back. She did a lot of fussing, but she hit me only a time or two. I knew that I had won, for I never got another whipping. I had learned the value of protest. And I, too, put my soul on ice. I had to, if I was to survive. (121)

The other members of the family denied her also, but in less dramatic ways. Her father was loving but distant and confusing to Mary. He died when she was fourteen, leaving her to live with her mother and brothers until they left home and she had graduated from college. Her brothers would not stand up for her in the hassles of adolescence, and, in the end, treated her cruelly and used her unfairly in their own affairs.

Mary grew up in a segregated world that made her life doubly denied. First, segregation meant she lived in a permanent state of jeopardy:

Most Americans have never had to live with terror. I had had to live with it all my life—the psychological terror of segregation, in which there was a special set of laws governing your movements. You violated them at your peril, for you knew that if you broke one of them, knowingly or not, physical terror was just around the corner, in the form of policemen and jails, and in some cases and places white vigilante mobs that formed for the exclusive purpose of keeping blacks in line. (158)

This, of course, is devastating to individuals, but the laws of segregation had another effect that was all too evident to Mary. They fixed African-American people at the "bottom of society"; in her experience, "it was a world without options" (158). It was also denying her a good education:

I knew that I wasn't being taught in school what I should have been taught. We didn't have the facilities. . . . Yet I wanted to do great things in life. How was I going to do them when I was being crippled from the start? (156)

Segregation meant cast-off books, few science facilities, and ill-equipped classrooms. White society and segregation were hurting her in many ways.

The denials associated with segregation went beyond exclusion from safety and a chance to better one's lot in life. Because segregation created a separate caste of people, Mary found she had to struggle against her own kind who replicated the injustices of segregation by presuming that social class and light-colored skin were associated with academic ability. She repeatedly observed that those of lighter color were seen as more beautiful and more talented. They received honors and opportunities the darker-skinned did not. Mary Mebane was not one of the lightest in skin color among African-Americans. As her friend told her: "You are *dark*, but not *too* dark" (220). Her color meant her being denied school honors such as "best girl scholar" (221), which she believed were due her based on school performance. Social class and skin color were also sufficient bases for her to be questioned repeatedly. Mary concluded from these and other incidents: "I've known for a long time that blacks are just as capable of exploiting blacks as whites are" (76). Given this, Mary came to realize: "They had reason to be appalled when they discovered that I planned to do not only well but better than my light-skinned peers" (219).

Mary Mebane gives us cues that the denials of segregation were coupled with many other obstacles. Mary knew that one solution to the problems in her elementary and secondary schooling was to go to a private boarding school. She also wanted to escape the African-American educational system when it came time to go to college. Of course, there was no money to allow either of these. In reality, she worked, lived at home while attending school and college, and had only the benefit of a small bequest from Aunt Jo for her higher education.

For young African-American women, another major obstacle comprised relationships with men, sex, and pregnancy. Mary recounts how her adolescent female friends found love and status through sexual activity. She also recounts the less desirable consequences that often ensued. Yet the temptation for such activity must have been great for a young woman who was denied love at home and whose success in education was repeatedly jeopardized by segregation and by the prejudices of her own teachers. There was only one way for her to overcome this obstacle: another denial, this time self-denial. She had to choose her dreams and loneliness over the possibility of love. However, her choice was not simply an exercise of will. She had learned that her desire for a different life would lead others to pull away also.

> I thought how terrible life was, that it could make people so cruel. I wondered about my own suffering, my painful awareness of how different I was from the people around me. Without knowing it, I had absorbed some of the basic structure of the English language and had added to my vocabulary. I had moved away from black speech patterns. But I didn't realize it then. I didn't want to be different. Why did doing what I liked make me different? (102)

Mary's stubborn will to reach a new pinnacle was not just the consequence of her response to being denied. She recounts encouragements also. Most of all, she had Aunt Jo as a role model. Aunt Jo had been North and had what Mary saw as class and poise, even if she had little money and was forced to live with her brother's family. She gave Mary the vision of another life beyond the one to which she was born. Aunt Jo, however, wanted Mary to have even more than she had had:

> Aunt Jo was also determined that I was going to college someday. Nobody on either side of the family had ever gone to college, but she knew that I would. She was going to send me herself. I didn't know what she wanted me to be. I doubt if even she knew. (39)

Aunt Jo gave Mary both a belief in herself and the modest means to help live up to that belief.

Mary's father loved her but was little involved in her schooling. There is a poignant scene, though, that reveals how she saw her father's encouragement. He found out she had won the award for best student in the primary grades. The scene reveals her uncertainty about how he would react, since he had mixed feelings about school based on his own experience. She was silent, unable to figure out how to respond to his knowing about the award. She was "overjoyed" with his response: "'That's mighty nice,' he said. 'I want you to win one every year'" (69).

Other encouragement came from some, but not all, of her teachers. First grade she found "bewildering" (50). It was so unlike home, and she became aware of the potential for conflict between home and school. She was "scared all of the time in second grade" (61). Her third-grade teacher, Mrs. Richardson, realizing that Mary had some potential, began special lessons for her and brought her stories to read at home. Her eighth-grade teacher certainly would win no awards for his curriculum or his instruction, but he did sponsor Mary's voracious appetite for reading, allowing her to go to the high school part of the building to spend most of the day reading in the library. Mary had played the piano by ear in church but wanted to learn more. She found "the best music teacher in town" (108) and arranged to trade housework for lessons. The music teacher allowed learning to take on a new meaning:

> I loved it. Scales to me were fun—to be able to go over the whole keyboard, first with one hand then with two, in key after key, major then minor, was a pleasure. I felt a sense of mastery. It was something new; that meant my world was opening up and I was very happy. (110)

In college, Mary found an African-American teacher of political science with whom she felt free to talk about her life. His encouragement was all to her. He listened to her and told her just what he thought. "He was the first person I had ever talked to, revealing my dreams, the pain of my life, exploring the possibilities for a larger life, a more meaningful one in a larger setting" (227). She had a philosophy professor who invited her to join a noncredit discussion group and took a personal interest in her. This was the first encouragement, she noted, ever received from outside her own ethnic group. She later reflects the bitter irony of this lesson for her life:

I didn't know it then, but the pattern for my life had been established: when help came, it would always be from the outside. (237)

Mary Mebane's autobiography is a story of struggle and ascension. Her life was not easy, and she had to make very difficult choices. Certainly, part of her will to ascend came from being denied the love and attachment she so wanted, but part of it came from the encouragement she received. Others wanted her to be able to separate from the past that had held them so mercilessly. This required taking a long view of ascension and accepting that there would be much uncertainty, suffering, and loneliness along the way. It also required a stubborn will, a will not daunted by the limits of her past, the pressures of growing up, or the wearing struggle to achieve a new life. She had to take the past, her background, and what she learned from her books, put them together with some vague vision of the future, and construct strategies for her own struggle.

Her autobiography reveals the strategies she employed. The primary strategy, of course, was a belief in herself and in the possibility that she could reach pinnacles she could not yet define. Yet this alone was not enough. She had to create her life every day out of what she was presented with. To do this, she had to have strategies to deal with family strife, adolescence, segregation, and African-American prejudices and stratification. Her strategy to overcome family strife was to tune it out and replace it with a life of her own from books, music, and education. Her strategy to avoid the pitfalls of adolescence entailed creating the reputation of someone who did not engage in sexual relations. She limited her dating and her male friendships, and invested in the activities that the school and church provided for adolescents. Here she worked against not only the social pressures of adolescence but also what she argues were the norms of African-American social life. Her strategy to overcome her segregation from white society was to be the best student she could be by topping out the African-American educational system, and then hope that an admission to white society would come from her merits as a student. This book ends before this strategy can be shown to be effective, but we know from the biographical sketch of the author that eventually she received her master's degree and doctorate from a traditionally white university, and went on to teach at a predominantly white Northern university. Her strategies to overcome African-American prejudice and stratification were much more involved. This is the reality she had to negotiate and re-create each day. Her first strategy was the one that was basic to overcoming the other obstacles: to be the best student she could be. Second, she had to deny herself outbursts of displeasure. She repeatedly recounts confrontations that she greeted with silence rather than letting it escalate into conflict. She put her "soul on ice" (121). However, when silence did not work, she learned that

> protest is the most effective way of stopping unfair treatment. People who treat you unfairly don't want others to know. (63)

As we read Mary Mebane's book, we saw what Rougemont might have been able to contribute to our society's discourse about education, had it had its own emblematic narrative. If Rougemont had a book about itself, we may have been able to read that the pinnacle is far from being achieved. There is much yet to be done. We may have read that education plays a vital role, but it requires *people* to use education as a strategy in the struggle to ascend, requiring us to appropriate our social institutions and pit ourselves against what Miss Dove so typified—the tendency of organizations to require us to suspend our will in deference to its authority. This, of course, is why stubborn will and sacrifice of personal comforts are so central to Mary Mebane's autobiography. A narrative of Rougemont might have let us read that in reaching a pinnacle you must face the unknown as well as the known. Emulating the past does not reach a pinnacle, but is a capitulation to the past. Finally, our reading may have let us see that ascension requires "truth-making," not "truth-seeking," behavior (Shackle 1966). We must see in our everyday lives the possibilities and use what is in our culture and society to make the truths we desire.

This, then, is the contribution to the discourse about education that Rougemont School might have contributed had it not come to an end. The lesson is that we have to learn from the past, yearn for a future, and construct a life that builds continuity between them.

Principle versus Struggle

The two books we have discussed here are, simultaneously, just books, good books, and great books. For us as authors, these are great books in that they led us to write our book, to construct some new meaning. For the people of College Park, *Good Morning, Miss Dove* is a good book. It affirms their lives as they have been. For Rougemont we cannot know, but it is likely that a book like *Mary* could have been a good book for them also. It may have had the same consequence *Miss Dove* had for College Park—a reification of their cultural beliefs, "fixing" them as the beliefs that should not be questioned. For the orators, they are simply books that, while popular, are not likely to survive the test of time, especially if the orators control the test.

Declaring them both great for our purposes does not make them the same, however. One narrative is about holding to principles, and the other about struggles, even though each addresses the other narrative as well. *Good Morning, Miss Dove* is about the virtue of having and holding fast to principles. The book extolls the virtues of doing your duty, finding your place in the existing scheme of things, and respecting authority. These virtues the novel treats as worthy of emulation, and emulation is clearly the pedagogy recommended: copying, drill, and rote memorization all serve to impart the knowledge and morality. Values in this way come from inculcation with knowledge. The message is clear: Ascension is achieved through emulating the virtuous. It is as precise as a fact and as certain as Miss Dove herself. In a world of fixed principles, the future is the past.

Mary offers us quite a different lesson. In this narrative, values come from life's adverse circumstances. They come from adversity and from encouragement. They come from will as well as reason. Knowledge can feed values, but only if they are already in fledgling form. We learn that ascension comes not from emulation of principles but from struggle and strategies employed in the struggle. The struggle is not just that of living up to the principles of the orators or of pursuing a pinnacle ahead, as with the philosophers, but that of using your past and a vision of the future to construct what you should do now. There is no definition, as in *Miss Dove*, of what is a moral life, only the idea that you must construct it out of circumstance and often in opposition to what others believe:

> What it was to take me many years to learn was that an absolute conformity to an abstract set of teachings is liable to lead you to great pain in the real world, for in the real world are many people who are not preforming to the principles you have set for yourself. (Mebane 1981: 147)

The orators would agree with the sentiment that a principled life is difficult, but would be worried about her principles emerging from her own efforts and her life's circumstances rather than from universal principles. The philosophers also will find little solace here. Mary's life got its meaning not from the process of discovery, for if the process was to teach anything, it would teach Mary to give up; the odds were against her. The meaning in Mary's life came from her constant and unrelenting efforts to make a link between who she was and had been and to create a vision of what she wanted. Her efforts were not only to re-create the past or only to invest in a future but to create a life that connected both, a life heavily invested in the now.

Mary also teaches the moral hollowness of the philosophical idea. She sought access to the wider world, the white world in this case. Each time she had an achievement, she learned it was not a pinnacle, for so much more was still to be done—a classic philosophical position. In the autobiography, her triumph in graduating from college is shown to be of little meaning:

> I walked across the stage and got my degree—and caught the bus home. I read the program again. I was summa cum laude. I wondered what that really meant—certainly nothing in my life. (237)

The philosophers propose that each accomplishment sets the stage for some future progress. However, what the philosophers miss that Mary Mebane poignantly understood is that such a position is literally *demoralizing*, leaving present action without a moral content.

The lost discourse that resulted from the closing of Rougemont, and the closings of so many African-American Schools, also feeds our critique of the orators' five key points about the Great Books or Ideas. By reclaiming the lost discourse via *Mary*, our critique can be extended. First, the test of time is no proof that the book is great now. The test of time can freeze beliefs when change is desirable, and it can make people assume their beliefs are beyond their control, as has happened in College Park. *Mary*, had it been about Rougemont, could well have done the same thing. It could have set an agenda that says these are the correct values and humans should leave them alone—the truth is already known. Second, the lost discourse shows us that particularistic narratives have much to teach us. Most importantly, they teach us what the orators want us to learn: People carry and create the beliefs we have (although the orators believe it takes the rare instances of Great Books or Ideas to make this possible). The universal ideas that the orators so revere do not teach us this lesson. By seeing them as universal, the orators reify these ideas and undercut the belief that human values, ideas, and beliefs are human constructions. Particularistic narratives offer a better chance that some readers will compare their own lives with lives that are different from their own and participate in the decisions about what should be maintained and what should change in their culture and society. Third, the power of *Good Morning, Miss Dove* and *Mary* derives not from any mental stretching but from the fact that readers can participate in them and feel invited to make decisions about the meaning of things. That is, these books allow people to participate in narrating their own lives and virtues. Constructing morality is true virtue. Being led by experts or traditions to conclusions about what is moral is not. Fourth, the common culture so important to the orators is not about the specific values we share or wish we shared. The common culture of the United States is better understood as the struggle over what beliefs we should share. This is what Francis Gray Patton, Mary E. Mebane, the orators, and the philosophers, taken together, teach us. Fifth, and final, is the explanation that our nation's decline is to be found in the devaluing of the everyday participation in the *struggle* over what will be the common culture. The orators and the philosophers have convinced us not that we should invest in the everyday construction of our culture but that we should either look to the past or search for the future. The lost discourse tells that the only way for our nation to reach new pinnacles is for people to participate in constructing today as a link between the past and the future.

American minds are not made by Great Books or by the pursuit of knowledge; they are made by active participation in the struggle over what will be our common culture. People do not need education to prepare them for this as much as they need to use education, in the form of ideas, narratives, and social institutions, as a strategy for such participation. Americans need to reclaim education and morality as things they are creating, not something that exists separately and independently. The power of American minds, and the strength of our nation, is our ability to use education today to link past pinnacles with pinnacles yet to be reached.

6

Reclaiming Moral Life with Schools

Virtue is much more complex than even moral philosophy has imagined. It is more than identifying dispositions and inculcating them. Indeed, it is not so much a product of reason and rational thought as it is a construction in everyday life. Morality may be a subject for moral philosophy, but moral philosophers are not needed for people to be moral. The people of College Park and Rougemont did not need orators or philosophers to construct virtue. Nonetheless, the ideas of orators and philosophers were part of what these communities used to make their moral tales. These ideas are sufficiently reified in our culture and in our beliefs about education that they would almost have to be part of the social construction of virtue. Yet there is a level of human and collective agency in this that is heartening. It suggests that what is universal about morality is that people are busy making it. Yet we do not wish to overplay this. The people of Rougemont and College Park were not "free" in their social and cultural constructions of virtue. As Giddens (1979) argues, every act of agency also structures, and every structured moment delineates the possibilities for agency. They were using their contexts to create morality, but context certainly was a limiting as well as an enabling factor for them. Temporally they relocated morality out of the past (as with the orators) and out of the future (as with the philosophers) and enjoined it in the present. In many ways, the central moral task of the peoples of College Park and Rougemont was to create in the present a continuity between the oratorical and philosophical ideas, between the past and the future.

However, we are getting ahead of ourselves. We must be careful that in concluding this book we do not end up proposing reifying some other set of ideas. Rather, our essential theme is that people in their everyday lives suggest possibilities for all of us to consider. This both helps to dereify ideas and suggests options that our own cultural contexts may not offer us. It is helpful to remember that the moral narratives of Rougemont and College Park did not end when we ceased our research. We will return to the special role of research projects such as ours later, but for now we return to the moral narratives of Rougemont and College Park to see what else they can teach us. We have told you that Rougemont School was closed in 1975 to desegregate Cedar Grove School. We also have told you that our research led to some written products in 1990. Let us close Rougemont and reopen the moral discourse of both schools and communities.

At this point we want to compare the accreditation self-studies that were presented by each of the schools in chapters 3 and 4. Each of the self-studies reflected the virtues important to each of the communities. The tone and language of the Rougemont self-study reinforced the strength of community within the school and the importance of collective struggle in the school's history. Those things that were held in high regard about the school were spoken of collectively, and those things that were not admired were handled in like fashion. The documents also reflected the "subject" nature of the Rougemont community and school, with the citizens, atmosphere, and identity of the community and school presented in many cases from the viewpoints of the constituents themselves.

The Cedar Grove School self-study presents quite a different tone and language, and one equally reflective of the virtues constructed over the history of the school. The Cedar Grove report identifies an elite and a group that does not belong in that elite, and refers to its student and parent population in ways that are divisive and not collective or communal. The self-study reinforces the importance not only of elitism and being part of the elite but also of authority, obedience, punctiliousness, and efficiency, much as had been done in other contexts throughout the history of the school.

Rougemont's Closing

The self-studies discussed were conducted in the 1973–1974 academic year, and immediately preceded probably the most important year in the history of both schools. In October 1974, the U.S. Middle District Court ordered that new desegregation plans for Treyburn be developed. In the new plan, four schools in the city were placed under consideration to be closed, Rougemont and Cedar Grove being two of them. In the final decision, Rougemont School was closed at the end of the 1974–1975 school year, and the community's children were redistricted into other schools, one of them being Cedar Grove. Cedar Grove School had once again used its power to protect its own interests. Given the history of school and community being so closely intertwined, the demise of Rougemont School would have a dramatic impact on its community. The Rougemont teacher in chapter 4 who recalled delivering coal to a student's home finished her story by reflecting on that decision:

You know, these are things I miss from Rougemont because it was really—that was a very good atmosphere to work [in]. I loved it. When that school closed I cried for almost a week.

Destroying the school led to the beginnings of community decline, as one community member described it:

The closing of Rougemont was the end of social organization; the end of home visits. Nobody knew what anyone else was doing. You didn't see people the way you did.

The person who was principal of the school in that last year poignantly described the impact on the community: "The kids in the heart of Rougemont went to Cedar Grove School."

Which schools would be closed was seen as a foregone conclusion. Many believed that because Cedar Grove was white and had always been an elite school, the historically African-American schools would not get a fair hearing, and that, indeed, seems to have been the case. A community member told us that the week before, as the decision was about to be made and it was evident the school would not survive, a school board member told him that for the board to consider leaving the school open, a large group of citizens would have to attend the board meeting and defend the school. Rougemont, however, had a different political structure, wrought in the throes of segregation. In a segregated society, it created the "Board of Directors" and "Bronze Mayor" to handle its political affairs with white society. For a large group of Rougemont citizens to attend an essentially white school board meeting would require it to re-create its political structure in less than a week. Efforts were made, of course, but the group of Rougemont residents who attended was evidently not "large" enough to influence the school board. The community did have a history of turning out at the school and did so for the school board's "explanation" of its decision. On a Sunday night after the decision to close Rougemont School was handed down, the school board met in the community to explain their three-to-two vote decision. One board member said that, having now witnessed the turnout of people to hear the board, if he could he would change his vote.

One Rougemont citizen lamented the closing of the school this way: "It hurt the community, everybody. We had one of the best schools in [the city]. We had good teachers. Why did they want to change it?" What had for decades made the school so strong may have been the reason for its demise: the integral and insular community that had made the school successful. The Rougemont School and its community had done a very effective job of defining itself as a community and—in the harsh political realities of desegregation—as an African-American community, despite being 50 percent white in 1974. In the end, the insularity that had for so long served Rougemont led to its downfall. The insularity meant that Rougemont was excluded by, and excluded itself from, the wider city's politics surrounding desegregation. Instead of being participants, they were the victims. The citizen who helped lead the community fight to save the school said:

> The school was good. It was new with new facilities. It was set up as one of the best schools. Being in a black community closed it. We had good teachers. They took interest in children.

It is also ironic, and tragic, that the best evidence of the power of the relationship between Rougemont School and the community came in both institutions' destruction. A former principal described the closing of the school as the "destruction of [the] community focal point." A Rougemont resident described the educational consequences:

> Being poor was not a stigma [at Rougemont]. They understood. [After the closing of Rougemont] people became afraid to come to school because of limited background or lack of education. Many students from the area stopped education after integration came. There wasn't a strong push. Things seemed to have broken down.

The teacher mentioned in chapter 4 who shared the story of the gathering in the park and the story of delivering coal and blankets to children and their grandmother said of the school's closing, "It was just like you were losing a friend, which I did."

Along with the decision to close Rougemont School came the decision to pair schools within the district. Under the plan, Cedar Grove School was paired with S. S. Paul Elementary, another historically African-American school serving the middle-class African-American section of Treyburn around Treyburn State College. Beginning in the fall of 1975, Cedar Grove would house kindergarten through second grade, and Paul Elementary would house third through sixth grade.

It was ironic that Cedar Grove School was already a desegregated school; by 1974 the student population included 109 African-American and 124 white students. Indeed, the president of the Cedar Grove PTA in 1973–1974 had been African-American, the first to serve in that capacity. Nevertheless, the desegregation of the entire school district demanded pairing. In the 1974 self-study, Cedar Grove School wrote that desegregation had not been a problem, but the writers had not planned on involuntary pairing. Teachers and students were assigned across the school to achieve racial balance, but it was apparent to many African-Americans in Treyburn that desegregation was closing African-American schools. About half the students that had attended Rougemont School in 1974–1975 came to Cedar Grove after the closure and pairing. In addition, four of Rougemont's teachers were transferred to Cedar Grove.

Some parents who had their schools closed chose to boycott the first three days of school at Cedar Grove School in the fall of 1975 to show their displeasure over the closing of their school as well as the failure of the city to provide busing for their children to Cedar Grove. Eventually most parents admitted their children to the new school, but the ill will did not so quickly disappear. Faced with the boycott, the principal of Cedar Grove, who was in her fifth year at the school, and the staff quickly moved to establish discipline and routines familiar to the students. But tensions were still evident at the school, and cohesiveness among the new faculty was not immediate. Those teachers who had been at Cedar Grove before desegregation remembered the lack of respect for the virtues historically constructed at the school, in particular those of efficiency:

Those teachers would use construction paper and cut a little piece out and throw it in the waste basket. Boy, soon as I caught that we had boxes. You put your scrap paper in there. There's a lot of pieces that'll do for your next project. And they had not done that.

The problem extended to matters far more serious than the wise use of resources. The virtues that were important in Rougemont failed to make the transition with the children. A member of the faculty in the desegregated Cedar Grove School had "some sense that parents feel disempowered over how the school functions." Another faculty member who worked at the school during desegregation described the role of the Rougemont community in their new school: "Rougemont people were so completely out of the picture. For whatever reason, they didn't really join in." She continued later, "They felt like they were left out. They felt like the white people were catered to."

In addition to feeling keenly the loss of their school, the most difficult part of the change for Rougemont parents was the sheer strangeness of Cedar Grove School. Rougemont School had had an intimate relationship with its community. Remember that former students recalled that if they misbehaved at school, a parent would be waiting at the street corner for them on the way home. Rougemont community celebrations revolved around the school. While Cedar Grove School may have had close ties with its community, it did not have such intimate associations with the Rougemont parents. Moreover, the PTA at Cedar Grove had a historically different role than that at Rougemont. Whereas the histories of both schools reveal a cooperation between their respective PTAs and their schools, the Cedar Grove PTA had sought to negotiate a greater role in the educational and administrative aspects of their school. The "strangeness" of Cedar Grove is evident in one Rougemont parent's recollection:

> It was hard at first. It was very hard. We were asked to work, you know, to join this and to do this. This was like going to a new thing with different people. Where will I fit in? At first I would come to the PTA meeting and [it seemed] like we were just sitting there and listening instead of being asked. And eventually we did receive flyers and different things inviting us to different activities. It was strange at first.

The "strangeness" continued throughout the 1970s and 1980s. The population òf Treyburn became increasingly African-American, and the end of legal segregation led African-Americans to engage in "block busting " While often thwarted and subsequently threatened, African-American families began to move into traditionally white neighborhoods. College Park was vulnerable, especially as real estate values declined in nearby neighborhoods. College Park residents banded together to protect their community by purchasing homes that became available. College Park residents also saw that the school was central to their community's identity and rallied around it. College Park parents were expected to send their children to the school and to be active in school affairs. This continues to this day. Thus, while the school became demographically African-American, it remained culturally and politically a white social institution.

This was not an easy achievement. The city, by the 1980s, was majority African-American, as was the school board. Cedar Grove School seemed to be under siege, and its community and desegregated teaching staff repeatedly overcame efforts to close or redistrict the school. The building itself is aged and costly to maintain, but a powerful vigilance kept the school protected.

In the mid 1980s, however, the turmoil entered the school walls. A long-standing principal retired and the school district selected a replacement. The replacement came in an improvement agenda, and threatened the power of the community to determine the fate of the school. The community appealed to the school board officially, while unofficially it engaged in covert political action. The principal was transferred in the middle of the year. A second principal failed to learn from lessons of her predecessor and was also subsequently "ejected." A third, interim principal, lasted less than a semester.

Mr. Michaels read the situation better than his predecessors, and used the project discussed in this book as one strategy to solidify his status with the community and the staff. Mr. Michaels also recognized an opportunity that we did not. He saw that something could be done with the oral history to unite the two communities. He commissioned a play.

A Morality Play

It was literally a dark and stormy night. The play was being performed at one of Treyburn's junior high schools because both a large stage was needed to accommodate all the actors and a large hall was expected to be needed to accommodate all those who would attend. The playwright had taken the celebratory history we had written, tapes of interviews, and our accounts of the meanings attached to the schools, and used them to write a script that had as its central device a wall of styrofoam blocks representing segregation, incorporated the moral icons of each school, and managed to get all of the children, some teachers, and many parents on stage at some point. It was a masterful script, and the play was a glorious success. Yet this must be put into context. Elementary school plays are blueprints for technical disasters, and this play was no exception. Using young children, busy parents, and teachers, and moving masses of children across the stage, created glitches of all sorts. Voice projection was a problem, timing was off, actors and actresses forgot lines, and so on. Entrances and exits were confused affairs. The audience was not that of a Broadway play either. The auditorium was large, filled with some six hundred people, roughly two for every student attending Cedar Grove School. Whole families attended; the children were noisy. The adults often called out to their children on stage, announced the identities of the characters too loudly, and then explained to whomever would listen the experiences they had with the character. No doubt technically it was a disaster. Morally and culturally it was a rousing success.

The stormy night did not keep extended families from attending. After all, children were all in the play and the play was about their own lives. Indeed, the play was the first time Rougemont families attended a Cedar Grove School function en masse. Relatives joined parents to see their own history, their own schools, their own teachers portrayed. The scenes were chronological, recounting events from each decade. Students re-created events and ceremonies we discussed in chapters 3 and 4. Adult actors and actresses played the teachers and principals of the time, saying and doing some of the things people had recalled in interviews with us. The stage was split in two, representing Cedar Grove and Rougemont, and action alternated between sides, showing the similarities and differences of the schools and communities over time. This in itself built a dramatic tension as the audience both identified with their respective communities and, for the first time, learned what was going on in the neighboring community. It was an educational experience unparalleled in the lives of these people. The split image was also united by the wall of styrofoam blocks. The play started with the wall high enough to divide the stage, and the end of most scenes on each side of the wall was a block being either added to or taken from the wall. Some scenes, especially early ones, ended with the actors simply considering the wall. Both communities were portrayed as adding to and subtracting from the wall. In the final scenes, the wall of segregation was fully dismantled, and a coming together was portrayed.

When lights faded at the end of the last scene, the audience cheered and gave standing ovations that continued through the presentation of the cast and through Mr. Michaels's giving of credits. Indeed, by this time the audience had pushed to the stage and surrounded him, cheering and laughing. Frankly, the research team was amazed by this response, and the scene of Mr. Michaels trying to give credit to the many people who had helped, while parents were celebrating and calling out, will remain with us forever. Something special had happened that evening.

The descriptive history itself had captured the attention of many, including alumni who now lived far away. It was a book that they could participate in, and many in their community directly had. They could legitimately complain when facts were incomplete or incorrect or when people important to them were not included in the text because we did not know about them. They could share with us other stories or mementos of their life at either of the schools. Some even took offense at some of the anonymous quotes we used, claiming we misquoted them only to find out that the quote was not from their interview but from someone else's. Yet even with all this, the descriptive history did not have the participative character of the school play.

As we discussed in the last chapter, a great book (or in this case, literary work) is better understood not as something that has stood the test of time but as something people use to help construct their everyday life. The play was clearly a "great" work by this definition, and it stood the test of the present. It involved a lot of people in its preparation and production, and asked people to play parts well known to them—their former teachers, parents, and fellow students. It also asked those same people to animate many of the cultural symbols and icons that were so important to them. The play had taken months to rehearse, and integrated the curriculum in language arts and social studies. The school and community literally hummed with activity around the play.

While both communities attended, more came from Rougemont than did from Cedar Grove. It was a major community event for Rougemont, and brought back memories of events at the old Rougemont School. Yet something else was going on here also. Cedar Grove, of course, had the book *Good Morning, Miss Dove* as an emblem of its history and significance. Rougemont, however, had no book, as we noted in the last chapter, and had no lasting testimony of its contribution to the discourse about education other than the descriptive history. The play, however, was a celebration of their heritage; signified that their discourse, however subjudicated (Foucault 1980), was still alive; and affirmed their presence in Cedar Grove School.

The audience ignored the gaffes and glitches. More importantly, however, the play was about the audience in ways that few works they had ever witnessed were. They recognized the characters: Mrs. Gregory, the Pursells, and many others they had told us about. They recognized that their own story was being told by the next generation, and they pointed to the characters on the stage, nudged each other, and talked during the production. They gave the play a standing ovation, and gave the principal his own curtain call, recognizing that under his leadership the school had done something for the community that few schools could ever imagine doing. The school gave both communities back to themselves and made a narrative of their lives for all to see. It recaptured their cultural discourse and celebrated it publicly. Rougemont now had its story told, revealing that their discourse was not lost as long as there was a school that could carry it forward. They became the subjects they had sought to be. Cedar Grove had a new narrative, a more participative and inclusive one than *Good Morning, Miss Dove* had ever been. They got the objective history they sought and much more. The communities also had a dramatic narrative of their integration.

It was, in many ways, this last narrative element that had been lacking in the school. They had the fact that they were desegregated and they had the fact that they were, according to test scores anyway, one of the top two elementary schools in the district. However, they had no narrative of community until the history was written and the play produced. Clearly, one play will not create an integral community where two have long existed because of prejudice and segregation. However, it seems difficult to achieve an integral community without developing such narratives. Here the two narratives, the descriptive history and the play, celebrated the cultures of both communities and also celebrated their coming together. These were narratives of continuity—of a past apart, of a present being constructed, and of hope for a future together. They were narratives that revealed the school to be the vehicle for representing the culture. All this was packed into a powerful and moving evening of moral construction replayed again and again in the video that had been made of the play.

The lesson of this school play is poignant yet simple. This play demonstrated to the communities that the school cared about them in ways forgotten. But this is not only a product of absent-mindedness—it has been the result of a century of educational policymaking that, step by step, has made schools creatures more of the state than of the community. The development of administrative rationality, the creation of a science of teaching, the consolidation of schools, school desegregation, and our most recent round of educational reform have all worked to separate schools from communities. Indeed, we would argue that educational reform, throughout this century, has at its base a distrust of local communities. Each successive wave of reform, each recycling of the oratorical and philosophical ideas, relies increasingly on experts and on political elites. The result is that school–community relations are essentially conceived of as a "problem" for reform. Public schools use parental involvement as a way of maintaining control over how the community relates to the school (Van Galen 1987). The public schools want communities to support them *as they wish to be supported* This is a one-way relationship, and, by definition, a one-way relationship cannot be a caring relationship (Noddings 1984). Yet Cedar Grove School discovered a way to nurture and sustain the community and, as a result, itself. The school became the agent in developing and fostering a moral dialogue about the communities itself.

This is a significant change in how to think about schools. Instead of trying to recapture a past pinnacle or searching for some future one, Cedar Grove School took upon itself the role of creating a continuity between the past and the future. It created a moral narrative that helped to establish a two-way relationship between the school and its communities. It sustained the communities by giving them voice, and, in so doing, established itself as a social institution instead of simply a public bureaucracy.

This, then, we see as an example of a different way to link education and morality than either the orators or philosophers intended. It sees morality not in holding to principles or in an unbridled search for truth but in creating relationships between people, between schools and communities, and between the past and the future. Even test scores went up that year; one teacher commented, "The test scores went up when we weren't even concentrating on them."

For us, this also suggests that schools can do much more for our culture than teach its great works and ideas or prepare people to be able to search out new understandings or ensure our international economic competitiveness, as important as all these might be. Schools can help communities reclaim their values by creating narratives that become the bases for moral dialogues. Schools can become agencies through which people can construct and reconstruct their moral lives.

Moral Reform of Education

So long as it is vital, the cultural tradition of a people—its symbols, ideals, and ways of feeling—is always an argument about the meaning of the destiny its members share. Cultures are dramatic conversations about things that matter to their participants, and American culture is no exception. (Bellah et al. 1985: 27)

Part of this book has been a critique of the major ideas that have shaped our recent discourse about how education has failed our nation and how, as a consequence, the nation has declined. Many authors have seen this debate as being about the American mind, its opening (Adler), and its closing (Bloom). We agree that the essential topic is the nature of the American mind, but we see the issue of central concern as being how the American mind is made. Its opening or closing seems dependent on this fundamental process. The question that remains is, How should we think about making the American mind?

We have an agenda, an alternative, but it did not exist prior to our experience with the schools and the books we have discussed here. They have taught us that much of what intellectuals value as important activity is not; much of what we thought will improve education will not; and much of what we assume attaches people to their nation does not. The American mind is based not in highly abstract thought but in everyday experience. Schools improve not because of policies set at state or national levels but because of what the school participants, parents, teachers, and students believe. The nation is in decline not because of the failure of such universals as nationalism but because of the failure of particularism. The American mind has been left to the mass media and to governmental policies, and is no longer wrought by the struggle over what we should believe. The American mind is a terrible thing to waste, to paraphrase the United Negro College Fund, but we are doing quite well at wasting it.

How should we make the American mind? Let us start by identifying the ways that it should *not* be made. First and foremost, there is not *one* way. American society is too diverse, and our educational system too decentralized, for this ever to be feasible. Many good and powerful ideas have been discredited by the attempts to spread them across the nation. For example, open schools worked quite well in some schools and communities, and still do, but our press to nationalize the idea showed us that open schools do not work in every place—sometimes they violate community beliefs about good education. The result of this press to nationalize, to make one policy the sole American way, is that we now believe the *idea* of open schools is no longer valid. The idea is valid; our expectations for the idea are not—no idea is good in all places and all times.

Second, the American mind cannot be made by laws. Certainly, much of our heritage is shaped by our unique legal structures and our faith in them. Yet laws are hard pressed to make something specific happen. They serve better to proscribe than to prescribe. In moral endeavors, we can outlaw behaviors but we cannot control beliefs. There are no fully deterministic conditions, although we would be the first to admit that social and cultural conditions are the stuff from which humans create their beliefs. Certainly we can and do try to shape the minds of our children by law and policy, but what results is not the desired uniform effect but, rather, diverse effects and unanticipated consequences (Giddens 1979). The role of law in the making of the American mind is best thought of as getting obstacles out of the way.

Third and relatedly, the American mind is not made by nationalism, a national language, or a national culture. Nationalism, rather, uses the minds for its own ends. It limits cultural construction by reifying a set of "first principles" that must not be violated. Proselytizing a belief such as nationalism is a poor way to develop commitment to the belief, as is well known by ministers who witness the short-term effects of revivals on those saved and on church attendance. Hirsch (1987) points to the early efforts of Webster and others to create a national culture, and finds that we need to renew this effort. What Hirsch misses is that the efforts of these well-intentioned early nationalists to justify a representative democracy defined citizenship as "passive citizenship" (Spring 1980), which accepts the obligations of being a citizen but defers to elected representatives the exercise of democracy. The New England town meeting, of course, sees citizenship quite differently, even though it has waned under the widespread definition of citizenship as passive. In the town meeting, citizenship is active. Everyday people exercise their rights and obligations in making decisions. While town meetings may not be the best vehicle for national decision making, they do suggest that active citizenship would engender a rather different form of nationalism. Further, pursuing a *national* culture obliterates both traditions and cultural possibilities for our society—it contributes to moral dislocation and the belief in national decline. Nationalism is better understood as one of the results of people struggling in their own communities and lives to attach themselves to others and to create beliefs that they can argue over, as the epigraph to this section, from Bellah and colleagues, so eloquently puts it. These arguments and struggles attach people to their society and give them a place in the nation. Nationalism results from people's participation in the affairs that, taken together, constitute national life, not from attempts to suppress the variety of views and interests. The orators' wish for a national culture and language in a democracy is conceptually possible only in gross abstractions of uniformity.

Fourth (and the thesis of this book), the American mind is not to be made either by looking to the past or by having faith in the fixture. The oratorical idea that the pinnacle is past is deadly to the mind. It conveys the message that there is no work left to be done other than to reproduce past ideas. Certainly we need to know the past and we need to use the past in making the American mind, but the past was not the pinnacle. The philosophical idea that the past and present are but imperfections along the way to some more ideal future is little better. It posits a future that is already out there waiting to be discovered, and encourages us to invest in this discovery. It forgets that in human affairs the future is to be constructed, not discovered. It forgets that any future is possible only by creating a continuity in the present between the past and the envisioned future. Certainly, to counteract a belief in decline we must envision new pinnacles for the future, but the present is what makes any future possible. Martin Luther King Jr. had a dream of a future of freedom and equality for people whose past had been slavery, but he also proposed nonviolent resistance as a strategy for the present—a continuity acceptable to both a Christian heritage and future visions of his people. The American mind is made in the struggle to create continuities between pasts and visions of fixtures.

Fifth, the making of the American mind should not be left to individuals. The orators are right that individualism creates problems for moral life. Clearly, American ideology supports a rugged individualism and self-reliance, but this also makes community and moral life quite difficult.

> If selves are defined by their preferences, but those preferences are arbitrary, then each self constitutes its own moral universe, and there is finally no way to reconcile conflicting claims about what is good in itself. (Bellah et al. 1985:76)

Individualism, as much as some Americans wish to revel in it, cannot lead to a mind that can make moral choices. To rely on solely the self makes even business impossible. Trade and commerce require a shared agreement that contracts will be upheld. Large corporations want people not to be individuals but to be part of the corporation. They transfer people and require them to move for advancement as a way to get people to attach to the corporation over other collectivities, including community and family. An American mind cannot be made alone. The mind, while owned by an individual, is the product of a life of connections with others. Without this, education would be impossible, socialization ineffective; there would be no possibility of an American mind or of cultural continuity. We can leave the American mind neither to nationalism nor to individualism. We must find some intermediary, some arena in which one can act as an individual and as part of a collectivity, some arena large enough to require social participation but small enough for individuals to feel their participation is necessary and productive.

Finally, the American mind is not to be made by intellectuals. This does not mean that education is not necessary, only that intellectuals should not control it. Jacoby (1987) argues that we have lost our public intellectuals to the university, where they have traded their public responsibility for teaching and research that speaks only to specialists. There is much to his argument. Yet, if the intellectuals lost to universities are experts and isolated from the world, the "public intellectuals" he so desires are elitists. The former focus their expertise on problems the public is not aware of. The latter take over the public's voice in the literary equivalent of passive citizenship. In either formulation, it is clear that we should not leave the American mind to intellectuals—they would likely make it in their own image. Intellectuals can help, and can learn a lot from helping people construct their culture, but they should not direct the making of the American mind.

The American mind is itself a gross abstraction, an attempt by the orators to get people to think beyond their particular interests and to think about the nation as a whole. The orators hope that a mind that is "common" is possible—that we are all alike in our values. Our hope is rather different. We see what is common as being the struggle over the definition of what will be the common culture. In the interviews we conducted that form the bases of chapters 3 and 4, people were telling us not only the facts of their histories but also, more importantly, what they wanted others to learn from their experience. They were both reciting the past and attempting to create the future. The opportunity we provided them was to create the linkage, the connection, between their lives and others and between the past and the future. Telling a history was not an individual act but an attempt to create a collective consequence of their experience. They were arguing against ideas they disagreed with and for ideas that they wished to be perpetuated—they were creating culture. They were about the moral act of creating a continuity between their past lives and lives yet to be lived. They were about creating the American mind.

How can we get people involved in making the American mind? Clearly the projects need to be small scale and locally focused, allowing for participation but not overwhelming people as in assigning them the responsibility to reverse national decline or correct America's moral inadequacies. What seems interesting and morally significant in Snow Camp, North Carolina, will be different from what is considered thus in Gary, Indiana. Strategically, the projects ought to involve the social institutions we normally use for socialization: the family, religious organizations, and the schools. Yet the family is in disarray, its meaning open to question, its commitments suspect and transient. The church is not as stable as it once was. Evangelicalism has led to congregations that lack traditions. Even Quaker meetings have become evangelical churches. Reform movements in Judaism have undercut the traditional bases of belief. Clearly the family and religion are credible institutions for cultural participation and construction, but they have limitations. What they lack is diversity. Families and synagogues or churches are seen as unities, collections of people who share similar commitments and heritages. Schools, however, are less unitary. Whether public or private, they are institutions that cross-cut family, social class, and religious beliefs. While some are more diverse than others, few schools are entirely homogeneous. The diversity and the traditions they represent are good bases for what we have in mind. Schools are where knowledge is consciously taught, even if it is currently taught in ways that undercut the participation, and the preparation for participation, of children in their moral life. Schools are institutions that we entrust with the socialization of our youth. The vast majority of our youth are enrolled in them. The schools also incorporate parents, even if currently in insidious ways, and are community institutions, as the ongoing debates over school closings show and as we graphically depicted in this chapter. They are caldrons of contemporary culture and generators of future beliefs. The public schools are especially democracy incarnate: they take all who come and try to make the most of them. In short, if we are to reclaim moral life, we must use the schools, public and private, as vehicles to create virtue, to create continuities between the past and future.

As ideal as the schools are for this, we should not be naive or overly idealistic. Not everyone sends their children to school, as the home schooling movement attests. Teachers are currently overwhelmed with executing the mandated curriculum, and our curriculum will require changes in ways they think about knowledge, as well as crowding the curriculum even more. Further, parents are fully committed with raising their children and making a living. Not everyone has time to participate in the kinds of projects we think are necessary. Also, there is no way to involve everyone in such projects—not everyone will find them of interest—nor to involve everyone in the same way as our egalitarian values would dictate; levels of involvement must be considered. Finally, we should not make the mistake of the philosophers in assuming that only studies that have pragmatic outcomes for students are valuable. Morality is best understood as the narratives that people use to create continuities between their pasts and futures. Pragmatism should not be the rule, nor should idealism. We should be creating possibilities for people to connect their pasts and their visions of their future. Yet they should make the decisions about whether to be idealistic or pragmatic. In this they control their destinies and the quality of their lives and the nation. To be sure, leadership is necessary on the national, state, and local levels. However, it is not just a leadership that establishes the codes for others to live up to but a more difficult leadership—a leadership that sets up the mechanisms for others to think about and create what they value, and to get governmental structures aligned to make these values possible. It is representative leadership in its best form.

Toward "Commoner" Cultures

To play on the oratorical idea of a common culture, we are about creating "cultures of commoners," cultures that the common people— rich, poor, Native American, African-American, Chicano, Asian, white, native, immigrant—have participated in creating. Efforts to create a culture common to all people have the effect of creating countercultures, cultures defined by resistance to the established belief system. America is the land of immigration, but we would replace the notion of a "melting pot" of assimilation with that of a "caldron of cultures." There historically has not been any cultural system that has assimilated all the others. Each new wave of immigration instead adds to the caldron, sharing only the struggle for a better life in the United States. All of us share in the myriad moral possibilities this allows, but all too often we silence possibilities, as was done with Rougemont.

Tocqueville saw the strong individualism of Americans as troublesome and potentially dangerous. It was balanced in the America he witnessed with strong community and church attachments, what Bellah and colleagues have called "associational life" (1985: 38). The modern American mind has no such balance, left to find solace, if not moral guidance and meaning, in "lifestyle enclaves" (Bellah et al. 1985). It is through small social institutions that individualism is tempered with commitment to others and through which shared values are created. Large institutions are not good at this—witness the ongoing efforts of large corporations to gain and sustain the commitment of their workers. Efforts to "massify" education undercut the possibility that schools may be able to make American minds that are not only knowledgeable and creative but also moral.

The recent "reform movement" in education has run its course. Its efforts for common core curricula in all schools, increased standards of performance on "objective" tests, and common teaching techniques are now seen as having undercut the commitment of teachers to their profession. The "massification" represented by these reforms is now being rejected in favor of more local autonomy. Obviously, this creates the possibility that moral participation and production can proceed through the schools. Yet local autonomy assumes that the locals have some way of determining what they should do with their autonomy— that they understand that with this freedom comes opportunities for schools to create virtue and morality. Schools can help in this by focusing on the people they serve, the "commoners," and by initiating efforts that (1) teach people that their cultural and moral history is theirs to maintain or change and (2) establish projects that reclaim the moral narratives in each school in such ways that people actively participate in the maintenance and change of their beliefs and social practices. They can be places where facts and values can intertwine productively, where one's own past can be discovered and compared to the pasts of others, where the future can be imagined, and where one not only participates, but also *learns how* to participate, in moral life.

The latter is the dual task that schools must undertake if we are to remedy the moral malaise of our country, the failures of education to prepare people in both knowledge and citizenship, and the perception that our nation is past its prime. The task is fourfold: (1) to prepare students to be active citizens and moral participants; (2) to organize projects that help the community and the students understand the heritages (the longstanding cultural arguments, as Bellah and colleagues

[1985] put it); (3) to project the visions of the future, the unrealized ideals that people have, and what of their lives they want others to carry forward; and (4) to engage in a shared enterprise that lets students and adults construct moralities that link the two. However, none of this will happen without a different conception of how the political process is to serve schools and the citizens, so let us start there.

The End of Educational Policy

There is a nostalgia about education that is hard to shake. The times people long for were times before we believed that educational policy could make schools effective. It was a time when administrative science was more an idea than a practice, a time before state and federal centralization of education via educational policy. Yet centralization has been touted as good in its own right. Larger schools, for example, were supposed to mean more diverse curriculum and better economies of scale, but, as Sher (1977) has so aptly demonstrated, many of these are "false economies." Administrative science and the politicization of education both want centralization so that control is maximized. In this logic, control is seen as good. It means that shirkers will be forced to carry their load and that the product can be standardized. However, control requires parents to be passive citizens and accept the largesse of the school district or state. We note that neither Cedar Grove nor Rougemont Schools would have come into existence if parents had accepted the passivity their government representatives wished them to accept. Neither neighborhood needed educational policy to control them—they needed it to represent them. Today this is harder and harder to ask of our public institutions. They have standard operating procedures, budget and funding guidelines, a hierarchy of regulations, and little responsiveness to what the citizens want.

Educational policy has become a way for politicians and government officials to control the public—to make schools do what is politically desirable. However, it is clear from decades of research that educational organizations are unique. They are not like businesses or the armed forces, for they must represent a host of constituencies with conflicting views about what education ought to be doing. Organizational analysts have come to call schools "loosely coupled organizations" (Weick 1976). In such organizations, efforts to enhance control over teaching escalates conflict and creates a diversity of interests instead of unifying and standardizing teaching and learning outcomes. This means that the way we have historically thought about educational policy does little to solve the problems of education; instead, it actually adds to them. The last two decades of educational reform have not led to dramatically different or better schools.

Indeed, reform has continually created new problems for the schools to solve, diverting the energies of educators and the public from the essential moral enterprise of schools. When the politicians begin to reverse the centralization of educational policy, they do not really understand what is going on. They just think things have gotten so standardized that initiative is being stifled. In this they are correct, but they neither understand why this is the case nor, more importantly, recognize that the existing approach to educational policy is now *the* largest problem American schools must face. Policy will not improve quality, because quality is an interpretation of the meaning of events. Moral values cannot be dictated. They are created in everyday life, in the relationships among people and in the tasks they share. Quality is fundamentally a "bottom-up" proposition. Our politicians and government officials have good reason not to admit this, for it means they cannot control the key mission of education. It also means that Americans should advocate for an end to educational policy, at least as we now conceive of it.

An end to educational policy does not mean an end to political and governmental action. It means, rather, that we must escape the policy logic that seeks to centralize and standardize education in the effort to reform it. Even where the policy logic has been most successful in education, in promoting educational equity, we can see the flaw in its conception. The policy logic is such that equity was and is defined as equal treatment, the same treatment even for people with dramatically different backgrounds. This logic of policy ends up preserving differences in academic performance because it does allow that people may need unequal treatment to catch up. Students who are not doing well in school need more than equal treatment; They need gifted and talented programs more than the academically gifted do. As we demonstrated in this book, policy resulted in ending the moral discourse of Rougemont. What is most disturbing is that equal treatment is the logic of almost all educational policy, even when the issue is not related to civil rights. Governments spend a lot of time trying to ensure that policy equalizes resources and constraints, except when politicians blatantly declare policy logic as irrelevant—what we call "pork barrel" legislation. The end of policy means that a new logic is needed for political and government action.

To us, the failure of educational policy is understandable. Policymaking reaffirms the authority and power of the policymakers. Compliance with policy does not get the desired ends—it gets more uncertainty and creates more problems that require solutions. Thus policymaking becomes a self-fulfilling policy. The more you make, the more is needed.

Corbett and Wilson (1991) show that there is an increasing awareness of the ineffectiveness of policy in resolving educational problems.

Indeed, they argue that policymakers have had the same realization, but instead of reconsidering their role they have decided to celebrate the establishment of policy rather than its effectiveness. Corbett and Wilson call this "front-end publicity" (3). We, of course, need not be overly cynical about our politicians and officials. They are caught in the same web as most of our citizenry. They play out the belief in educational policy, because they are not communicatively competent themselves (Bowers defined "communicative competence" as "the ability to negotiate meanings and purposes instead of passively accepting the social realities defined by others" [1984: 2]). They have been led to believe that there are objective solutions to our problems and that their actions are more effective than those of the citizens they represent. They actually believe that there are shortcuts to educational quality, that if people would comply with policy then education would improve. This of course is nonsense. There is no shortcut to people participating directly, investing their time and effort in what they believe is important. Unfortunately, politicians and officials are pawns of the cultural belief that making educational policy actually improves education.

We think that instead of policy we should have possibilities. Law and regulation should be geared so that schools are encouraged to examine their own narratives, traditions, beliefs, and what they want for the future. They should also be encouraged to create a today they believe in that will connect the two. We have many words for how this may be accomplished. "Facilitation" is a common term for decisions that clear the way for people to decide what is important for them to do. "Decentralization" is a word we use to say that we will let decisions be made by the people who are directly concerned. "Citizen participation" is a term we use to indicate that people wish to exercise directly their rights. The end of policy should be coupled with such processes. Policymakers should be thinking about how to use government to help people learn from their pasts and yearn for their futures and to enable them to connect the two in everyday life.

Our colleagues and critics have told us this is a pipe dream. Our politicians are too driven by special interests to let the citizenry decide how to act. Our governments are too bureaucratic to surrender their authority to control and regulate. Thankfully, human affairs are not so deterministic, as the orators ironically have taught us. They are created by people and can be changed by people. This is expressed well in our educational organizations. This is why we call them "loosely coupled." We do not have to wait for politicians and governments for us to act. We have plenty of room for action now. Unfortunately, it means that we can simply ignore our politicians and government—insouciance is the order of the day.

The end of educational policy would ask politicians and government officials to make substantive decisions. It would require them to ask, "Does this legislation or regulation promote citizens and educators participating in decisions about what is to be valued in their schools?" Participation is the base, but clearly not the end all. In order for schools to be vehicles of moral construction, people must be involved in making sense of their histories, their desires, and their daily lives. Policies in the past have focused on participation in decision making. We have no objection to this, but we think the prior issue is participation in moral construction. Before one can make good decisions, one has to have a grasp of context: the histories, values, and desires of the people in the school. This comes through work on cultural projects such as school and community histories; artistic expressions such as stories, novels, plays, murals, music; educational parks about the environment, nature, and science; journalism; documentary projects such as community photography exhibits, oral histories, biographies, and autobiographies; and so on. Participation in these lets people share their traditions and the futures they want, and creates cultural artifacts that link the two. Substantive legislation would foster possibilities for people to reclaim moral life with schooling.

Moral Possibilities and Schools as Communities of Memory

If schools are to be about moral life, then we need to do more than shed our current way of thinking about educational policy and reform—we must conceive of schools as places for moral construction. We cannot offer ideas that will invariably allow this to happen. We must avoid replacing the ideas we have dereified with other reified ideas—remember that the problem with the ideas we have discussed here is not so much their content as their reification. They have much to offer when they are treated as possibilities to be considered for moral construction. When reified, they blind us to other possibilities and we are pawns of them. When we viewed them as possibilities, we retain the capacity to consider them, to find points of agreement and critique, to join them with other ideas, and to employ them or not in the social construction of moral life. Given what Rougemont and Cedar Grove Schools taught us, we would offer five possibilities: schools as communities of memory; schools as places for constructing moral narratives, schools as places for constructive canon-making, schools as places for imagined futures, schools as places for continuity construction, and schools as places with curriculum for moral participation.

Bellah and colleagues write: "Where history and hope are forgotten and community means only the gathering of the similar, community degenerates into lifestyle enclave" (1985: 154). In this we see the irony of the recent calls by orators for curricula that promote a common culture. Being similar leaves little room for community. There is little chance that one's taken-for-granted assumptions will be challenged. Community is different from consensus. To have a community, there must be struggles, trials, successes, and failures. These are things that life, history, and hope are made of. These are things that give values their depth and separates them from mere opinions.

The public schools are sufficiently diverse for community to be possible. Yet schools today all too often view that diversity as problematic, and seek to silence it (Weis and Fine 1993). When they do silence it, they have no history of overcoming adversity to give participants hope in difficult times. Even if diversity is not silenced, our public schools are largely ahistorical organizations. If there is a remembered past, it is all too often that of being a sports power. We have few heroes and heroines, few pivotal events, few lessons to learn from.

Moreover, schools tend to view communities as external entities that should primarily support the school. They have little awareness that schools are embedded in communities and serve as a key social institution in the community. We should ask, How does a school help construct the community within which it is embedded? In todays' schools, the task is often to take neighborhoods that are geographically separate and to make a community where none would otherwise exist. This is a large task but not insurmountable, as we learned in our work with these schools. The key attribute of a school serving as a community of memory is that the school facilitates the remembering and the retelling of the histories that make up its moral narrative. Oral history projects are just one of many possibilities; The key is that the medium be about recollecting and remembering the community's past.

There is some danger in retelling history, for it forces us to face issues that have been silenced rather than resolved. Bellah and colleagues write: "And if the community is completely honest, it will remember stories not only of suffering received but of suffering inflicted—dangerous memories, for they call the community to alter ancient evils" (1985: 153). Without such honesty, there seems little chance for schools to reclaim themselves as moral enterprises.

Constructing Moral Narratives

It is no accident that we are seeing a revival of interest in narrative forms of expression. The moral crisis that Purpel (1989) identifies in education is shared by all our social institutions. As MacIntyre puts it, the "language of morality" is in "grave disorder" (1981: 2). Philosophers and academics will not be able to put things right. Rather, morality and virtue, as we have argued here, are the province of everyday people and everyday life. The moral crisis can be eased only by people in their everyday lives consciously engaging in the construction of morality and virtue. We have emphasized that it is the participative element in moral constructions that is important. People re-collect, participate in selecting and assembling, and re-member, giving new meaning and salience, their moral tales—that is, moral work is essentially narrative work. "The unity of a human life is the unity of a narrative quest" (MacIntyre 1981: 219).

MacIntyre also argues that the narratives of individuals are also part of the narratives of others and others' are part of the individual's. Moral life, then, is found not in principles derived from the past as argued by the orators nor in the search for future truths as argued by the philosophers but, rather, in the stories that people tell in the present about themselves and others. It matters little if the stories themselves are true to a set of actual historical occurrences. What matters is that people engage in the constructing and telling of tales, for this is how people may locate themselves as moral beings and create moral communities to which they and others belong. The Rougemont and College Park communities were telling something of their past; but, more importantly, they were engaged in creating morality as they told their stories to us, and sharing it with us resulted in their stories being available for others to appropriate in their everyday discourse—and in such works as this book.

A second possibility for schools is seriously to consider storytelling a central part of their mission. Teachers rarely tell their students their life stories, let alone stories about former students, colleagues, or community members. Teachers rarely ask students to tell their stories. These are reserved for the lunch table, bus ride, or stolen moments "off task." Elders are rarely invited to tell about life "back when." We rarely relate our life stories to stories by Shakespeare or other authors. Rather, we pursue some efferent understanding of the text read.

Our research team was leery of sending the fourth- and fifth-graders out to interview adults in Rougemont and College Park. Now it is clear that this was important moral activity. The failing was that we did nothing other than collect the narratives the kids were told. We should have spent considerable time discussing and comparing the narratives they collected and their own lives. We now see this as a moral failure on our part. Storytelling is central to the moral enterprise of schooling and thus should be seen as part of the curricula for students. However, for this to be sufficient to create and sustain a community of memory, storytelling must include and be about the community around the school.

Constructive Canon Making

There is much to learn from the oratorical idea, as long as one considers it just an idea and not a statement of what should be. While we mercilessly critiqued the orators' use of Great Books, there is much to be gained by having an individual school considering what texts, ideas, works, and experiences are central to understanding the peoples that have been brought together in that specific school. Constructive canon making would seem to involve an ongoing discourse about this. The focus is on the *making*, not on the canon itself. As we have seen in recent years, any canon can incite conflict, especially when the canon is taken to define what is American or Western culture. This level of argument is essentially unresolvable, because there is no ground shared by the disputants. Each group has a different basis for its claims.

A school that has taken on the project of becoming a community of memory for those it serves has sponsored and helped construct moral narratives, and has retold the stories for public consumption, as Cedar Grove School did with the play, and has constructed different grounds than we have seen in the canon conflicts to date. The important point is that ground needs to be constructed, and a community created that has available to it the "dangerous stories" that Bellah and colleagues regard as the mainstay of community moral life (1985: 153). Such grounds are particularistic, to be sure, but MacIntyre (1984) suggests it is through such particularism that we join our wider cultural and societal narrative. The complaint against particularism often offered by orators ignores the embedded nature of cultural beliefs. Our particularism both plays out our wider culture and creates new possibilities for moral life, education, and our nation. We join the wider discourse not by learning it but by participating in discourse itself.

It seems reasonable to adopt the process Adler (1990) describes for his identification of Great Books as a process for individual schools. A school may wish to set up broadly representative canon-making committees. They may wish to canvass the parents, teachers, students, academics, and other groups to get nominations for the canon. Then a process of reading (if a written text) or viewing (if a work of art or experience) and considering the nominated texts, ideas, works, and experiences may allow people to argue for those things that speak to them and/or suggest morally and culturally constructing possibilities to them. This process should include students, parents, and teachers, at a minimum. This is in itself a moral discourse and can be regarded as an end in itself. Instituting this as an ongoing process may make sense. There will be points where selections will need to be made, and we would suggest using the moral narratives that the school has sponsored as one ground for the decision. If the construction of these narratives has not involved the silencing of some stories, then this ground should be inclusive of the various peoples in the school. Yet, as we will argue next, the philosophical idea also has something to contribute.

Imagined Futures

The philosophical idea suggests another basis for constructive canon making. While we have critiqued this idea for positing the existence of some ultimate truth, even if difficult to attain, the consideration of possible futures binds us not only to our own community but also to the wider world. We escape our particular context and use our cultural beliefs to imagine possibilities for ourselves individually and collectively. We do not think it is necessary to employ the new genre of thought called "futures research" to engage in imagining futures for ourselves. What is needed is simply to engage in an expansive process of imagining your school, your community, your nation, and your world as you would wish it to be. This can be followed by asking people to temper these imaginings by considering what futures are somehow probable. Both of these exercises construct moral narratives and community for a school.

Again, such moral work will engage people in the arguments that lead to moral and cultural construction. Imagining futures should also lead to nominations for additions to the school's canon. It seems reasonable that schools should make available to their students and their communities those works that suggest possibilities for the future. Some works may be simply demographic projections of the compositions of the school, community, state, nation, and world. Others may be clearly futuristic in the sense that they are projections, real and fictitious at the same time. It also seems realistic to ask students and others to examine works of and about the past for what they offer and suggest for the future. Again, expansive imaginings may then be coupled with dialogues about what is more or less likely and more or less desirable. The future adds to the canon and gives a second ground for decisions about what the canon should comprise.

Constructing Continuities

The moral narratives we related in chapters 3, 4, and 5 all point to the moral blindness that comes from the refication of the oratorical and philosophical ideas and their opposition. We are blind to the fact that moral action is fundamentally in the present. Instead of the present being morally suspect, as it is in each of the reified ideas, the present is the moral moment in human life. We cannot act in the past or in the future. In the present, we construct morality and virtue. Miss Dove's virtues of respect for authority, efficiency, obedience, and punctiliousness were College Park's present virtues. The virtues of respect for others, responsibility for others, discipline as a community endeavor, struggle and suffering, excellence for its own sake, and standing firm with faith were Rougemont's offerings to the current moral discourse. Both were constructions in the present, employing both pasts and futures. In short, the present should be the morally revered time for it.

But precisely what is the present, in moral terms? The present can be defined only in the presence, not the absence, of the past and the future. Moral theories have largely overlooked what this means for schools. However, it is clear that feminists in their work of dereifying ideas based on the study of men suggest some possibilities (Gilligan 1982; Noddings 1984, 1992) for a useful conception of what is moral and how the present can be conceived. Gilligan's classic statement puts it well: The moral may be seen as "making connections" (1982). As she, Noddings, and others have argued, our existing ideas about the moral are blind to people making moral decisions based on their connections to others. The ethic of caring is about developing reciprocal relationships that nurture and sustain the parties to that relationship (Noddings 1984). This is a complex moral concept that we cannot do justice to here, but we can see that one way we are moral in the present is through our connections to others in caring relationships. This is the point of moral narratives. They unite us with those we tell of and tell to. This is what we are about accomplishing in communities of memory, in constructive canon making, and in imagining futures together. In the narratives we have related in this book, people constructed their moral tales out of relationships with others, the moral icons they portrayed, their friends in times being discussed, the interviewers to whom they told the tales, and the imagined others who would hear the tales.

Noddings (1992) has extended the notion of making connections as moral activity in a manner we think is useful to consider further. Building on Dewey (1963), she sees connection as being about continuity. A moral relationship is more than a single interaction. It has a past, a present, and an implied future. Noddings offers at least four types of continuity that are important in the moral education of children: continuity of place, people, purpose, and curriculum. She elaborates each of these in suggesting how schools should be reorganized to achieve continuity for children. We find her suggestions compelling, but here we wish to offer another form of continuity, the continuity between the oratorical and philosophical ideas.

As noted above, these ideas do have much to offer us *as moral and cultural participants*. When we understand these ideas as possibilities for social construction of virtue and moral life, we control their use and application (rather than them controlling us). We can then use them to create narratives of continuity that reclaim morality and virtue. The people we interviewed constituted the present as the moral continuity between the recollected pasts and the imagined futures. This construction reclaims the present as the primary scene of moral action. The virtues assigned to the teachers in both schools were created in a present, recollected from the past, and given to us to be carried forward in time, changing the notion of "timeless virtues" to "time-full virtues."

Schools may wish, then, to facilitate discussions of what continuities are possible between the constructed canons and the imagined futures. This invites people to participate in deciding what the schools and communities should be doing now. Under current conditions in schools, this type of discussion leads to divisiveness, for power is the only means for deciding which view will prevail. Yet when schools become places that support us with a grounding in narratives, communities of memory, constructive canon making, imagined futures, and continuity construction, a discussion of values is possible and disagreements have comprehensible bases. Reclaiming the moral life of schools will not eliminate differences, but it will make differences understandable and unite them in narratives.

A Curriculum for Moral Participation

In chapter 1, we argued that curricular approaches to moral education seemed both to succumb to instrumentalism and to ignore the larger issues about the role schools play in the moral lives of adults and communities. However, this should be not taken as a wholesale rejection of curricular approaches. Clearly, reclaiming the moral life of schools would have to involve rethinking curricula along the lines discussed above. As Noddings (1992) has suggested, in order to emphasize the construction of morality, it is necessary to displace the centrality of the traditional subjects in a curriculum. This does not necessarily mean that we would not teach the relevant content of the traditional subjects, but it does mean that we should not teach them as reified knowledge. It also means that the what and how of instruction should serve the construction of narratives, community of memory, constructive canon making, imagining futures, and constructing continuities as decided by an individual school and the community and/or communities it helps to create.

We should, of course, remember that all of these possibilities are about being moral participants in our schools and communities. Education can promote developing the communicative competence necessary for moral participation by

(1) providing an understanding of the cultural forces that foster change; (2) providing a knowledge of cultural traditions that will enable students to exercise judgement about those elements of the culture that are worth preserving; and (3) providing a method of thinking that enables students to see decisions in social life in terms of relationships, continuities, disjunctions, and tradeoffs. (Bowers 1984: 2)

Without such understandings, we will remain pawns of our culture, the moral life of schools will be held captive by reified ideas, and reforms will continue to recycle. Perhaps worse, we will remain blind to the possibilities in our own lives for constructing virtue and morality. But with the promise of such communicative competence, we will become participants in the construction of our cultures, the moral life of schools will be the product of our ownership of ideas, and we will construct new forms of schooling. In these lie our possibilities for the social construction of virtue.

REFERENCES

Adler, M. 1940. *How to read a book*. New York: Simon and Schuster.

———. 1982. *The paideia proposal*. New York: Collier Books.

———. 1990. *Reforming education: The opening of the American mind*. New York: Collier Books.

———. 1990. "This Prewar Generation. In G. Van Doren, (Ed). Reforming Education: The Opening of the American Mind. NY: Westview Press (pp. 3–20).

Apple, M. 1986. *Teachers and texts*. New York: Routledge.

Bellah, R., et al. 1985. *Habits of the heart*. Berkeley: University of California Press.

Berger, P., and T. Luckmann. 1967. *The social construction of Reality*. Garden City, NY: Doubleday.

Blair, H. 1965. *Lectures on rhetoric and belle lettres*. Ed. H. Harding. Carbondale, IL: Southern Illinois University Press.

Bloom, A. 1987. *The closing of the American mind*. New York: Simon and Schuster.

Bowers, C. 1984. *The promise of theory*. New York: Teachers College Press.

———. 1987. *Elements of a post-liberal theory of education*. New York: Teachers College Press.

Butchart, R. E. 1976. *Local schools: Exploring their history*. Nashville, TN: American Association for State and Local History.

Campbell, R., T. Fleming, L. Newell, and J. Bennion. 1986. *A history of thought and practice in educational administration*. New York: Teachers College Press.

Carlton, P. 1991. Oral history at Virginia Tech documents experience of public school principals. *Oral History in the Mid-Atlantic Region Newsletter* 4:1 (Spring): 1–14.

Carnegie Forum on Education and the Economy. 1986. A nation prepared: *Teachers for the twenty-first century*. New York: Carnegie Forum on Education and the Economy.

Clifford, J., and G. Marcus (eds.). 1986. *Writing culture*. Berkeley: University of California Press.

Collins, R. 1982. *Sociological insight*. New York: Oxford University Press.

Commission on the Reorganization of Secondary Education. 1918. *Cardinal principles of secondary education*. Washington, DC: Government Printing Office.

Corbett, H. D., and B. L. Wilson. 1991. *Testing, reform, and rebellion*. Norwood, NJ: Ablex.

Cuban, L. 1988. Why do some reforms persist? *Educational Administration Quarterly* 24(3): 137–50.

———. 1990. Reforming again, again and again. *Educational Researcher* 9 (1): 3–12.

Dempsey, V., and G. Noblit. 1993a. Cultural ignorance and school desegregation: Reconstructing a silenced narrative. *Educational Policy* 7(4): 318–39.

———. 1993b. The demise of caring in an African American community: One consequence of school desegregation. *Urban Review* 25(1): 47–62.

Dewey, J. 1902. *The child and the curriculum*. Chicago: University of Chicago Press.

———. 1915. *The school and society*. Chicago: University of Chicago Press.

———. 1916. *Democracy and education*. New York: The Free Press.

———. 1963. *Experience and education*. New York: Collier Books.

Dilthey, W. 1977. *Descriptive psychology and historical understanding*. The Hague: Martinus Nijhoff.

Du Bois, W. E. B. 1965. *The souls of black folk*. In *Three negro classics*, ed. J. Franklin, 207–390. New York: Avon.

Emerson, R. W. 1876. *Society and solitude*. Boston: James R. Osgood.

Finnegan, R. 1992. *Oral traditions and the verbal arts*. New York: Routledge.

Fish, S. E. 1980. *Is there a text in this class? The authority of interpretive communities*. Cambridge: Harvard University Press.

Foucault, M. 1980. *Power and knowledge*. Ed. C. Gordon. New York: Pantheon.

Frankena, W. A. 1963. *Ethics*. Englewood Cliffs, NJ: Prentice Hall.

Freire, P. 1985. *The politics of education*. New York: Bergin and Garvey.

Geertz, C. 1973. *The interpretation of cultures*. New York: Basic Books.

———. 1983. *Local knowledge*. New York: Basic Books.

Gellner, E. 1983. *Nations and Nationalism*. Ithaca, NY: Cornell University Press.

Giddens, A. 1979. *Central problems of social theory.* London: Macmillan.

Gilligan, C. 1982. *In a different voice.* Cambridge: Harvard University Press.

Goetz, J., and M. LeCompte. 1984. *Ethnography and qualitative design in educational research.* Orlando, FL: Academic Press.

Habermas, J. 1971. *Knowledge and human interests.* Boston: Beacon Press.

Halbwachs, M. 1992. *On collective memory.* Ed. L. Coser. Chicago: University of Chicago Press.

Hall, J. D. 1987. *Like a family: The making of a southern cotton mill world.* Chapel Hill: University of North Carolina Press.

Hawley, R. A. 1982. Miss Dove redivivus. *Phi Delta Kappan* (September): 34–6.

Hirsch, E. 1987. *Cultural literacy.* Boston: Houghton Mifflin.

Hirsch, E. et al. 1993. *Dictionary of cultural literacy.* Boston: Houghton Mifflin.

Jackson, P. W., R. E. Bootstrom and D. T. Hansen. 1993. *The Moral Life of Schools.* San Francisco: Jossey Bass.

Jacoby, R. 1987. *The last intellectuals.* New York: Basic Books.

Jarret, J. 1991. *The teaching of values: Caring and appreciation.* New York: Routledge.

Johnson, J. 1986. An historical review of the role of black parents and the black community played in providing schooling for black children in the South, 1865–1954. Ed.D. dissertation, University of Massachusetts.

Kennedy, P. 1989. Can the U.S. remain number one? *New York Times Review of Books* (16 March, 36–42).

Kent, J. D. 1987. A Not Too Distant Past. *The Educational Forum* (24): 329–35.

Kimball, B. 1986. *Orators and philosophers: A history of the idea of liberal education.* New York: Teachers College Press.

Kuhn, T. 1962. *The structure of scientific revolutions.* Chicago: University of Chicago Press.

Lyotard, J. 1979. *The postmodern condition.* Trans. G. Bennington and B. Massumi. Minneapolis: University of Minnesota Press.

MacIntyre, A. 1984. *After virtue.* Notre Dame: University of Notre Dame Press.

Malinowski, B. 1922. *Argonauts of the Western Pacific.* New York: E. P. Dutton.

Mannheim, K. 1936. *Ideology and utopia.* New York: Harcourt, Brace.

Marcus, G. E., and M. J. Fischer. *Anthropology as cultural critique: An experimental moment in the human sciences.* Chicago: University of Chicago Press.

Mebane, M. 1956. *Proud Shoes: The Story of an American Family.* NY: Harper.

Mebane, M. 1981. *Mary.* New York: Fawcett.

National Commission on Excellence in Education. 1983. *A nation at risk: The imperative for educational reform.* Washington, DC: Government Printing Office.

National Education Association. 1983. The NEA Report of the Committee of Ten on Secondary School Studies. Washington, DC: Government Printing Office.

Noblit, G., and W. Pink (eds.). *Schooling in social context.* Norwood, NJ: Ablex.

Noddings, N. 1984. *Caring.* Berkeley: University of California Press.

———. 1992. *The challenge to care in schools.* New York. Teachers College Press.

Popkewitz, T. 1991. *A political sociology of educational reform.* New York: Teachers College Press.

Pater, W. 1910. *The Renaissance.* London: New Library Edition.

Patton, F. 1947. *Good morning, Miss Dove.* New York: Dodd, Mead.

Patton, M. 1992. *Qualitative research and evaluation methods.* Newbury Park, CA: Sage.

Peacock, J. L. 1984. Religion and life history: An explanation in cultural psychology. In *Text, play, and story: The construction and reconstruction of self and society,* ed. E. Bruner, 94–116. Washington, DC: American Ethnological Society.

Precourt, W. 1982. Ethnohistorical analysis of an Appalachian settlement school. In *Doing the ethnography of schooling,* ed. G. Spindler and L. Spindler. New York: Holt, Rinehart and Winston.

Purpel, D. 1989. *The moral and spiritual crisis in education.* New York: Bergin and Garvey.

Quinn, N., and D. Holland. 1987. Culture and cognition. In *Cultural models in language and thought,* ed. D. Holland and N. Quinn, 3–40. New York: Cambridge University Press.

Relph, E. 1976. *Place and placelessness.* London: Pion.

Rosenblatt, L. 1978. *The reader, the text, the poem.* Carbondale, IL: Southern Illinois University Press.

Rosenfeld, S., and J. Sher. 1977. The urbanization of rural schools, 1840–1970. In *Education in rural America*, ed. J. Sher. Boulder: Westview.

Shackle, G. L. S. 1966. Policy poetry and success. *The Economic Journal*. (Dec.) pp. 755–767.

Schlechty, P., and G. Noblit. 1982. Some uses of sociological theory in educational evaluation. In *Policy Research*, ed. R. Corwin, 283–306. Greenwich, CT: JAI Press.

Sher, J. 1977. *Education in Rural America*. Boulder: Westview Press.

Sichel, B. 1988. *Moral education*. Philadelphia: Temple University Press.

Siddle-Walker, E. V. 1993. Caswell County Training School, 1933–1969. *Harvard Educational Review* 63(2): 161–81.

Sizemore, B. 1987. The effective African American elementary school. In *The Social Context of Schooling*, ed. W. Pink and G. Noblit, 175–202. Norwood, NJ: Ablex.

Southworth, C. 1988. Geometry, fir trees, and princes. Ph.D. dissertation, University of North Carolina at Chapel Hill.

Spring, J. 1980. *Educating the worker-citizen*. New York: Longman.

Straughan, R. 1982. *Can we teach children to be good?* Philadelphia: Milton Keynes.

Thompson, P. 1988. *The voice of the past: Oral history*. New York: Oxford University Press.

Tyack, D., and E. Hansot. 1980. From social movement to professional management. *American Journal of Education* 88(3): 291–319.

Van Galen, J. 1987. Maintaining Control: The Structuring of Parent Involvement. In G. Noblit and W. Pink (eds.) *Schooling in Social Context*, 78–90. Norwood, NJ: Ablex.

van Gennep, A. 1975. *The rites of passage*. Chicago: University of Chicago Press.

Vansina, J. 1985. *Oral tradition as history*. Madison: University of Wisconsin Press.

Washington, B. T. 1965. *Up from slavery*. In *Three negro classics*, ed. J. Franklin, 23–206. New York: Avon.

Weber, M. 1947. *The theory of social and economic organization*. New York: Oxford University Press.

Weick, K. 1976. Educational organizations as loosely coupled systems. *Administrative Science Quarterly* (21): 1–19.

Weis, L., and M. Fine (eds.). 1993. *Beyond silenced voices.* Albany: State University of New York Press.

Wexler, P. 1987. *The social analysis of education.* New York: Routledge.

Whitman, W. 1964. Democratic vistas. In *Prose works 1892,* ed. F. Stovall. New York: New York University Press.

Witherell, C., and N. Noddings (eds.). 1991. *Stories lives tell: Narrative and dialogue in education.* New York: Teachers College Press.

Young, M. F. D. 1971. *Knowledge and control: New directions for the sociology of education.* London: Collier-Macmillan.

Zeichner, K. M. 1991. Contradictions and tensions in the professionalization of teaching and the democratization of schools. *Teachers College Record* 92 (3): 363–79.

Index